Growing
AT THE
Speed
OF Life

Growing
AT THE
Speed
OF Life

A Year in the Life of
My First Kitchen Garden

GRAHAM KERR

A Perigee Book

A PERIGEE BOOK
Published by the Penguin Group
Penguin Group (USA) Inc.
375 Hudson Street, New York, New York 10014, USA
Penguin Group (Canada), 90 Eglinton Avenue East, Suite 700, Toronto, Ontario M4P 2Y3, Canada
(a division of Pearson Penguin Canada Inc.)
Penguin Books Ltd., 80 Strand, London WC2R 0RL, England
Penguin Group Ireland, 25 St. Stephen's Green, Dublin 2, Ireland (a division of Penguin Books Ltd.)
Penguin Group (Australia), 250 Camberwell Road, Camberwell, Victoria 3124, Australia
(a division of Pearson Australia Group Pty. Ltd.)
Penguin Books India Pvt. Ltd., 11 Community Centre, Panchsheel Park, New Delhi—110 017, India
Penguin Group (NZ), 67 Apollo Drive, Rosedale, North Shore 0632, New Zealand
(a division of Pearson New Zealand Ltd.)
Penguin Books (South Africa) (Pty.) Ltd., 24 Sturdee Avenue, Rosebank, Johannesburg 2196, South
Africa
Penguin Books Ltd., Registered Offices: 80 Strand, London WC2R 0RL, England

While the author has made every effort to provide accurate telephone numbers and Internet addresses at
the time of publication, neither the publisher nor the author assumes any responsibility for errors or for
changes that occur after publication. Further, the publisher does not have any control over and does not
assume any responsibility for author or third-party websites or their content.

GROWING AT THE SPEED OF LIFE

First edition: March 2011

ISBN: 978-0-399-53612-0

An application to file this book for cataloging has been submitted to the Library of Congress.

PRINTED IN THE UNITED STATES OF AMERICA

10   9   8   7   6   5   4   3   2   1

The recipes contained in this book are to be followed exactly as written. The publisher is not responsible
for your specific health or allergy needs that may require medical supervision. The publisher is not
responsible for any adverse reactions to the recipes contained in this book.

Most Perigee books are available at special quantity discounts for bulk purchases for sales promotions,
premiums, fund-raising, or educational use. Special books, or book excerpts, can also be created to fit
specific needs. For details, write: Special Markets, Penguin Group (USA) Inc., 375 Hudson Street, New
York, New York 10014.

Stand at the crossroads and look;
ask for the ancient paths,
ask where the good way is, and walk in it,
and you will find rest for your souls.

—JEREMIAH 6:16

For Treena
The one who shares my table and my bed, the absolute love of my life.
She has chosen the path to wellness rather than going out on her
genetic tide. It is to her that I dedicate my garden and this book with
my ongoing love and care.

And for Gracious Gardeners
My present enthusiasm was made possible by my many
newfound friends and neighbors, who shared their lifetimes
of gardening experience with me.
Please don't let it stop there!

I have much to learn (and welcome learning) from everyone
who has proven experience. If my newfound ideas are different from
yours, then I really want to hear from you.

Remember contribution to the common good beats criticism every
time. And the common good is the good we can do in common.

To contribute, please go to www.grahamkerr.com/speedoflife.

—GK

CONTENTS

ACKNOWLEDGMENTS

I owe my understanding of greenhouses to Charley Yaw. Charley Yaw passed me on to Scott Titus, who heads up the Center for Holistic Advanced Organic Studies (CHAOS)—and yes, he really does have a good sense of humor—from whom I got a new perspective on topsoil.

Both Charley and Scott have become dear friends, and together with Deb Mitchell—a delightful master gardener/lecturer connected to Washington State University—I have a rich source of local knowledge and continual advice.

While in the midst of reading twenty-four excellent reference books, from which I wanted to extract useful snippets of information to offer in this book, I came across Stephen Albert's *Kitchen Garden Grower's Guide* and his website, Harvest to Table (www .harvesttotable.com). Steve had already done my homework, having researched each plant *comprehensively* with the practiced eye of a true expert. My sketch pages for each plant were greatly aided by all his hard work.

Sandy Silverthorne went beyond his usual cartoon whimsy and outlined all my plants with his customary economy of strokes. I love his work!

The nutritional numbers have been through multiple layers of analysis, with a final pass under the eagle eye of my very long-term friend and culinary associate Suzanne Butler—or "Butters," as I often call her. It's as close as she ever gets to being saturated!

Every word, indeed every keystroke, was the work of our personal, private, and confidential secretary, Wendy, and without her, our little world would be snow white blank pages, without a digital stroke in sight.

Then there's my dear friend John Duff, with whom I have created six books. I strayed for a season of three more literary efforts, and now I'm happily back in the fold and benefiting from his understanding of good food, good gardening, good books, and, as a result, the truly good life.

PREFACE

L et's try starting this book with a mild confession. Until this year I'd never met a plant that I couldn't kill. I was my very own herbicide.

I now understand the problem. I never gave them a reasonable amount of my undivided attention. I even used to suggest that there was no point in going back to smell the flowers inasmuch as I had blown the petals off as I flew past on my way to who knows where!

Almost all of this has now changed. I'm still very active, but I don't leave my plants unattended. Now they don't die (at least not from lack of attention). Not only do they survive, but they actually thrive! And here I am with my 29th book, written at the speed of this new *inclusive* life.

I'm finding a new rhythm, with fewer fits and starts, a more even—almost predictable—adventure that is nonetheless filled with unexpected natural challenges and great joy from sharing the eventual harvest. May our kitchen gardens help us understand what it means to keep growing personally at the speed of life.

Graham Kerr
Nonsuch Cottage and Garden
Mount Vernon, WA

Growing
AT THE
Speed
OF Life

CHAPTER ONE

Why I Decided to Grow a Garden

For almost 60 years I have been running the final stretch of the relay race to put healthful food on the table, which means I was the last one to carry the baton of fresh fruits and vegetables, preparing them for the plate, which is the finish line. It's not an uncommon role for most cooks, professional or otherwise.

Another member of the team started the race by selecting and germinating the seeds. Another followed by preparing good soil and transplanting the vegetable "starts." A third and fourth nurtured those plants through their maturity and got them to market to be handed over to me—the cook.

Being from another planet

In my long career as a gourmet/nutrition teacher, I have cooked just about everything that grows, but I've never grown a thing I've cooked. So what got me thinking about the earth-to-table process?

You have to be from another planet not to have heard that a diet made up of mostly fruits and vegetables is a first-line defense against so many of the avoidable chronic diseases of our time, such as obesity, heart disease, type 2 diabetes, and some cancers. I've been looking at this issue in our own family since 1975, when the National Institutes of Health first introduced the "5 A Day" concept—the idea of consuming five or more servings of fruits and vegetables every day. In fact, I worked with the institutes to promote this initiative. But curiously, and disappointingly, as one set of records shows, the $24 million campaign resulted in an increase of only half a serving (from 3 to 3.5) among American consumers between 1975 and 2008.

The National Health and Nutrition Examination Survey (NHANES) 2001–2006 (compared to NHANES 1988–1994) revealed the following for consumers aged 40–74: The number of those who even attempt the "5 A Day" concept has dropped from 42 percent to 26 percent, and at the same time the obesity rate has risen from 28 percent to 36 percent. Also, the engagement in exercise (12 times per month was used as the benchmark) has fallen from 53 percent to 43 percent.

Nothing about these numbers is good news for our nation's future health. But *please* notice that the fruit and vegetable decline is way ahead of the rest by at least 6 percent.

Now that might seem to be a pretty boring statistic, but the way it hit me was far from boring. Any greater release of energy, and I would have gone into orbit.

For my small part in the "5 A Day" program—I had done nearly 500 newscasts on the subject—I saw consumption go from only 3 servings to 3.5 servings. I took this personally, even though I was far from the only one urging folks to consume more.

Why was this happening? And what more could be done to achieve the needed 300 percent increase to between 9 and 11 servings a day that most experts (according to the OmniHeart Study) believe to be the amount needed to truly make a difference in diabetes, heart disease, and of course obesity?

I decided to go back to the starting line and begin to run the whole race by doing something entirely new. During my earlier TV career as the Galloping Gourmet, I was awarded the Broken Wooden Spoon by Weight Watchers International. The company described me as public enemy number one to all those making healthy choices.

Clearly, in the 1,000 new TV programs we've made since 1987, we have changed—and Weight Watchers did eventually send me an unbroken spoon! However, even those changes had not made the adjustments that our modern world now needs.

I wondered if I could help others to reach these goals with a little sweat equity in my own backyard and enthusiastically pass my experiences on.

The home that my wife, Treena, and I built and moved into in April 2001 is

situated with views facing to the west and south over the fabulous Skagit Valley, one of the most productive agricultural delta valleys in the world, just halfway between Seattle, Washington, and Vancouver, British Columbia. The design of the house was inspired by our love of boats—it's a mere 1,400-square-foot "cabin" that uses its limited space in much the same way as a maritime architect might have designed it. Called Nonsuch Cottage, after a small sailboat we once owned (and, purely coincidentally, after the infamously overembellished castle built by King Henry VIII in the south of England), our cottage sits on an acre of land that falls off rapidly to the west, giving us up to 16 hours of sunshine on our south side in midsummer. For the longest time, we lived with a south lawn that gradually became a sea of dandelions. (Had I only known that springtime organic dandelions can fetch $7 a pound at market I might have entered the earth-to-table race sooner!)

I've always loved the word *serendipity*—it sounds like something a hairdresser might do to create one of those finger-in-a-light-socket hairstyles. In our case, it was First Lady Michelle Obama putting spade to turf on the White House lawn—yes, it was the *south* lawn!

Surely it was serendipity that had me plunge my spade into our south lawn within days of the First Lady? And now there are two southern lawn kitchen gardens—and there I believe any comparisons should cease!

Our plans called for three styles, or types, of gardens, all edible. Along one of our docks (there's that nautical influence again), we would grow each separately in a container called an EarthBox.

The second project, for which we'd join the food race in selecting and germinating seeds, came in the shape of a greenhouse. We watched in awe as a great local company with a worldwide reach (Charley's Greenhouses) raised our 16×8-foot structure in just 7 hours! Here we would get a head start on the short Pacific Northwest growing season and, we hoped, grow vegetables all year round.

Our final and most labor-intensive garden would be a tenth of an acre of raised beds for peas, beans, chard, cabbage, tomatoes, peppers, eggplant, carrots, parsnips, and a whole raft of lettuce busily keeping down the weeds among the red beets and summer and winter squash—all in all, more than 30 plants under the supervision and care of a man with *absolutely no prior experience*!

While it wasn't completely clear to me what impact the experience of creating this garden would have on my life, my neighbors, and even, to a small but vital degree, our community, I recognized early on that I would want to share the lessons learned. And so I started to document my year with the kitchen garden in a series of short videos, since television had always been my most compelling platform when it came to proselytizing about food and well-being—and now even more so since the Internet has provided us with a whole new community of viewers (many of whom have only the vague recollections of their parents recounting the tales of *The Galloping Gourmet* from the 1970s). Gradually it occurred to me that there would be a book in all this. And it be-

came my intention that this book would not only be of value to the armchair gardener but also serve as an introduction to gardening for the person who had the wherewithal to pick up a spade and dig into his or her own version of the south lawn, be it a few square yards in a suburban backyard, a couple of pots on a balcony in the city, or an acre or so in the country.

But beyond sharing my back-to-the-land experience with readers (along with growing and cooking information for 60 or so garden fruits and vegetables, which makes up the bulk of this book), there are a few other key elements in my quest to inform and entertain viewers and readers. And, as a long-time student of food and food culture, it would be remiss of me to try to convey not only the *what* of eating healthfully but also the *why*. In other words, I want to give you the ammunition to become inspired to increase your own intake of fruits and vegetables from that low point of 3.5 to 9–11 per day.

For many readers, the health benefits of simply eating fresh and organic may be

> So what if some of my store-bought, "fresh" produce was picked 7 days ago and then trucked over 1,000 miles to be sorted and distributed and stored and finally put out on display? Food loses its ability to nourish my body every hour after it leaves the soil. How do I feel about the possible 151 hours during which the food that I am eating has been losing its value?
>
> And how do I respond to the idea that modern transcontinental or even transglobal transportation of produce, shipped off-season, is a major contributor to global warming? Is my off-season shopping increasing my personal carbon footprint?
>
> *Answer:* I could grow my own and enjoy the enormous nutritional benefits of eating that food within 1 hour after harvesting. And I can contribute to cutting back on agribusiness's need for oil as well as my own trips to the market.

enough. For the gourmets among you, I hope that the information about common and not-so-common vegetables and the accompanying recipes will provide you with the impetus to cook from scratch, even if you aren't yet willing or able to put that spade into the ground. For others, it will be thinking about the way our food comes to the table and the mostly negative impact that transporting, storing, and processing food has on our environment.

CHAPTER TWO

The Garden-to-Kitchen Connection

In the 2008 Olympic Games in Beijing, China, the United States male and female relay race teams both dropped the baton and were disqualified. During the past two generations, since perhaps the early 1970s, we have dropped another two batons: *home cooking* and *the kitchen garden*.

I need no detailed statistics to back up this claim, only a simple observation of the way most of us live, even as I tried to follow and teach a healthier way to eat.

I have worked with food and public communications every single day for more than 50 years and watched as people appeared to eat fewer plants that they had grown or cooked from scratch.

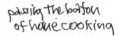

passing the baton of home cooking

I'm not surprised that our overall health has worsened! Notwithstanding great scientific leaps in medical intervention, our level of appropriate preventive behavior has fallen, and the evidence is plain for

everyone to see. We've gained weight at an alarming rate, and weight is a prime precursor of ill health, especially for coronary disease, type 2 diabetes, and some cancers. Strangely, our retreat from the scratch kitchen *and* the kitchen garden really does provide an interesting opportunity for a combined synergistic turnaround.

Throughout this, my first year as a gardener, I've noticed a clear improvement in both our family meals and my perception of life itself. To grow a vegetable, harvest it in its prime, and cook and eat it on *that* day is to relish food in a whole new way.

I thought that I had always eaten *intentionally* and valued the overall experience, but I was amazed at my increased appreciation of each plant, just because I had tended it as it grew and watched it carefully as it was more perfectly cooked. It looked better, tasted better, and even felt like a far better choice for my body.

From seed to soil to plate was now a continuous experience, and at no stage had I been indifferent. Of course, all this had taken time, and this is where I went from being amazed to becoming astounded.

I've always felt that I never had enough time for everything I've tried to do, and because of that stress, I've been robbed of the joy that comes from completing a job that I consider to be really well done. I've never enjoyed cutting corners, even though they may never be seen by a casual observer. But they would be more than obvious to me, the perpetrator, who must labor on and often leave a trail of regrets.

I've discovered that as a gardener, I really cannot cut corners. At least I can't if I want to grow the plants as naturally as possible. It takes time and effort, consistently applied. While there is a sacrifice, there is also the ample reward as the seed breaks open and new life appears and grows and grows—at times I've found it almost breathtaking . . . and yet it is slow, and it demands my patience and commitment.

I've described this for myself and others as the *speed of life*. And I've adjusted to that speed in my own day-to-day habits, and in many ways I've stopped trying to *win* the race with a competitive drive. It's enough for me that I can, with greater confidence, see a race—or way of life—marked out for me, and if I persevere and run it patiently, then I may be able to finish well, if not to finish first or even try to do so!

The Benefit to the Body

I've been on a consistent search for the past 38 years. It's not for the fountain of youth (I have no illusions about life's normal course); however, it has seemed only reasonable to want to be well enough to celebrate life and its opportunities for as long as possible.

So my search has been for my wife, Treena, who has been sick and wants to be well, and for myself, who is well and doesn't want to be sick. We have become partners in purpose where our goals overlap: simple, reasonable wellness.

I must now have read at least 600 research papers on the subject and followed the relevant nutritional and behavioral sciences closely. Everywhere I see a consistency—not in percentages of fats to calories and the like, which always seem to move up and down, albeit slightly, but in the apparent widespread benefits of the freshest and best (most natural and sustainable) vegetables and fruits. The more, it seems, the merrier!

Nudge-Nudge: The Law of
Intended Consequences

I've now lived long enough to have seen politicians manipulate the nutritional sciences by only gradually ratcheting up their recommendations for how many servings of fruits and vegetables we should consume each day. Exactly what is one serving is known by only less than 1 percent of the population, so either you are part of that small group or you will increase its membership by reading the following explanation:

> 1 serving = 100 grams

Scientists speak in grams because metric measurements are much less likely to cause error or misunderstanding. The cup measure can change in multiple ways, resulting in substantial changes in taste, texture, and nutrition. Sometime in the future, the United States may go metric; but in the meantime, let me translate those 100 grams into a measure that most readers will understand.

Try to get 100 grams (3.5 ounces) into a cup measure and it *almost* fills a half cup (usually 4 ounces). So, you see, consumers already have to make some adjustments to line up with the scientists—and those small adjustments can add up over time.

This is how most readers will understand a single serving size:

Diced hard fruits and vegetables	½ cup
Leafy greens (pressed down)	1 cup
100% fruit or vegetable juice (6 fluid ounces)	⅔ cup
Whole fruit (1 medium piece)	4 ounces
Dried fruit	¼ cup

½ cup

Let's see how this might work over a typical day of your life, adding up to 10–12 servings a day.

BREAKFAST

(Cereal with either)

1 banana = 1 serving

And/or ¼ cup dried fruit = 1 serving

And/or ½ cup berries = 1 serving

100% fruit juice, ¾ cup = 1 serving

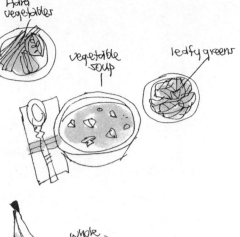

LUNCH

(Soup and/or Salad)

1 cup vegetable soup = 1–2 servings

1 cup leafy greens = 1 serving

½ cup hard vegetables (tomatoes, beets, celery,
   onions, etc.) = 1 serving

EVENING MEAL

½ cup vegetables = 1 serving

½ cup potatoes = 1 serving

DESSERT

½ cup berries (or other fruit) = 1 serving

The History

The U.S. government began to make quantitative suggestions about diet, including nutritional guidelines, in a white paper in 1974. The "5 A Day" program emerged from those suggestions. (It is noteworthy to record that Canada introduced a program calling for 9 servings a day around the same time.) Now fast-forward to the recent OmniHeart Study and the recommendation for 11 servings a day.

All of these visionary objectives should be compared to the present estimated actual U.S. consumption of 3.5 servings, one of which is said to be french fries.

Upon review, I'd call this a fairly typical example of "Nudge-nudge, wink-wink . . . say no more," to co-opt the famous line from *Monty Python's Flying Circus*.

Recently, one of President Obama's largely behind-the-scenes advisers coauthored a book called *Nudge*, which suggests that government's role is to encourage change with gentle pressure through small positive legislative initiatives (nudges) that will get the greater ball of intended consequences moving in a positive direction.

Hence, we used to consume 3 servings and we have been "nudged" by 5- or 9- or 11-a-day programs to arrive at only 3.5 servings in 2010!

The Canadian program resulted in 4.964 servings a day in 2008, up from 4.277 servings in 1974—almost 1⅔ servings more than the U.S. achievement during the same period.

I wonder where we would be now if we had grasped the nettle that science understood and began in 1974 with a "9 A Day" program. As it now stands, we apparently need to increase our consumption from 3.5 to 9–11 servings, which is at least a 300 percent increase. The consequences for such an increase could be interesting. For example:

■ We would become substantially part-vegetarian. Meat (and its saturated fat levels) would fall by at least 50 percent, as they have in my household.

■ Low-density lipoprotein (LDL) cholesterol levels would fall, along with triglycerides, and high-density lipoprotein (HDL) levels would rise, reducing heart disease.

- We would likely lose weight, reducing type 2 diabetes.

- We might also see a reduction in some cancers.

It is instructive to look at a major study (Adventist Health Study-2, 1976–1988) conducted among California Seventh-Day Adventists, who practice a predominantly vegetarian lifestyle. (The results were quite similar to other Adventist groups worldwide.) Among their vegetarian members, researchers noted increased longevity compared to the general population of the state. The men and women lived 9.1 and 6.1 years longer, respectively. In another study, California Seventh-Day Adventists were shown to take fewer medications and had fewer overnight hospital stays and surgical procedures. Based on a 1992 comparison, they were the longest living formally described population in the world.

Since we as a nation are trying to reduce our healthcare costs, it is clear that the adoption of such a lifestyle, even if modified, could cause substantial economic savings. However, could we produce enough plants to meet such a goal? The answer is a qualified yes, but other major changes would be required, among which would be:

- A vast increase in fresh and best in season (FABIS)—that is, locally grown, sustainable food

- A conversion of monocrops into multicropping

- Smaller farms using intensive agricultural techniques and marketing concepts, such as community supported agriculture (CSA)

- Projects in urban settings (in the 1800s, 6 percent of Paris consisted of kitchen gardens)

These changes would open up small-scale farming to millions of people who may prefer to live a simpler life to that offered in the high-tech, high-pressured, and polluted urban sprawl. Such change would reduce carbon emissions because local and smaller producers use less oil. But it would also increase the price to the consumer. As prices rose, so would the number of people who saw the advantage of growing their own. And such a movement would give birth to a whole raft of revived industries, from seed producers to nurseries, greenhouses, natural fertilizers, and garden tools.

There seems little doubt that such a domino effect would result in us eating better and eating less. By doing so, we might live longer, healthier, and more active lives, with much lower healthcare costs.

Utopian? Well, yes, I suppose so, but isn't that really more appropriate than the "Nudge-nudge, wink-wink . . . say no more" that, with its political procrastination, seems to have had barely any impact on our ever-increasing addiction to convenience and to pharmaceuticals to somehow keep us going?

Add to the swing toward plant life the concept of reduced portions—*especially as we age*—and the business of eating is ripe for massive change.

Changing a food habit, however, is considered by some experts to be harder than breaking a heroin addiction—largely because we *must* continue to eat!

One thing that may help us is a random factor that would appear to be just over the horizon but surely coming soon to a table like yours: our economy and the impact of higher oil prices on our artificially low food prices. When we get substantially higher gas prices, the present road transport system that brings produce over a thousand miles in the off-season may well be severely curtailed, and local, sustainable, seasonal agriculture may take its place.

Even then, the actual farming overhead costs will become painfully obvious,

Yeah, give me a cauliflower, a couple of rhutabagas and some rhubarb

and when that happens, the kitchen garden may well be the most logical and cost-effective way to go.

By the mid-2010s, say 2015–2017, I strongly suspect that we will see a definite return to home-grown vegetables and, along with that change, an improvement in the quality of the lives we have left.

To some degree, I'm now in the midst of making that change, and in every sense, it's really working out just fine. I didn't make the change out of a fear of the future, but rather out of the certain knowledge that tomorrow's communities will be much more independently sustainable for their food supplies, and I simply wanted to know what would need to be done to help it along.

CHAPTER THREE

My Need-to-Know List

I know of literally dozens of great books on gardening that go to enormous lengths to cover the fascinating subject of growing your own food. They appear to leave nothing out, and there—especially for the novice gardener—lies the problem.

For me, all the available information was overkill. To settle down to read a book on improving soil that had at least 50,000 words (the size of this entire book) was more than I could do in year one. Although I do intend to read it later, what I wanted in the short term was sufficient guidance to keep me out of trouble and bring me enough reward to fuel a lasting enthusiasm to know more and to keep on digging!

I reduced my need-to-know list to a baker's dozen of topics, which I believe most novice gardeners—and not a few more experienced ones—will find of primary interest:

1. **Soil:** how to sample, test for pH, adjust for rainfall runoff
2. **Turf:** preparation and removal

3. **Soil Improvement:** fertilizer, soil-less mixes, manure, stones
4. **Raised Beds:** layout, pathways, crop plan, critter control
5. **EarthBox:** containers, operation, location
6. **Seed Germination and Vegetable Starts:** how-to, care
7. **Transplanting:** when, how
8. **Watering:** how much, how often
9. **Feeding:** how much, when
10. **Pest Control and Plant Diseases:** organic-related, main concerns, evidence
11. **Composting:** using leftovers, preparing for next season
12. **Seasonal Replanting:** getting a second crop
13. **The Greenhouse:** size, location, layout, operation

These subjects became my game plan, and my *local knowledge* gardeners guided me in their practical application. Nothing was theoretical; it was all hands-on practical.

So, this is where I record what I did and provide you with references and recommendations to get you started on your own quest. You may even want to take my topic checklist to your own *local knowledge* kitchen gardeners, who will have had experience with your particular microclimate.

1. Soil

Scott Titus, my neighborhood soil expert, arrived at our soggy site in early March carrying what looked like a giant apple corer. He proceeded to plunge it into several parts of our lawn and deposited these earthen cores into a plastic bag, to be sent away for analysis.

On our property, the soil depth, before reaching substantial stones, was less than 10 inches. There was also green plastic netting, used by sod farmers to hold together the instant lawn, that had been there for eight years.

We've got clay and some silt, so the ground's wet, and our driveway slopes, dumping all the surface water directly onto our sunny gardening site.

Our first task was to redirect the surface water by digging out an 8-inch-deep trench to intercept the runoff. We buried a 4-inch perforated drainage pipe and then covered it in ½-inch gravel. All this is what I was told is called a *French drain*. Exactly why it's French I've been unable to discover. Everyone with an English background usually questions why things are dubbed "French"!

Our lawn/soil turned out to be pH 5.77, quite possibly because of the leaching effect of rain over the concrete driveway. (For more on pH, see "Feeding" on page 35.) At this stage I wanted a sustainable garden in which I'd do my best naturally, but I also didn't want to fail by immediately pursuing an organic-only project and risking my already fragile expectations of success.

I began with the thought that I might have to use some chemical intervention to avoid yet another failure in my hitherto history of gardening misdeeds. As it turned out, going organic was less of a problem and more of a benefit. Healthy soil begets healthy plants.

I have now read enough about soil to be better informed and yet still relatively clueless. I know enough to be awestruck at the complexity of nature and convinced that I need to do much more to leave it alone!

I have neither the space nor the expertise (yet) to give you specific guidance on how to adjust your own share of the 7 inches of topsoil that wrap our world in the raw material of life itself, because without it all life would fail. What I can do is share my enthusiasm to know more and then do more to preserve the soil . . . the way it was designed to function.

The word *natural* has, like all good, simple words, been abused until almost unrecognizable. The natural world is, to my mind, that which is left entirely on its own.

We have an island close to our home called Camano. The First Nation peoples of the Northwest used to call it the Island of the Berries. They would come by canoe to harvest natural berries that had survived, even flourished, without the slightest intervention by humankind.

The moment that we clear that kind of land and even scratch the surface, it ceases to be natural. We have disturbed the natural habitat of a whole ecosystem of truly abundant, vigorous, and sustainable life.

Now I'm also a realist, and I understand that the growing population needs to be fed and sheltered and must therefore displace the natural order to some degree. I've been told that if the present 1–2 percent of organically farmed produce were to become the norm, then we would need about 40 million people to return to the soil as a full-time way of life.

Neither is even a remote possibility, but we can still move in that direction as we become convinced of its basic good sense.

As a result of my personal research, I've become convinced enough to find out what I need to know in order to do what I need to do to return my own small garden space, as near as possible, to a natural habitat, where healthy plants grow without necessarily growing faster or larger than those of my neighbors.

Surely we can admire each other's gardens without entering into yet another commercially inspired competition?

What I now know and am endeavoring to apply in my second year is quite basic, but it has allowed me to undertake a bold experiment. I really want to have an abundant garden that owes its vitality to very few inputs that have been contrived by man.

In a real sense, I want it to mimic what Treena and I try to do with our pharmaceuticals. There are medications that we understand are necessary for Treena (so far no prescription drugs for me). That means it's on an individual basis, in the same way your soil is quite likely to be different from mine—and even different from one side of your property to the other!

Notwithstanding those often quite sharp differences, there are some similarities; just as both Treena and I need protein, carbohydrates, and fats, so do our soils need nitrogen, potassium, and phosphate.

On a much smaller scale, there are also micronutrients that play as important a part as do vitamins, minerals, and antioxidants.

The plants that grow in our increasingly rich soil will draw energy and health from this abundant goodness. The same plants will eventually become our nutrition. It must therefore be obvious that a best-practices, "deep" organic garden will be the best possible choice for our daily food.

So now, may I encourage you to explore what *your* soil needs in order to be well suited to growing nourishing vegetables!

So what if there are more than 5,000 chemicals added to our food that are generally regarded as safe (GRAS) until occasionally proven unsafe? What if they gradually accumulate in certain tissues throughout my body? How does this affect my enjoyment of food?

Answer: If I grew my own with minimal input, as in low-input sustainable agriculture (LISA), I could eat with a smile on my face.

2. Turf

The first challenge in preparing for our garden was to deal with the grass, or rather the dandelion patch that passed for a lawn. I began to kill it with an organic preparation, but that showed no apparent effect. Scott suggested Roundup. At this stage it felt like every good intention to go organic had just evaporated. How could I use *that* stuff on a kitchen garden? I was given to understand that there was no risk because Roundup's active ingredients have a relatively short half-life, and I had no living edible plant even close to the patch. Ironically, I had to fertilize the grass first to get it to grow vigorously before adding Roundup, so that it would more effectively kill the grass, roots and all. (As a Scot, I found the additional cost for fertilizer hard to take, but I did what I was told.)

Within a week, my lawn was dead. I had succeeded in my very first task of killing everything on site in a very inorganic way. Not exactly what I had imagined!

I need to add, at this point, that I didn't know that I could have achieved the same result by covering the area with large sheets of cardboard, the kind that protect mattresses in transit. I've since experimented with that method, and it does work over time. Allow 2–3 months to effectively smother an area. The cardboard will decompose, adding another layer of organic material.

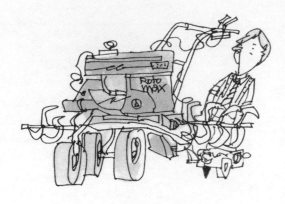

When the entire grass area was certified as truly dead, the next step was to churn up the whole mess.

Our soil was wet clay with a dense dead topping—sounds almost like a commercially packaged carrot cake!—and needed at least an 8-inch scoop. My pal at the rent-all place recommended a 9-horsepower rototiller that weighed in at about 200 pounds! It arrived on a flatbed truck, and after a very brief demonstration, the rental man left with the encouraging words, "My wife used it last week, and she's only five feet four. She found it easy." And he was gone. The machine sat there solidly, and I imagined that it was growling at me, but then I have a rather active imagination when it comes to machinery, with which I have had some issues in the past.

I managed to get this monster started and engaged the forward gear. As the tiller blades flashed down, my rental beast leaped forward, pawing at the ground like a bull in search of a matador. As this massive, self-willed machine dug in, it started to gather speed, heading down our steeply sloping land, coming perilously close to the edge. My feet sank into the slippery, freshly turned clay as I reached wildly for the kill button, within only a foot or so of the point of no return. The monster died among the dead grass. I breathed deeply; the monster steamed silently.

I had obviously taken on more than the machine could chew. Always the optimist—and forever in search of my local knowledge experts when my own intelligence fails me—I remembered my neighbor Kurt, a tall, broad-backed guy who also happened to drive a backhoe. So together we manhandled the beast around and around the lawn, which now looked like a scene from a World War I movie: dead grass garnished with bright green plastic netting set against a slick mud gray background relieved only by the odd startled worm.

We had begun to prepare the soil!

I was left wondering how anything that wet gets to be dry enough to even look like plantable soil.

"Cover it with plastic sheeting. The sun will warm the earth and evaporate the moisture," suggested Scott. And so I draped the whole thing and dumped stray timbers on it to hold the plastic down. The sun disappeared—it does that for months on end in the Pacific Northwest—and it rained hard, which it also does, and then it blew a gale. The plastic blew off, and the rain saturated the ground. I eventually found and replaced the plastic and nailed it down with wooden stakes.

It rained for days; a weak sun got the soil temperature just over 60°F. At least the runoff was redirected through the French drain.

I learned later on in the year that the drying out of such soggy soil is hastened by removing the plastic in the early afternoon to let the steam roll off and then replacing it just before sunset.

3. Soil Improvement

We ordered 2 yards of steer manure and six bags of Coco-Coir; sprinkled it liberally over the clay; rented a small, almost feminine rototiller; and proceeded to mix it all up into what looked like a wild rice pilaf that had been left on the stove way too long! We bounced the clumped clay up and down using a six-pronged composting fork, removing stones and bits of green netting, gradually reducing the clumps to a rough granular texture. Finally, we nailed the plastic sheeting back in place with long wooden pegs and prayed for the sun.

In a real sense, this was an emergency action designed to move from sod to kitchen-garden-ready in one fell swoop. There would be more to come, as discussed under "Feeding" on page 35.

4. Raised Beds

When I first heard the term *raised beds*, my mind raced to multiple berths in World War II troop ships and then straight on to wooden-sided grow beds made with railroad ties (so popular in urban landscaping in the 1970s) or even adobe bricks. But my friend Scott Titus isn't at all shy about any of his choices. "I won't have a piece of stone in my garden, and I also avoid large lumps of wood," he declared. "Keep it as natural as possible. Build the beds with earth. It's much easier to manage."

graham and Treendis first attempt at raised beds

And so out went the *Better Homes and Gardens*–inspired brick or crazy paver pathways; the 2-foot-wide pathways between the beds would be covered in 2–3 inches of cedar sawdust. The beds would be a reachable width, which to my stretch (with a moderately poor back) was 3 feet.

Our plot of land enjoys mostly all-day sun, except a small shed casts some shade—perhaps the right place for peas and lettuce?

Around this neck of the woods (why do we say *neck*?), folks try to get their vegetable starts in the soil around Memorial Day (in late May), and this became our goal.

We drew out a plan (see the illustration on page 25), drove in some stakes at carefully measured intervals, strung some line, and began to fork the somewhat dried-out earth into heaps, which began to take on the shape of raised beds.

It was at this stage that I fully understood Charles Dudley Warner's 1870 dictum: "What a man needs in gardening is a cast-iron back, with a hinge on it." Scott Titus brought the saying up-to-date with his take on the labor of digging: "I take three Tylenol *before* I begin!"

My efforts paled alongside those of Scott, who appeared to be tireless and at

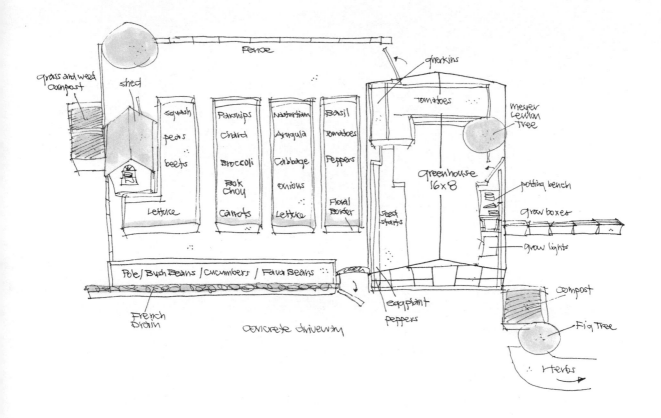

the same time fully engaged in bringing some form out of chaos. The most physical effort I've undertaken over the past many years has been wielding a pen and a whisk. Mid bend I wondered if I was, in fact, digging my own grave. (Later, the effort lessened as my body adapted and gained both flexibility and strength. For both, I am amazed and grateful!)

When all the beds were mildly raised, we covered them again with plastic to rid the soil mix of its additional wetness, since it had rained solidly during the entire exercise. Then we got the 3 yards of cedar sawdust for filling in the pathways. My but it looked good when dry and yellow, but then, this too would pass! We determined the locations of the plants we'd try and stepped out the fence line we'd need to keep the critters out.

Enter my next new friend: Richard Mattreus, a local expert at excluding deer, rabbits, and other charming wildlife that were well

fence to keep the critters out

used to our property. For them it was like an African wild game park without boundaries—a place to eat every one of Treena's roses and rub their antlers on our new apple trees, having first snacked on the fruit.

We strung 8-foot-wide plastic netting on 12-foot-high posts. "Deer have bad eyesight," explained Richard. "They see the posts and assume the net goes that high." We buried 12 inches of net (for the critters that like to burrow) and put in a solid pair of gates.

Now we could plant!

5. EarthBox

For several years I've served as a member on a United Nations advisory board called the Growing Connection. Our focus has been on equipping villagers 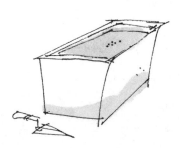 and their schools with devices that grow abundant food with very low water use. Clearly sub-Saharan Africa was central to our concern, but so were other drought-stricken areas around the globe. The sturdy plastic box (28×14×10 inches) has a perforated floor above a water reservoir, a filler tube, an overflow, and a plastic shower cap.

Its sister box, made for the U.S. market, comes complete with castors, earth, and fertilizer, and very good, simple instructions. In a matter of minutes you can be in business, growing a small crop of edibles in a very limited space that gets 7 or more hours of sun on a clear day.

I included this concept in my most-wanted list because it occurred to me that there might be a lot of people like me who feel the growing urge but who may not be ready to tackle a bigger project or may simply not have the space. The Earth-Box can provide that perfect solution. The small crops and very low maintenance make an excellent way of getting a taste for the difference that fresh makes.

In my first year, I used two boxes in the greenhouse (although they can be used outside as soon as the weather permits). I filled one with the provided soil and fertilizer and the other, by way of my own need to experiment, with Coco-Coir and Intrepid organic fertilizer. I put three identical tomato starts in each box. (I did this to test the included fertilizer against my own input into my own soil selection. I wanted to be able to continue to use the container without depending on the manufacturer's special extras.) The only difference was that I placed the box in which I'd used the Coco-Coir mixture closer to the sun.

My experiment was interesting. I got more pounds of fruit earlier from the Coco-Coir box. From the box using the supplied provisions, I got huge vigorous growth but a little less fruit. Next year I'll put them side by side, so that they get equal sun exposure.

I also planted a cluster of lettuces—red leaf, oak leaf, romaine (cos), and curly endive—in one EarthBox and filled two others with basil and late-season strawberries. Everything burst forth and was, to my mind, hugely successful. I should add that the instructions are very clear, but I still didn't get everything right. I put too many tomatoes in each box. Two plants is plenty; three get in each other's way.

One of my pals, an expert in all things, had never worked with an EarthBox before and so mixed the fertilizer into the potting mix instead of laying it in a shal-

Two's company...

graham and his
Earth Box

low trench, as clearly specified. The result was a massive jungle and less fruit! So please do exactly as the instructions say.

The third error, another of mine, was to leave off the plastic caps on two tomato boxes; this greatly increased evaporation and provided an open breeding ground for unwanted insects. The rest were covered and used much less water and showed fewer signs of pests.

It looks so simple—and it is—so don't cut corners and potentially miss out on the real thrill these boxes provide. These boxes would be especially good if you live in the city and want to introduce your children to gardening.

6. Seed Germination and Vegetable Starts

Since this was my first year, I had, of course, no prior experience with seeds that succeeded. While I focused my attention on finding heirloom seeds for produce with great tastes and textures, my local knowledge pals were more concerned with myriad sustainability issues.

A tomato, for example, had to fit our short growing season and resist certain diseases and pests that love the Pacific Northwest as much as we do. Viva Italia tomatoes resist blight (a common problem caused by late summer showers), but they are a Roma (plum) that ripens en masse, unlike the Brandywine cultivar—a large, rudely shaped fleshy tomato with a deep passionate sweetness—which maintains its greenness until the season is almost over.

Time was against us, so we used the seeds that were known to work well—and taste and texture were left for a time when I would have more experience. Hence, my seed choices for next year will be made with the help of a local heirloom seed provider, having due regard for the microclimate we worked with this year. Of course, once the selection is made, the rest of the handling is basically the same.

The seed packet tells us all we need to know (or should do), and once again, be sure to follow the fine print. For example, I purchased seed for Scarlet Nantes carrots. The packet told me it would take the seeds about 2 weeks to germinate at 60°F and 68 days to mature. They went into the bed in May, just after Memorial Day, and were wonderfully ready (if not fully grown) by mid-July—just 60 days.

I was told to plant 2–4 inches apart in my 3-foot-wide row. So I went for 3 inches (ever the middle-of-the-road decision!). I thinned them when the tops reached 4 inches, allowing about 2 inches between the remaining plants.

Now comes the tough part. Here are all these growing baby carrots, and I was ripping them out to make room for their fellows to mature. What I'm pleased about is that it felt bad, so it wasn't done without emotion, but I was able to use all of the thinned-out plants in my rapidly increasing compost.

The package went on to tell me that I could plant carrots every 2–3 weeks for a continual harvest up until mid-July, to have fresh supplies in the fall and winter.

The seed packs for other plants can have all manner of coded messages that relate to hybrids or heirlooms and disease *resistance* rather than complete *avoidance*.

I'm really excited about the years that I hope spin out ahead of me, because each year I'll keep the packages on file and journal each plant's progress until I've matched up my little microclimate to the taste I find most satisfactory.

I have been the happy—although sometimes late—recipient of excellent advice about greenhouse and indoor seed germination and the journey to the great outdoors, which I pass along in "byte"-size pieces. There is no specific need for a greenhouse. Seeds can be started on window ledges from February on. All my notes are equally applicable.

■ **Pots:** You can reuse old plastic pots, but you must wash them well in detergent with a little bleach. You can also use paper cups that are biodegradable. (I think

that clay pots are too expensive for this phase and take up too much storage space out of season.)

- **Potting Soil:** Purchase a good potting soil from your garden center. Alternatively, you can sterilize garden soil. Place the soil in an aluminum foil roasting pan to 3 inches in depth, cover with foil, and bake at 200°F for 20 minutes—at which point all disease and seeds are dead, and your soil is ready to use without contaminants, weeds, or other un-wanted seeds. Or place the garden soil in about 2-pound batches in an unsealed plastic roasting bag, and microwave each bag for 3 minutes. It'll create a horrid smell, but it is fast and effective. Before planting, do a porosity test. Start with damp soil in a small pot. Add water to the top of the pot and count slowly to five. If the water drains in 3–4 seconds, the soil is too porous. If it takes 7–8 seconds, it's too dense. That's one reason I like to use the Coco-Coir: it drains perfectly every time, and it's more like the consistency of the raised-bed soil, into which the seedlings will be transplanted.

- **Planting Depth:** The rule of thumb is the smaller the seed, the shallower the planting depth. That means that the seeds should be planted at a depth of about two to three times their width.

- **Watering:** Keep the planted seeds moistened by misting, not flooding, until just gently dampened. I have a 2-quart misting jar that pumps up a small pressure and does the job very well. I've added a timer mister system (see page 34), so we'll see how this pans out. Frequent misting also prevents the thin layer of soil that covers the seeds from drying out, which robs the soil of the moisture it needs to give the seeds a good start.

- **Drainage:** All my pots and trays have drain holes, allowing for the regular mist-ing (twice a day) not to accumulate and permitting the seeds to breath. I found this

graham learns the hard way about flooding the plants..

concept hard to grasp; surely when smothered in soil there's no air? But here I was so wrong: the whole point of fine soil is that there is plenty of air, providing it isn't saturated with water that has nowhere to drain.

■ **Temperature:** To keep the germinating seeds at the right temperature, you can use a specially designed heat-pad arrangement that is thoroughly waterproof (don't use the one you bought for that back pain!) and linked to a temperature-sensing device, allowing you to regulate the soil temperature. There's a range between 63°F and 75°F that works best on vegetable seeds. All you have to do is set your tray of freshly planted seeds directly on top of the waterproof pad and plunge the ceramic sensor into one of the small pots. When the soil temperature reaches 70°F, the pad will turn off; it'll kick back on when the soil cools slightly.

■ **Light:** Some seeds, especially really small ones like lettuce, need some kind of light source to help them germinate. Without light they will emerge, but they reach out for whatever glimmer they see and get tall and straggly instead of developing sturdy stems. Good greenhouse centers have excellent *safe* grow lights, very important in a watery environment!

plant searching for light

■ **Feeding:** At their earliest stage, the seed has its own life support system and needs no added boost from outside until it has six leaves. It is at this time that the transplanting should take place.

7. Transplanting

Once I have a greenhouse or a sunny indoor window ledge, I can program my seed-starting schedule backward from the approximate date that a seedling can be put out in the raised bed. I say *approximate* because so much depends on local conditions that hard and fast dates don't always work. Take Swiss chard, for example:

Plant in raised bed: May 20–30

Harden off (discussed in a bit): May 13–17

Early growth (about 6 weeks): April 15–20

Germinate seeds: early March indoors, in a greenhouse, in a heated cold frame, or on a sunny windowsill

My good friends advised me to always wait for the first true leaves after the *cotyledons* drop before attempting any transplant. "The what?" I questioned, as if those "coties" (as I called them) were some kind of elfin brigade that shelter under toadstools in a downpour and function like helpful bacteria.

I learned that these are the very first, purely altruistic leaves, which are used as food by the emerging, growing plant. They often turn yellow and fall off after giving their lives for the true leaves that follow.

Having just enough space in their 2-inch-square plastic pots, the seedlings begin their 4–12 weeks of growth. Some of the larger species may need a second

home in a 4-inch pot. If so, grab the seedling by its leaf, never by the stalk (a crushed stalk is often terminal; a crushed leaf is expendable). Ease it out of moist soil and very carefully tease the roots away from a close neighbor's roots, and make a suitable hole (about the size of a medium cigar) for the roots and the soil clinging to them. And again, gently shift the earth to cover the roots well and then mist the new arrival.

When it's time to shift the starts outdoors, the plants may need to be hardened off. This takes about 1 week. The plants need to be exposed to wind and sun after their greenhouse home, but they should be sheltered from direct sun and need *less* watering, *never* more! They need oxygen around their roots, and overwatering starves them of air and makes their leaves go yellow.

Seed packets list the amount of sun needed and how to sow the seeds, including distance apart and depth. This is all well and good, but like everything in our nanosecond world, the information is too abbreviated.

I wanted more—really, as much as I could take! Fortunately, I found the Harvest to Table website (www.harvesttotable.com) and the admirable Stephen Albert, who has boldly gone where nobody (that I can find) has gone before: he has listed more than 30 need-to-know specifications that help the novice and expert alike. For all my selections, I had done 6 weeks of research on my 60 plants before even ordering his *Kitchen Garden Grower's Guide*. I could have saved so much time, but it is a great source for confirming sometimes conflicting data!

In my first year, I adopted a kind of all-at-once approach to sowing directly into the raised bed just after Memorial Day. I marked out rows 4 inches apart *across* my 3-foot-wide beds and sowed carrot, parsnip, Swiss chard, and beets. They all flourished and left no room for weeds, but they were so difficult to thin!

I talked this over with Scott Titus, and we decided to change the direction

and plant in longer rows (north–south) instead of short (east–west) rows. That should make thinning easier because one could reach a long line with greater consistency.

8. Watering

If you listen to Pacific Northwest stories about our annual rainfall, you might wonder why watering was even on my radarscope (so to speak). Well, this past year was a triumph—lots and lots of sun. My friend Scott called it "the best growing year I've ever experienced"—and here I had thought it was my newfound skills!

Regardless of my soil's natural tendency to retain water, I did need a regular supply of water about twice per week. Since I had a pre-existing sprinkler on a timer for the grass, I found yet another local expert to adjust the coverage to match the planting choices I had made in each bed I had prepared.

A few plants, like beets, did better receiving misting from above, but most of my plants benefited from ground up watering. We thought about this as we did the overall plan and decided to use drip irrigation, three lines to a 4-foot-wide bed.

It all worked out fine except for the large winter squash leaves, which eventually developed a powdery mildew because they had already gotten too much overhead water (a situation not helped by the fact that they were growing in partial shade, which is not advised).

My suggestion is to get advice from someone who really knows, and bite the bullet on cost. Once it's done—and you understand what was done and why—then your approach to watering can remain flexible year after year with only you in charge.

In the greenhouse, it was more complex. I put in a special timer and rigged an irrigation line into which I could tap a variety of misting or drip feeds. It took time, but it will be much better than having to ask our neighbor to fill in for me when I find myself away from home for any length of time.

At this point I need to speak in a LOUDER VOICE because it's *so* important.

Because I'm on the road unpredictably, I had always dismissed the idea of an edible garden and greenhouse because they would need attention, especially proper watering on a daily basis. But with a good timer and both light and heat sensors, the plants will still get their basic daily attention, albeit mechanically (and, perhaps, more reliably).

graham speaking with a louder voice

You've already made an investment (especially if you've got a greenhouse), so go the extra mile on the watering system and see that it's done right! However, don't allow automation to take over. Your plants need your personal attention.

My last units that needed watering were the EarthBoxes, which I watered by hand each day through the box's reservoir filler tube. There is an automatic overflow system to prevent overwatering that worked fine, but since the boxes need help when unattended, I linked them into the greenhouse irrigation device to eliminate a potential source of failure.

9. Feeding

With the watering working well, I then had to turn to a far more complex issue: feeding. My local knowledge experts told me that there were two major errors made by gardeners: adding too much or too little fertilizer. I found this unhelpful. "So," I asked, "what is the Goldilocks quantity—the *just right* amount?"

"It depends," they replied.

And so it went on—with me getting no wiser and, if anything, more confused!

Goldilocks

Too Little   Too much   Just Right

I know that my body needs a mix of pro-tein, carbohydrates, and fats, and over the years I've learned enough to adjust how much of each I eat, but I don't do this by numbers. I've learned to size it up with my eyes, and I know what a portion of leafy greens looks like (it's a cupful when pressed down lightly) or what a ¼ cup of raisins looks like or a medium apple. Since I weigh myself daily, I know if my calorie intake and energy output is balanced (or unbalanced).

So, since *I* seem to be doing okay, why shouldn't I think of my plants in the same way and avoid confusion?

There is one single marker for the Goldilocks equation, and that's pH, a scale measuring from 0 to 14, with 0 representing pure acid and 14 representing pure lye. The neutral point is, logically, 7.

Wouldn't it be nice if all plants loved growing in neutral soil? Unfortunately, they do not. But here we can still pull off a reasonable compromise, since most plants do well enough between 5.5 and 7.5. (A notable exception is the potato, which requires a pH of between 4.8 and 6.5, but which I don't plant in my garden due to lack of space.)

At the very least you should get a start-out baseline reading of your soil (see page 18) and perhaps an annual check up in the late fall, when most of the har-vesting has been done. A 1-pint sample is enough, taken from several parts of the garden from holes dug down 6–8 inches and scraped from the wall of the hole in a thin downward slice. Consult your local county extension agent or refer to the Yellow Pages under "Soil Testing" to find out where and how to send your samples.

I was told to add peat moss or good compost to add acidity and ground lime-stone to increase alkalinity. But frankly, this is where I bowed to my friends and their local knowledge. Most textbooks speak of 50–80 pounds of lime to change 1,000 square feet of soil by 1 pH point (from 5.5 to 6.5, for instance), but that's not what I saw being done. Because I've got only about 400 square feet of raised beds, I figured that 10 pounds would do it, but Scott did it by eye (like I eat), and it was more like 7 pounds, according to my obsessive–compulsive observation! This is another of those areas where local knowledge is king. No amount of technical estimation can take the place of experienced organic growers in your area who work with similar soil and climate.

Scott added fertilizer with the same practical eye and told me to watch the leaves. "If they yellow, feed 'em." He handed me a container of his own organic fertilizer, Intrepid, and left. (Should you be unable to find his fertilizer, I'm sure you'll be able to locate a good natural alternative at your nearest nursery supply store.)

In my search for what (on earth!) to do next, I ran headlong into a whole catalog full of nifty instruments that promised to take all the guesswork out of watering and feeding. You just stick the various pronged devices into the soil and, bingo, they tell you what to do. My first reaction was relief. At least I've got a solution! But I had learned through ample experience not to jump at technology on its face (advertised) value. I decided to think it through for a couple of days before ordering.

One week later I was convinced that I'd prefer to follow the billions of farmers who observe how their plants are doing and through years of experience know instinctively how to respond. If I began my journey with a reliance on high tech, it might mean that I'd never know what "high touch" was like—and machines would have created a dependency that could have reduced my direct involvement with the plants, which I'd gain through observation. So I decided to buy the tester and do *both* and keep a good record.

Over the first year, I added fertilizer twice—about 5 weeks apart—using beet leaves, Swiss chard, and peppers as a visual guide. If their leaves wilted and discolored, I responded. I added a third feeding for the winter squash.

I also tried a fish-based liquid (see the Glossary on page 58) that comes in concentrated form. Just add water and apply every couple of weeks. I'd walk about with a long wand-like watering device attached to a pressurized tank, directing the spray just at the union between soil and plant. Since my plants flourished, I can only assume this helped.

So far, this observation with technical support has worked, but I'm still feeling the need to more clearly understand how to give my plants the best feeding possible within natural sustainable guidelines.

My local knowledge friends tell me that I may never really understand, because the health of an individual plant can be affected by weather, pests, and windborne disease, and the best soil in the world, while it will definitely help, isn't an absolute guarantee of a healthy plant.

So I observe and I measure and I record the results. I'm concerned. I weed and I feed, and in so doing, I've discovered a truly rewarding connection to my garden.

10. Pest Control and Plant Diseases

Of course, I'm not the only one who looks hungrily at my beautiful plants. There's an army out there with tiny legs, furry bodies, scampering feet, fluttering wings, and bright slimy trails.

Since we have deer and rabbits, we put up a fence with 12-foot-high posts and 8-foot-high plastic netting. As I mentioned earlier, I'm told that deer have poor eyesight and see only the 12-foot posts, not the top of the net at only 8 feet. We also buried 2 feet of plastic netting in a trench, since, I am told, rabbits don't burrow any deeper than 2 feet.

Slugs can be drowned in beer (an apparently organic death) by setting out small paper cups of your least favorite brew on their happy trails. A simpler answer is Sluggo, an aptly named organic substance.

I was advised to patrol the garden each morning and look out for bugs 'n' beetles on and under leaves. These can be handpicked into a small pail and destroyed. As it happens, I usually take a morning walk in the longer-light days at 8 a.m. and simply extended my routine with a 10-minute patrol.

I've also been introduced to orange sticky cards to catch small flying pests like aphids and white flies. I've also used diluted neem oil as greenhouse spray—especially on tomatoes. This spray worked well—though, once again, don't expect perfection. Absolute death to all critters means using chemicals that kill the good and the bad and may even accumulate in fat cells in your own body. A good home remedy is boiling two cigarettes in some beer, straining it well, and spraying it on the leaves; nicotine kills!

There are any number of reasons why plants fail—both obvious (lack of water or fertilizer) and mysterious (diseases). There is no real alternative to *observation*, and nothing beats a brief daily inspection.

If a plant looks strange compared to its neighbors—shriveled darkened leaves, all droopy and tired—and I can't determine any specific reason, I pull it out, put it into a plastic bag, and take it immediately to our local extension service to get an opinion. Just like a person with the flu, a diseased plant may be contagious and *must* be removed, but you can learn why it suffered and perhaps prevent the mishap from spreading.

11. Composting

Now here's a subject that every green-minded reader will find essential: what to do with the heap of discarded leaves, old root stock, stalks and vegetable trimmings, coffee grounds, and tea bags—those by-products of growing and cooking that made up my own ever-mounting compost heap. Frankly, I simply assumed that any organic material would rot if I left it alone. But it didn't work out that way!

At first, I was more concerned about the aesthetics of my compost, in that my initial pile at one end of the garden looked untidy. So I asked Richard, who had done such a good job building the fence and gates, if he could build me a two-bin unit outside

compost pile

the fenced area, behind the greenhouse. He managed to find some discarded mahogany and built it with slats that allowed air circulation. This worked out to be cheaper than some of the plastic tumbler bins.

With all well and good, I began to pile in the waste—avoiding weeds with seeds, meat, and fat. This was a vegan heap!

I knew enough to understand that for the bacteria to work, the compost needed air and moisture. So I sprayed the heap each morning and plunged my spade through it on an almost daily basis. Still, after a time there didn't seem to be signs of decomposition. I was getting anxious.

Scott Titus suggested I add some of his miraculous fertilizer, but it didn't seem to do the trick either. At least I needed signs of it heating up.

It was time to rethink the pile-it-all-on process I'd adopted, so I had to find a way to mix the compost up and get the larger pieces much smaller. I eventually found a tree nursery that had a small chipper; I blended the whole pile with 2 yards of good topsoil—what a splendid sight.

To avoid having to rent a chipper in the future, I began to use an old kitchen blender set aside for this purpose to mix up kitchen scraps, tea bags, and so on. When the container looked fairly full, I simply added water, ran it on the mix setting for a couple of minutes, poured it onto the heap, and raked it into the compost.

Try building your compost in three layers. Scratch up the bare soil to allow the microorganisms an easy route to gain access to the party, then pile on kitchen waste, weeds, leaves, and other garden trash on top of a gallon of rotted manure. Try for a recipe based on 1 gallon of scraps to 1½ bushels (12 gallons) of leaves and grass clippings. Then add 1 cup of lime, 1 cup of bonemeal, and 2 shovelfuls of soil.

It helps if you shred harder organic matter like pruned twigs. This can be done by lowering a rotary lawn mower onto a pile of leaves (for example) and letting the machine eject the shreds against a hard upright surface or carton to be easily collected. Be sure to wear gloves, safety glasses, and long slacks.

As you put your compost together, be sure to spray each layer with water, as it needs to be damp throughout. It's described as 50 percent moisture, but I don't know how that can be measured other than being just . . . damp!

There only remains the need for air. I recommend the use of a composting pole (for example, the compost aerator from www.territorialseed.com). It has a pair of folding hinged blades that drive easily into the heap and then open up on their way out to aerate.

12. Seasonal Replanting

Right from the get-go I was keen on getting fresh produce all year round, both to eat and to share. While there are certainly places in the continental United States where this is possible outdoors, it certainly isn't so in the Pacific Northwest. But there are ways to extend the season by replanting crops and using a greenhouse.

To start, I marked my diary in bold words:

PLANT NOW FOR FALL/WINTER CROPS
Beware of procrastination . . . plan ahead.

In our outside beds, once the peas and runner beans had been harvested, I replanted with a variety of salad greens: arugula, mesclun mix, and mâche (corn salad) as well as bok choy, mustard greens, New Zealand spinach, broccoli, and savoy cabbage. My early plantings of beets, carrots, and Swiss chard were all depleted, so I filled those spaces with lettuce and broccoli starts.

Since I had the advantage of the greenhouse to extend my growing season year round, I aimed for a greenhouse planting from seed to begin the first of September, when I could keep the greenhouse temperature from dropping below 40°F.

Rather than simply use the greenhouse as a nursery for my seasonal planting, I set about to create grow beds inside, built with sturdy yellow pine sides. (I read up on woods that could be used in greenhouses and elsewhere in the garden and was extremely surprised to discover just how toxic some could be—leaching arsenic and chromium into the beds and plants.)

My selection included beets (various colors), broccoli, cantaloupe (on a high trellis), garlic, lettuce, green onions, parsley (Italian), New Zealand spinach (on a trellis), Swiss chard, garden cress, mâche, bok choy, and spring raab (also called broccoli rabe). I also decided to have a section for herbs, including basil, rosemary, dill, cilantro, marjoram, and mint.

I also chose a fair sprinkling of flowers to interact with the vegetables, as well as to entice Treena into the greenhouse to join me for a cup of tea on a blustery afternoon. I knew that she'd find joy in a few cold-tolerant flowers, such as pansies, sweetpeas, nasturtiums, snapdragons, marigolds, geraniums, chrysanthemums, primroses, and cyclamen. There are also some hardy bulbs that do well, like hyacinth, crocus, and snowdrops.

As it turned out, the winter crop was disappointing but a great learning experience. I now have a more modest plan for next winter, which includes spring raab and mâche plus a *few* flowers, and several vegetables for food bank donations, such as broccoli and Swiss chard. I've already added two citrus trees: a kefir lime and a Meyer lemon. These will go out in the summer and return in the fall in 16-inch-diameter containers. But afternoon teas with Treena remain firmly planted.

13. The Greenhouse

A while back we had invested heavily in one of those above-ground swimming pools (with a water pump) that sat on a concrete slab. It didn't work for us.

Fortunately, we found a buyer who profited hugely by our mistake, and we were left with a grand slab of concrete (about 16×8 feet), a water and an electrical supply, and a small but gratefully received check.

Serendipity strikes again! The slab turned out to be just the size for a greenhouse and in exactly the right spot. A greenhouse, I thought, would help me make the most of a short growing season—and be a worthwhile investment.

I stopped by at Charley's Greenhouses and picked up a catalog. At first I simply looked for one that would fit my ready-made foundation, but there were so many options, it was impossible to choose without—yes, you've guessed it—*local knowledge!*

Charley and Carol Yaw have been selling greenhouses and their apparatus for over 32 years. They have a devoted following of avid gardeners who want to get a head start on the short Pacific Northwest growing season and to have flowers and food for the longer winter months.

I met with Charley to discuss the site and what might best meet our needs. We settled on a 16x8-foot Traditional model. Charley explained that almost everyone eventually wound up wanting more space, but he felt this would meet our needs for our own table, to share with our neighbors, and to donate a small but regular supply to the food bank.

We live about 500 feet above the Skagit Valley, with Puget Sound and the Peninsular Mountains in the far distance and the San Juan Islands off to our right. It's a grand view, and I wanted to be able to look at it through plain glass, which isn't the best insulation or price, but I had it firmly in my mind that we could take afternoon tea and the occasional breakfast at one end, amid the warmth, color, and sweet aroma of our verdant winter garden.

Charley helped us plan it out, and we equipped it with three long wooden benches and several overhead wire racks. We found an English potting tray and, again with local knowledge, added the following:

■ Automatic overhead ventilation panels (the heat expands oil in a cylinder that cranks open the panels; when the air cools, they close). *I should warn you here to get equally automatic spring stops in case the wind blows up, as ours did and blew the otherwise robust fittings clean off the roof!*

Treena joins graham in a cup of tea

■ A waterproof heat pad to slip under the seedlings, with a ceramic probe that craftily takes the soil temperature and lets you adjust it to awaken the seeds' ambition to become a future dinner.

■ Trays upon trays of little black pots that nested into black trays, some that drain and others that don't. (Apparently some seedling plants benefit from the more humid environment of the nondraining bottom tray. Also, they are less messy.)

■ Black Gold potting mix and a sack or two of Coco-Coir from Scott Titus, along with his Intrepid organic fertilizer.

"Do you want to build it yourself?" asked Charley. "You've got to be kidding!" I replied, and I told him of a recent debacle with a filing cabinet I'd ordered from a catalog that promised "some easy assembly needed."

A three-man crew arrived on site, and within 6 hours the greenhouse was up and ready to grow. Had I chosen to build it, I just may have gotten it up . . . but I am not confident that essentials such as doors opening and closing would have been achieved.

For those of you with a more robust self-confidence (and more experience), the do-it-yourself kit will cost you about two-thirds of my 6-hour wonder (although you'll probably have the expense of the foundation, which I already had in place from the former pool).

But the greenhouse kit itself is only part of the investment. Creating this "un-

natural" natural environment also demanded looking at issues of heat and light.

While it crossed my mind to get very ambitious and try my hand at cultivating the likes of bananas and pineapple, I quickly dispensed with that notion, given the cost of heating even my modest-size greenhouse to tropical levels. It isn't worth it unless you are growing vanilla as a cash crop!

So we settled for cool, but not below 40ºF.

The standard low-cost domestic indoor heaters are not designed or built for these adverse conditions. Charley had a robust fan-driven heater that was controlled by a good thermostat and designed to be used in damp greenhouse conditions.

Taking due regard for what I choose to call *minimal electronics*, I had our electrician install three power sources: one overhead for lighting and two at waist height for bench operations, with ground fault interrupters (GFIs) all round for safety. Now I had a place for the radio/CD player, a boiling kettle, a toaster, a romantic Tiffany-style overhead light . . . oh yeah—and outlets for the plants, too!

Of course, one assumes that living in a glass house will mean plenty of light, but that's relative when it comes to seeding, germinating, and growing.

I quickly discovered that my vegetables needed somewhere between 700 and 1,000 foot-candles (a measure of illuminance). And that was where the simplicity ended! Nowhere in all my diggings and siftings have I encountered such complexity—so many choices and such apparent cost differentials.

The whole business of light may be very important for commercial growers, but really, I asked myself, do I need an HID bulb or an MH or the latest fluorescent . . . or simply move into the new neutron 16 that uses microwave technology?

Time again for local knowledge and my pal Charley because I knew this was another choice I couldn't make on my own!

graham realizes he
"overdid it" in lighting his
start

We finally settled on a six-light fixture, 4 feet long and 18 inches wide. The fluorescent tubes are T5 daylight (6,400K), which is very close to natural sunlight (5,000 lumens per lamp equals 30,000 lumens). This still doesn't mean much to me, but if you copy the description and take it to a greenhouse supplier, the people there will nod wisely and sell you the exact same unit.

If the garden were just for our private use, it would be easy to look forward to cleaning out the beds, testing the soil, adding nutrients and compost, doing other chores, and then having a well-deserved rest. However, if one has committed 50 percent of the crop to neighbors and food banks, those folk don't stop eating when the season begins to slow down. It was because of this special use (very dear to my heart from the get-go) that I did some detailed homework on how to use my small greenhouse to the max—not just to get a head start on the short growing season but also to learn how to extend the season through the fall and into the winter.

CHAPTER FOUR

Cooking Methods for Maximum Flavor and Nutrition

Thanks to the Internet, recipes are a dime a dozen, but their availability doesn't mean they will teach you *how* to cook. That's because cooking is more about method than about measured ingredients. When you know how to cook, the ingredients you choose become a matter of personal taste—and seasonal availability.

The enjoyment of food is, of course, a sensual pleasure that I've spelled out for years using the acronym TACT: taste, aroma, color, and texture. It's true that all plants have those attributes in their raw state, and most can be relished just as they are or in combination with others.

The entire purpose of *cooking* means you submit raw foods to heat, either dry, such as roasting, or moist, as in steaming. Heat releases different flavors and aromas and changes the food's color and texture. And over the past 50 years, I have made it my business to study and compare these dry and moist cooking methods, seeking out those that provide the most *balanced* results. Note that I didn't say most *enjoyable*.

The biggest challenges in cooking come with what we add to raw ingredients, either by way of the cooking method (see "Deep-Fry" on page 56) or by flavor enhancers. Unfortunately, in too many cases the results can be detrimental to our efforts to retain as much nutritional value as possible.

The senses are so easily seduced by adding, for example, salt, fats, sugars, alcohol, and well-textured wrappings made from refined starch. The results can be pleasing enough to become addictive and, if consumed frequently in unwise quantities, can turn a treat into an eventual threat. Note that only the letter *H* separates the words *treat* and *threat*—and both end in *eat*. For me, this H factor is the harm done by high volume and high repetition.

When dealing with grown foods, the imbalance comes largely from the added fats from butter, cheese, cream, bacon, and, to a lesser extent, oils. This does not mean that any of these should be eliminated (unless you're a vegan and eschew animal products). However, it does mean that each of us needs to have a very firm idea of how much to add and when.

To some degree, the *how much* will be determined by your individual risk factors. However, it has been well proven for decades that it is unwise to exceed 10 percent of our daily calories from saturated fat, or 200 calories out of an average 2,000-calorie daily diet. In fact, we may see this recommendation move to less than 7 percent of calories from saturated fat (this recommendation is being considered for the upcoming U.S. Dietary Guidelines to be posted late in 2010).

Given that there are 9 calories in every gram of fat, the 200-calorie limit on saturated fat per day translates to about 20 grams (or less) each day. Not all fatty foods are pure fat (only oil is 100 percent fat), so compare the following "fat-rich enhancers," which are often added to vegetables to boost their flavor:

Fat Source	Common Measurement	Saturated Fat Amount (Grams)
Butter	1 Tbs (~½ oz)	7.2 grams
Heavy Whipping Cream	2 Tbs (~1 oz)	7 grams
Cheese*	1 oz.	4.15 grams

*Changes by cheese type

Source: *Bowes & Church's Food Values of Portions Commonly Used*, 18th Edition, copyright © 2005 by Jean T. A. Pennington; Lippincott Williams & Wilkins, Baltimore, MD

As you can see in the table, these fat sources quickly add up. Butter is commonly used in cooking and just 3 tablespoons can put you over your maximum goal of 20 grams or less each day! Cream can add up, too. Cheese adds a lot of flavor and with so many delicious varieties, when used sparingly, may be a very good use of your saturated fat grams.

One simple way of getting a "somewhat" butter flavor is to use the small I Can't Believe It's Not Butter spray bottle to spritz vegetables just before serving.

Over the years, I have added more than my share of saturated fat—and other potentially negative flavor additions, such as salt and sugar—almost by habit and always for the pleasure that they unquestionably bring. But they have reduced to some extent the benefits provided by grown food. However, when these additions are reduced in volume—again, *not* eliminated—they do their part in contributing to our enjoyment in the way that a good perfume applied carefully does its enhancement.

Seasonings of any kind need to support and enhance the flavor of the food itself and *never* become an overwhelming presence.

Now . . . let's take a look at cooking methods before we get into the recipes.

Blanch (Parboil)

Blanching is a method that can be used as part of the preparation before actual cooking to reduce the cooking time needed for another method. In some cases, it helps retain the color of the vegetable, especially for green beans and peas.

Blanching is the very swift process of dunking the vegetables—all at once—into plenty of boiling water for about 1 minute and then turning them directly into ice cold water.

While blanching will reduce both the water-soluble and heat-sensitive vitamins in the food, the loss is certainly not likely to cause any serious deficiency.

In my judgment, the ease and the color and texture enhancement gained by blanching help raise the volume of vegetables served and reverse the traditional proportions, making the meat/protein the garnish for a change.

Boil

When foods undergo a complete immersion in boiling water or stock, there is definitely a leaching of soluble vitamins, but there are textural and flavor (stocks) benefits as well as simplicity!

I infinitely prefer steaming (discussed next), which avoids the loss of nutrients and involves about the same amount of time; steaming also seems to provide a more even result. There are, however, a couple of exceptions: boiled new potatoes and green peas. New potatoes can be boiled for about 10 minutes and drained, then covered with a towel (pressed down onto the potatoes) and left on a low heat for about 5 minutes to draw off the surplus water. This method avoids that waterlogged texture that often accompanies straightforward boiling.

And a favorite of mine: peas tightly covered and boiled in ¼ cup of water with a few leaves of fresh mint and just a touch of sugar.

In addition to the obvious flavor benefits, there is also the water itself, which now contains some of the leached vitamins. This I always add to my ever-present stockpot of trimmings so that I don't lose those nutrients (see the Vegetable Stock recipe on page 288).

Add just enough salt to the water to avoid the need to add more at the table.

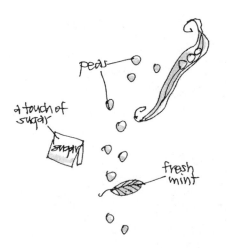

peas

a touch of sugar

sugar

fresh mint

Steam

Steaming is swift and offers good retention of flavor, color, and nutrients, provided that the food is not steamed for too long. Every unnecessary minute on the heat will seriously reduce this method's benefits. So I urge you to use a timer every time you steam.

The vegetable is placed in a perforated basket that is suspended over vigorously boiling water and covered tightly with a lid to contain the steam. The best material is stainless steel. The most useful size for a small family is 9 inches in diameter by about 3 inches deep. There are times when I use two baskets: root vegetables, which take up to 20 minutes, are cooked in the lower tray, and their leaves, which take only about 5 minutes, are added to the top tray at the 15-minute mark.

graham makes the discovery that some times work better than others...

Steamed vegetables are dull surfaced—they do not reflect light. A very light spritz of olive oil from a manual spray will help enhance the color, or try a scattering of fresh herbs and perhaps a light dusting of smoked paprika to make them look much more appealing as well as add flavor without compromise.

I add a light sifting of sea salt to the vegetables before they are steamed. Some salt will dissolve on the surface and some will be lost, but it's better to control the amount than to succumb to the top dressing assault so often used at the dinner table.

Drip-Stew

Drip-stewing is one of the oldest known cooking methods, dating back thousands of years to ancient China. A three-legged clay vessel with hollow legs supports a bowl, into which meats and vegetables are piled along with enough water to at least fill the legs. The covered pot was traditionally placed in the hot cinders of a fire. The water boiled in the legs, releasing steam and indirect heat to the foods in the bowl. You can duplicate this method using a large pot and a kugel-hopf cake pan.

Microwave

Much has been said about fiber-agitating cooking by microwave. Some suggest that because of its speed and lack of water/steam exposure, this method retains the most nutrients. Others counter that while that may be marginally true, it is equally true that the texture of the plant is changed. *Both are true.*

Heat is developed by the microwaves' rubbing fiber on fiber. It's cooking by friction, and for plants, the entire piece cooks at exactly the same time all the way through. This process is what changes the texture. Because normal heat penetrates gradually, you tend to get a softer exterior and a firmer center. Microwaving provides a slight change from what we know as normal.

I most often use my microwave to partially cook—or start—certain foods. For instance, I take a good-size russet potato (8 ounces) and cook at full power for 7 minutes, then turn it over for a further 1 minute. I let it rest for another minute and then cut it in half lengthwise. I then cut deeply into the exposed (still *just* undercooked) flesh, brush it with olive oil and sprinkle on paprika and sea salt, and slip it under a broiler to brown for about 5 minutes. In 15 minutes, I have a quick and attractive alternative to a baked potato in its jacket, which would have taken about 1 hour. I do the same with winter squash to ease the cutting process; I then seed, season, and roast.

Using this method, I save time while allowing for a more natural texture and the addition of browning and seasoning absorption that would otherwise be lost by straight-through microwaving.

I must add here that the microwave promises speed and to some extent delivers. But if speed becomes the central goal, then much of what we know to be the great sensual benefits of cooking could be lost, and eventually we will hand over our entire food supply to those who will do it for us. When speed rules, it quite logically blazes a path for convenience, which in turn eventually displaces scratch cooking and its fresh ingredients.

Thermal (Hay Box) Cooking

For thermal cooking, you will definitely need a piece of equipment currently made by Thermos. I own two units, which I find extremely useful as an alternative to the slow cookers that tend, in my opinion, to overcook, especially vegetables. Since I use it often, I've included it for interest's sake; it is by no means a recommended essential.

The hay box is a well-insulated thermal container that can hold two stainless-steel covered saucepans of 20-cup capacity. Vegetables are brought to a boil in a carefully (lightly) seasoned broth or water. (I love to leave the vegetables in large—2- to 3-inch—chunks.) The container is sealed with a very thick lid. You can then go to work—and 6–7 hours later return to vegetables cooked entirely (quite soft) but still in their original shape. The cooking liquid is superb as a clear soup, and each vegetable—say, carrot, parsnip, turnip, rutabaga, or cabbage—will have shared its flavor with its neighbor—lovely stuff.

Again, a spritz of olive oil or a sprinkling of fresh herbs will be enough to serve them as is. Any surplus can be mashed together for a perfect creamed (without cream) side dish of absolute smoothness or a good soup base.

Braise

This moist-heat method starts with browning the vegetables in oil, then cooking covered in the oven or on the stovetop (also known as poële) with liquid. Particularly when a stock is used, as the liquid and herbs are added, the flavors combine and penetrate the vegetables *and* enrich the cooking liquid as it reduces.

I cut the vegetables into about a 1-inch dice and briefly shallow fry (see "Sauté" on page 54) in just enough ordinary olive oil to stop them from sticking, about 2 teaspoons for four portions in a nonstick or well-seasoned cast-iron skillet. When just lightly browned, I add a clove or two of chopped garlic and 1 level tablespoon of grated gingerroot, stir briefly, and then add a good vegetable stock (see page 288) to half cover. Add a dusting of sea salt and a fresh herb of your choice, such as oregano. Cover tightly and allow the vegetables to part simmer/part steam over medium heat (300°F) until just tender; for root vegetables, about 35 minutes. I finish the dish with a very small amount of arrowroot mixed with cold water to a thin cream, called a *slurry*; take the hot pan off the heat, drizzle in the slurry, and stir until it just becomes glossy, reflecting the light. Overdone thickening is ghastly!

Roast

By far my favorite dry-heat method is to oven-roast root vegetables and some greens like Brussels sprouts, preferably in a convection oven. Clear glass oven-proof baking dishes do really well; cast iron is also good, but the enameled varieties can be costly and heavy to work with.

As with the moist-heat methods, root vegetables should be evenly diced to ½ to 1 inch. (Some vegetables, like beets, can be roasted whole, wrapped in aluminum foil.) I season lightly with sea salt and smoked paprika (for color and flavor) and often add some powdered rosemary. I then spray the surface with olive oil and place the dish in a preheated oven, generally at 375°F. Depending on your choice of vegetables, you should allow just 40 minutes, with one good toss and stir after the first 20 minutes.

The dry heat (especially if using convection) will evaporate a good deal of the water content, causing a concentration of flavors with a slight caramelization of the plant sugars. There should be no need to add oil or fat to help the vegetables glisten, but fresh green parsley always enhances the eye appeal.

Sauté

Sauté sounds so much nicer than pan-fry, but that's about what it is—but with more flourish. With a medium to hot pan surface, food is cooked using a small amount of oil.

The key to effective sautéing lies in the pan heat. It can take a good 5 minutes for a pan to reach 350°F—and I strongly suspect that most pans fail to reach this surface heat. As a result, food tends to leak water as it heats, boiling rather than frying, which holds back the browning effect and the release of natural volatile oils in such vegetables as onions, garlic, and peppers.

One way to know just how long it takes for a pan to be effective is to buy a small surface thermometer usually used for outdoor grills. You put it in the skillet and it reads the surface temperature. After a while you will know when the pan is hot, but the temperature gauge is a good way to learn. Sautéed foods can be tossed (great fun to learn) or stirred carefully and infrequently . . . allowing time for the food to settle and get the browning effect. Again, season lightly and add fresh parsley. Added oil or fat is not needed.

Stir-Fry

When Danny Kaye was alive, I used to cook with him on his full-size professional gas range at his home in Beverly Hills, and I have a memory of his using a large wok—a steel bowl-shaped pan that fit well on the large gas flame. Because I've seldom met anyone else with a similar installation, I've adjusted the stir-fry method to be done in a large flat skillet with reasonable sides, 2–3 inches. (There are, however, lots of styles of woks that are suited to both cooking on gas and electric stoves. There's even an electric wok, if you are so inclined to purchase another appliance.)

Like in sautéing, the pan has got to be hot—but not incandescent! I prefer good-quality nonstick, well-sealed cast aluminum that's got a reasonably heavy base. At about 350°F and using just 1 tablespoon of olive oil for four portions, add diced (to about ½ inch) foods in order of their texture: carrots first and bean sprouts last. Avoid scorching the likes of garlic, green onions, and ginger by adding these later, after some fluids have been released.

It really isn't necessary or beneficial to continuously toss and stir. In fact, it's better to let the ingredients settle and brown a little. Two wooden spatulas work exceptionally well for tossing. The Chinese use large chopsticks. Metal tools will play havoc on nonstick material.

As with all other methods, I very lightly season with sea salt before stir-frying because I like to add soy sauces or other Asian seasonings, and there is plenty of sodium to go around. MSG and added fats or oils are, in my opinion, absolutely unnecessary.

I almost always make a small sauce to add at the last moment, with a reduced vegetable stock mixed with miso and a little cornstarch or arrowroot. But always be ultra-cautious with starch additions—too much is truly awful; however, it can quickly be thinned down with added stock.

Deep-Fry

I'm listing the deep-frying method because I need to explain why I'm *not* giving you some cooking guidelines. To immerse a food in hot oil, especially after it has been coated with batters or breading, is an attractive idea sensually. To avoid noting its almost universal enjoyment would be crass.

Having said that, I find that keeping a relatively large quantity of oil in a pot with the expectation of using it only occasionally is naive. Set it up and, like the baseball field in the movie *Field of Dreams*, you may find yourself coming back to the fat pot with more frequency than is good for you. Which, of course, means more fat. And fats that are exposed to oxidation through heating increase the presence of free radicals, which offset the nutritional benefits of the vegetables you are cooking.

Oh—and when we eat out, my wife, Treena, orders only six french fries if they are offered. *Nothing is banned*—but a reasonable moderate quantity must be the first and firm rule.

Treena's 6 french fries

CHAPTER FIVE

How to Grow, How to Cook

In my first year with the garden, I grew 34 plants, and I plan to introduce a further 26 in year two. All 60 are described in this section of the book. Since many entries do not benefit—or suffer—from my personal experience, I relied on the wisdom of others, such as my local knowledge posse and writers and gardeners such as Steve Albert, whose *The Kitchen Garden Grower's Guide* has become my companion along the way, and should be yours as well. With Steve's brilliant encyclopedia at my side and the advice of my other experienced gardening friends—Scott Titus, Charlie Yaw, and Debbie Mitchell, among others—I was able to gather a few important growing characteristics for each plant as well.

What I have tried to do is give you just enough information to get you started and to encourage you to go that extra mile for any particular plant. There are so many resources for you to call on, and I have included some of those in the reference section at the back of the book. But you will, no doubt, find your own local knowledge sources, which will be invaluable to you as they have been to me.

For each vegetable, I've given a nutrition profile that clearly shows the benefits you get from that plant. I loved getting this information down on paper and rejoice in the fact that not only did the plants provide an incredible array of tastes, aromas, colors, and texture, but these very attributes announce the presence of the truly remarkable combination of nutrients needed for our vibrant health.

Oh yes, you need to know that I've rounded off many of the numbers, since they seem less bothersome when, say, protein is shown as 1 or 2 grams rather than 1.36 or 1.95 grams.

My kitchen has taken on a whole new feeling, as the garden provided such unrivaled freshness, seasonal variety, and the adventure that can come only through observing the miracle of growth at the speed of life.

Each plant, therefore, goes from seed to harvest and then to the kitchen with a selection of recipes, both simple and more complex yet always seeking to provide the most enjoyable nourishment possible.

Glossary

The following list of gardening/growing terms includes explanations and notes on terms used throughout the book. Here, too, are those terms used as shorthand in the captions to the illustrations that accompany each plant listing.

Annual: a plant whose entire life cycle occurs within 1 year.

Biennial: a plant with a 2-year life cycle that seeds in the second year.

Blanch: sheltering the plant (usually the stem) from sunlight by heaping earth or mulch up to the leaves (used for celery and leeks, for example).

Blight: leaves suddenly wither; begins with yellow spots that go gray and then black. Remove the plant ASAP.

Bloodmeal: dried blood; comes from meat-processing plants (abattoirs) and is usually mixed with water. It is a very high-nitrogen fertilizer.

Bolting: a plant's response to too little water, too much heat, and/or poor soil; going into flower or seed.

Cloche: glass or plastic cover to protect plants in the beginning of a growing season; plastic milk jugs can be used.

Companion planting (con): plants that will not grow well in the same vicinity.

Companion planting (pro): plant characteristics benefit side-by-side plantings.

Compost: ideally 50 percent nitrogen, 25 percent phosphorus, and 25 percent potassium, with a pH of 7.

Compost tea: watered-down compost. An easy way to mix is to half fill a watering can with well-matured compost. Add the same quantity of water and let it sit for a day in the sun (hence the term *tea*). Let it settle before pouring the tea onto the soil (not over the plants). You can replenish the water three times using the same compost.

Cool season: a plant thriving at 60°F–65°F; doesn't do well in warm summers (75°F plus).

Cottonseed meal: a useful slow-release fertilizer with 7 percent nitrogen, 3 percent phosphoric acid, and 2 percent potash.

Depth: to some degree, a shallow-rooted plant will do well next to one with deep roots, as they don't draw nutrients from the same level of soil.

Determinate: plants that stop growth with a flower at their apex; the fruit of these plants usually matures all at the same time.

Feeding/fertilizer: organic material used to increase nutrients for plant growth.

Fish emulsion: a fertilizer made from the by-products of the fish-processing industry, which is considered acceptable for use in organic horticulture and adds micronutrients to the soil.

Floating row covers: usually fabric but also fine netting suspended over wire hoops to protect plants from flying pests and low temperatures.

Germination: the number of days from planting to the first evidence of a shoot breaking out of the soil.

Green manure: made up from leaves that mature quickly; used to add structure to the soil (organic contents).

Harden off: tender plants grown indoors are taken outside for 2–4 hours a day for up to 7 days to help them adjust to cooler temperatures before planting outside.

Harvest: The number of days from seeding (and sometimes transplanting) until you can expect to harvest. This can guide you in setting out subsequent plantings.

Height: Tall plants can partly shade smaller plants, so if the lower plants need full sun, be careful about the positioning, On the other hand, a plant requiring partly shady conditions may do well with a tall companion.

Humus: decomposed plant material (compost) added to clay soil to help bonding and to help sandy soil retain water.

Intercropping: sowing or planting fast-growing plants between slow-growing plants (for example, mâche and radishes with peppers and tomatoes); also deep-rooted plants alongside shallow-rooted ones.

Lime: used to lower the acidity of soil that is too acid (7 pH upward); it is a calcium compound.

Loam: medium texture with good organic matter that includes no silt, clay, or stones; retains moisture.

Lodge: when a long-stemmed plant (like onions or garlic) is bent over toward the ground; helps provide extra growth to the bulb.

Mildew: caused by various fungi; manifests as a white discoloration.

Mulch: a layer of usually organic material added around plants to control weeds, retain moisture, and protect from heat and pests.

Nitrogen (N): stimulates leaf growth and stems; found in bloodmeal, guano (bird/bat droppings), hoof and horn meal, soybean meal, and cottonseed meal.

Organic: substances obtained from natural sources; soil developed without manufactured chemicals.

Perennial: a plant can survive for three or more seasons.

Pests and diseases: only a few are mentioned; for a fuller discussion, see the resource at the back of the book.

pH: scale of acidity or alkalinity of soil; plants can be particular.

Phosphorus (P): provides cell division and tissue development; good sources are mushroom compost, rock phosphate, and bonemeal.

Planting: how deeply to plant the seed and at what time; how much space to give the germinated seed so that it can attain its proper size without crowding.

Pollination: moving pollen from one plant to another to enable fertilization.

Potassium (K): promotes plant metabolism; found in wood ash, sawdust, granite dust, cocoa shell dust, and fish emulsion.

Rhizobia: bacteria found in legume roots that helps convert atmospheric nitrogen, enhancing plant growth.

Rotation: a means to avoid the buildup of pests, diseases, and so on, that are attracted to certain plant families by periodically changing location. Also, some plants take from the soil, some return to the soil; rotating crops improves the soil quality overall.

Sets: usually purchased in small bundles, these are immature plants, usually onions.

Side dressing: fertilizer sprinkled to one side of a plant and scratched lightly into the surface; liquids can be sprayed (such as fish fertilizer and compost tea).

Soil/fertile: many plant nutrients, well-drained and aerated.

Thinning: fine seeds (like lettuce and carrots) are removed when young to provide space and nutrition to those remaining.

Tilth: soil surface that is fine, crumbles easily, but is not dry; very suitable for seed germination.

Warm season: plants that need 75°F for minimum growth; soil temperature between 65°F and 80°F.

Whitefly: a tiny white moth-like insect that hides in colonies under green leaves, which turn yellow and wilt; use orange sticky card traps or spray with neem oil.

Width: air circulation is a necessity; don't risk overcrowding; allow enough space for plant to reach full maturity.

Yellows: a range of diseases that cause stunted growth and yellow leaves.

Zones: temperature range best suited to plant, based on first and last frost predictions.

Apple

There is a well-established myth that in the midst of the Garden of Eden, there was an apple tree, and that this may have been the so-called forbidden fruit. While I know of nobody who can prove or disprove this (since the fruit itself is never described), it is unlikely that Adam and Eve would have made it in a climate that featured up to 1,000 "chilling hours" without clothing!

I was delighted to learn that our plot of land is a more-or-less (nothing is perfect) ideal spot on which to grow a small orchard of highly prized apples. And so, with the guidance of the experts from the Washington State University Extension Service, Horticultural Division, in Mt. Vernon, Washington, I have planted six dwarf trees of the Honeycrisp cultivar and six other trees of a mix of apples that are well proven in this area and appear to be able to coexist.

I wanted trees that would not grow above 10 feet, so that their fruit would be easy to reach; that were good bearers; and, I hoped, that would make it without harsh chemical sprays during the fruiting season. So I have planted Jonagold, Gravenstein, Spartan, and Akane, all dwarves that can be topped at 8–10 feet.

Apple trees can tolerate winter temperatures as low as −40°F. In fact, each variety requires a certain number of chilling hours each winter, which is the number of hours at 45°F or below. Chilling hours can vary from 1,000 or more to as few as 400 hours. Choose an apple variety suited to your climate and winter temperatures.

Trees can be purchased bare root, balled and burlapped, or in a container. Bare-root and balled-and-burlapped trees are available in the winter and early spring, when the trees are dormant and without leaves. A container-grown tree can be planted any time during the growing season. Remove the container carefully and plant the root ball at the same depth as the container.

Once correctly planted and supported with a good 2-inch-diameter stake, there is little to do but spread good compost around the tree in the spring and water well. Please seek good local advice on how and when to prune.

You will need two trees that cross-pollinate. Again, your nursery will help with your perfect choice.

The Numbers

Per 100 g raw (3.5 oz; 1 medium): 52 calories, 0 g fat, 0 g saturated fat, 14 g carbohydrate, 0 g protein, 2 g dietary fiber, 1 mg sodium

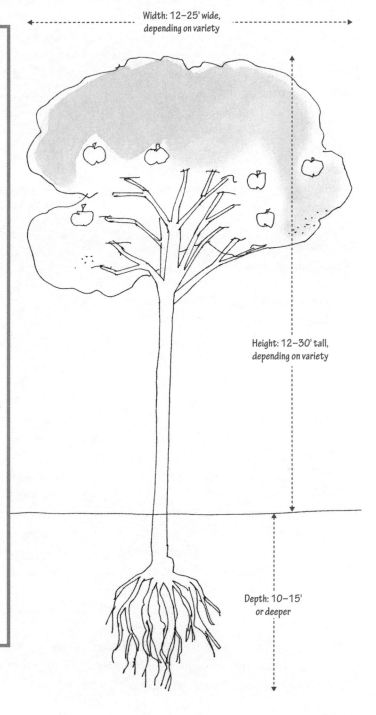

Width: 12–25' wide,
depending on variety

Height: 12–30' tall,
depending on variety

Depth: 10–15'
or deeper

Perennial

Water: Newly planted trees, moderate watering weekly; established trees, infrequent watering except during prolonged dry periods

Sun: Full

Pests: Susceptible to a number of insects that are very difficult to control without preventive spraying during the dormant season. Among the pests that attack are scale, apple maggots, codling moths, fruitworms, and mites. Many pests can be controlled with pheromone-bated insect traps.

Diseases: Susceptible to many fungal diseases that are difficult to control without use of preventive spraying. Choose varieties that are resistant to the diseases in your region.

Soil: Well-drained, loamy, sandy, and clay soils

Fertilizer: Aged compost around trees each year

pH: 6.0–7.0

Varieties: There are nearly 10,000 different kinds, or varieties, of apples, of which about 7,000 grow in North America. Only about 1,000 of these are grown commercially or in home gardens. The most popular: Red Delicious, Golden Delicious, Granny Smith, and McIntosh.

Zones: 3–9

Planting: Plant bare root trees in spring as soon as soil can be worked.

Harvest: From bloom to harvest, 95–180 days, depending on variety. Should bear fruit in the second year.

Spacing: 15–30 feet, depending on variety

Edible: Flesh of fruit

APPLE AND PEAR CRISP

This is an opportunity to reduce portion size because this dessert is so full of flavor you'll only need a modest helping.

SERVES 9

FOR THE FRUIT
3 cooking apples (Jonagold, Winesap, Northern Spy, or other tart flavorful apple)
3 Bosc pears
½ cup golden raisins
2 cups dealcoholized fruity white wine
⅛ teaspoon ground cloves

FOR THE TOPPING
½ cup old-fashioned oats
½ cup low-fat graham cracker crumbs or whole-grain flour
3 tablespoons sliced almonds
½ cup packed dark brown sugar
1 teaspoon ground cinnamon
¼ teaspoon ground nutmeg
3 tablespoons butter

½ cup low-fat vanilla yogurt

Preheat the oven to 350°F.

Peel and core the apples and cut into eighths. Peel and core the pears and cut into quarters. Place in a large skillet; add the raisins, wine, and cloves, and cover with a piece of waxed paper cut to fit. Bring to a boil, lower the heat, and poach gently 15 minutes or until tender but not mushy. Drain, reserving the liquid, and lay the fruit in a 12×12-inch baking dish.

Combine the oats, graham cracker crumbs, almonds, brown sugar, cinnamon, and nutmeg in a bowl. Cut in the butter until the mixture holds together in a crumble. Scatter over the fruit and bake, uncovered, 30 minutes or until golden and crisp on top.

Meanwhile, pour the reserved liquid back into the large skillet and boil vigorously until reduced to about 2 tablespoons. Take off the heat and stir in the yogurt. Cut the crisp into 9 pieces and serve with the yogurt sauce.

Per serving: 226 calories, 6 g fat, 3 g saturated fat (4% calories from saturated fat), 41 g carbohydrate, 2 g protein, 4 g dietary fiber, 72 mg sodium. Exchanges: ½ Fat, 3 Carbohydrate

BAKED APPLES

A fruit lover's dessert. The spice is like a perfume that makes the apple all the more desirable.

SERVES 4

4 medium cooking apples (Jonagold, Northern Spy, Rome, or Winesap)
1 cup unsweetened apple juice or water
½ teaspoon ground cinnamon
¼ teaspoon ground allspice
Pinch ground cloves
¼ cup packed dark brown sugar
¼ cup low-fat vanilla yogurt

Preheat the oven to 350°F.

Core the apples with a spoon or apple corer and cut shallowly in a line around the fruit about 1 inch from the top. Set in a baking pan and pour on the juice. Lay a sheet of aluminum foil on top and bake 30–40 minutes or until the apples are tender.

Set the apples on dessert plates and pour the cooking liquid into a small saucepan. Stir in the cinnamon, allspice, cloves, and brown sugar. Bring to a boil and cook down until the sauce is a thick syrup. Pour over the apples and serve with a dollop of the yogurt.

Per serving: 186 calories, 1 g fat, 0 g saturated fat, 47 g carbohydrate, 1 g protein, 4 g dietary fiber, 18 mg sodium. Exchanges: 2 Fruit, 1 Carbohydrate

TARTE TATIN

This is the forerunner of all upside-down fruit desserts. It's grand and glossy and begs the question, "How did you do *that?!"*

SERVES 8

½ recipe Pie Crust (see page 289)
4½ Jonagold or other soft cooking apples
¼ cup water
⅓ cup sugar
¼ cup butter
1 teaspoon freshly grated lemon zest
Flour for dusting

Roll out dough for 1 pie crust to a 9-inch circle. Lay a cloth over it and set aside. Core, peel, and halve the apples. Leaving the apples in halves, lay them on a plate the same size as the pan you are going to use and trim the apples to fit together in a circle of 8 halves, with 1 in the center. Set aside.

Preheat the oven to 425°F.

Combine the water, sugar, and butter in an 8-inch chef's pan or heavy-bottomed ovenproof skillet. (If yours is larger, then increase the pie crust so that it is 1 inch larger than the diameter of your pan.) Bring to a boil and stir until it turns golden brown. Pull off the heat and lay the trimmed-to-fit apples in the pan, round side down. Scatter the lemon zest over the top. Reduce the heat to medium. Place a lid, 1 size smaller than the lip of the pan, right down on top of the apples. Cook, gently shaking occasionally, 15 minutes or until the apples are tender. Remove from the heat and cool 10 minutes.

Dust the prepared crust lightly with flour. Fold in quarters and lay on top of the apples, unfolding to cover completely. Tuck the edges down around the hot apples and prick the crust a few times with a fork. Bake 20–30 minutes or until the crust is brown. Set on a rack and cool slightly, about 10 minutes. Place a large inverted plate on top of the crust. Hold with a cloth in both hands and smartly turn the pan and plate upside down. (You *can* do it, *really*!) Lift off the pan. Cut the tart in wedges and serve warm or cold.

Per serving: 191 calories, 10 g fat, 0 g saturated fat, 26 g carbohydrate, 1 g protein, 1 g dietary fiber, 100 mg sodium. Exchanges: 2 Fat, 1½ Carbohydrate

Artichoke

Cynara scolymus

Since my first-year garden was both small and (in my case) totally experimental, I really didn't have the space or inclination to grow artichokes, a fairly massive plant that winds up with so little to eat!

Artichokes come from southern Europe, and there is some genetic evidence that they came out of the wild cardoon, a naturally occurring thistle-like plant popular in ancient Greek and Roman cuisine.

It's really quite regional as far as quality is concerned because the artichoke thrives in coolish, moist summers with mild winters. It also demands a degree of patience, as most plants don't bloom and fruit until the second year. Although it's a perennial that can last for up to 15 years (with good winter mulching), it may bear its fruit for only 4 or 5 of those years.

For my money, this is really a commercial grower's crop, given its space and complexity. On the other hand, it's one of those sunny corner plants for which a dozen or so can produce a sudden rush of admiration from those timid souls who are just moving beyond lettuce and parsley, like me!

I've had two over-the-top opportunities to savor artichokes: One was the fairly typical pluck-'n'-dunk the cooked leaves from the globe into a rich hollandaise (butter, lemon, and egg yolk) sauce. The other involved removing the choke/heart and filling the space with pâté de foie gras (goose liver paste). Both these very gourmet delicacies came complete with concentrated saturated fat and high calories, and accompaniments that, in my judgment, obscured the flavors of the plant itself. My purpose in the recipes that follow is to do everything possible to enhance the natural flavors of the individual plant while retaining its maximum nourishment.

The Numbers

Per 100 g boiled (3.5 oz; 1 large head): 53 calories, 0 g fat, 0 g saturated fat, 12 g carbohydrate, 3 g protein, 9 g dietary fiber, 60 mg sodium

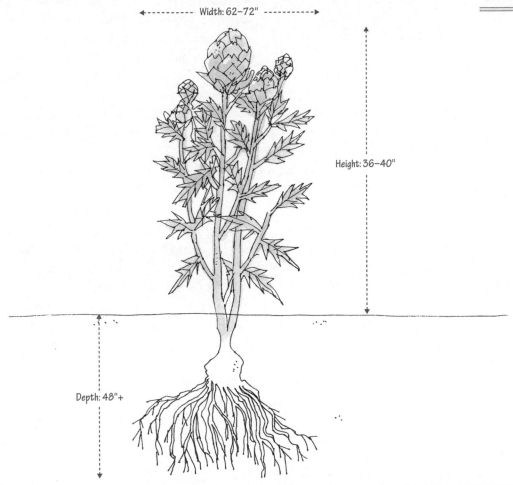

Width: 62–72"

Height: 36–40"

Depth: 48"+

Perennial
Water: Moist
Sun: Full (8 hours minimum)
Companion Planting:
PRO: Asparagus, cabbage family
CON: Pole beans, cucumbers, tomatoes
Pests: Aphids, plume moths, slugs, snails
Diseases: Crown fungus rot
Soil: Bloodmeal and compost before planting out
Fertilizer: Spring/autumn with Microbesoft or fish emulsion every 14 days
pH: 6.0–6.8
Varieties: Green Globe (second season), Imperial Star (180 days from seed in first year)

Zones: 8–9
Planting: ¼-inch deep indoors, 10 weeks before last frost; transplant to 6 inches apart, then thin to 4 inches apart at 6–8 weeks. Won't flower in first year; after summer harvest, prune back to 12 inches for second crop in autumn.
Germinate: 10–14 days
Blooms: Mid-autumn (if not harvested)
Harvest: Summer; 150–180 days from seed, 50–100 days from suckers (offshoots or divisions)
Rotation: Don't follow sunflowers
Edible: Soft part of leaves and heart

ARTICHOKE

Basic Preparation

Journalists and other students of the English language should be required to describe the preparation and cooking method of an artichoke (the globe variety) so that a cook who has never seen one could manage the task.

Every cookbook I could find simply assumes too much. They describe *spines*, *bottom*, *heart*, and *choke* as though each were obvious. As a result, they are mostly ignored!

So here is my attempt to remedy this situation.

The globe artichoke is really an enormous bud that has yet to blossom and is a large baseball-size globe of tough, green, sometimes *spine*-tipped overlapping leaves that sits on top of an inedible stalk.

When cut in half lengthwise, you can see that the stalk's entry is surrounded by a dense gray-green collar about ½ inch thick, which forms the *bottom*. Immediately above the bottom is a fuzzy mass of fine fibers called the *choke*, which, like the stalk, is inedible and always removed.

Surrounding the choke are about four tender inner leaves that make up the *heart*, which includes the bottom.

A fair-size artichoke can weigh in at 12–15 ounces. The heart will provide 4–5 ounces max.

There are two basic methods of preparing the artichoke:

Whole: Trim the stalk off flat and lower the globe into boiling salted water, to which you've added 1 tablespoon freshly squeezed lemon juice for every 1 pint of water. Cover and boil for 20 minutes. To test for doneness, tug out one central leaf; if it comes out easily, the artichoke is done. Remove, turn the globe upside down to drain, and cool. When the artichoke has cooled, pinch several leaves together at the top and twist sharply, remove, and set aside. Using a teaspoon, dig out the choke but leave the bottom.

Drizzle about a tablespoon of Treena's Vinaigrette (see page 74) inside the globe. It will season the leaf ends when pulled out and those previously removed from the top. You eat only the fleshy end pieces that attach to the bottom.

Hearts: Cut the globe lengthwise in quarters with a large sharp knife. You will clearly see all the parts in cross-section. Put each piece bottom down into a bowl of freshly squeezed lemon juice *immediately* to prevent the flesh from blackening. Put a steamer on the stovetop and heat the water. Strip off all the outer leaves, leaving three or four of the tender inside leaves, and cook covered in the steamer as hearts for 20 minutes. When cooled, detach the choke and stalk, and trim the outside of the bottom. Use as described in the recipes that follow.

ARTICHOKE OMELET

Artichoke hearts always provide a deep, smooth, rich texture and make this omelet a good candidate for brunch.

SERVES 6

1 tablespoon olive oil

1 bunch (about 6) green onions

3 garlic cloves, chopped

½ cup chopped red bell pepper

1 cup chopped zucchini, ½-inch pieces

1 cup shredded collard greens

8 Greek olives, pitted and chopped

1 cup frozen or canned artichoke heart
quarters (or prepared fresh, as on page 68)

½ teaspoon dried oregano

½ teaspoon dried basil

2 Roma or Viva Italia tomatoes, seeded and
chopped

¼ teaspoon freshly ground black pepper

⅛ teaspoon salt

2 tablespoons chopped fresh parsley

2 tablespoons plus 1 teaspoon freshly grated
Parmesan cheese

1¾ cups egg substitute* or 1 cup egg substitute
plus 3 whole eggs for added texture

*I prefer Egg Beaters Southwestern Style. If you use
whole eggs for added texture, you'll increase the
saturated fat content.

Heat 1 teaspoon of the oil in a heavy, oven-proof skillet on medium. Slice the white ends of the green onions and finely chop the green parts. Sauté the white parts with the garlic about 1 minute to release the flavors. Add the red pepper, zucchini, collard greens, olives, artichoke hearts, oregano, and basil, and cook 8 minutes or until the vegetables are crisp tender and colorful.

Stir in the tomatoes, black pepper, salt, and 1 tablespoon each of the parsley and Parmesan cheese. Pour the egg substitute into the vegetables, shaking the pan to distribute it evenly.

Scatter 1 tablespoon of Parmesan cheese over the top. Cook on medium about 6 minutes or until the bottom is done and the top is still runny. Place under the broiler for 2 minutes to finish cooking. Scatter the remaining Parmesan cheese and parsley on top along with a tablespoon of the green onion tops; drizzle with the remaining olive oil. Cut into four wedges and serve.

Per serving: 110 calories, 5 g fat, 1 g saturated fat, 8 g carbohydrate, 10 g protein, 3 g dietary fiber, 283 mg sodium. Exchanges: 2 Very Lean Meat, 3 Vegetable, 1 Fat

ARTICHOKES, ASPARAGUS, AND PEAS WITH TARRAGON

A most elegant combination side dish that goes very well with either seafood or poultry.
SERVES 4

½ cup low-sodium vegetable stock (see
page 288)

8 ounces frozen or canned artichoke hearts or
6 fresh hearts (as prepared on page 68)

1 cup chopped asparagus

1 cup fresh or frozen peas

1 teaspoon dried tarragon

¼ teaspoon salt

¼ teaspoon freshly ground black pepper

½ teaspoon arrowroot or cornstarch mixed
with 1 tablespoon stock (slurry)

2 tablespoons freshly grated Parmesan cheese

Heat the stock in a large skillet. Add the artichoke hearts and simmer 5 minutes. Add the asparagus and peas, and cook 3 minutes more or until the vegetables are tender.

Season with the tarragon, salt, and black pepper, and stir in the slurry. Heat until stock is thickened and glossy. Scatter the Parmesan cheese over the top and serve.

Per serving: 89 calories, 1 g fat, 1 g saturated fat (10% calories from saturated fat), 14 g carbohydrate, 5 g protein, 6 g dietary fiber, 306 mg sodium. Exchanges: ½ Starch, 2 Vegetable

HERB BROILED ARTICHOKES

This recipe can be used as an appetizer or as a main dish (served with couscous or brown rice), but the added carbohydrates will obviously increase calories and carbs.

SERVES 4

8 fresh artichoke hearts, precooked
¼ teaspoon dried tarragon or 1 teaspoon chopped fresh
¼ teaspoon dried basil or 1 teaspoon chopped fresh
1 tablespoon chopped fresh parsley
1 tablespoon chopped fresh chives
Extra-virgin olive oil cooking spray
Brown rice or couscous (see page 293)
¼ cup mango chutney*

Major Grey's is a good type.

Turn the broiler on to preheat.

Lay the artichoke hearts on a broiler pan in a single layer. Combine the tarragon, basil, parsley, and chives in a bowl. Coat the artichokes lightly with the cooking spray. Scatter the herbs over the top and spray with oil again.

Broil 4 inches from heat until heated through and slightly browned. Place 2 hearts on top of a small scoop of rice or couscous and garnish with 1 tablespoon of chutney.

Per serving: 111 calories, 0 g fat, 0 g saturated fat, 26 g carbohydrate, 3 g protein, 10 g dietary fiber, 382 mg sodium. Exchanges: 2 Vegetable

PASTA PRIMAVERA

I always use frozen or canned artichokes for this excellent kitchen-garden pasta dish. My very few experimental fresh ones are always served whole.

SERVES 4

8 ounces penne pasta
1 tablespoon olive oil
2 large garlic cloves, bashed and chopped
1 (8-ounce) package frozen artichoke hearts, thawed
8 medium mushrooms, trimmed and cut in half
3 cups fresh or 1 (10-ounce) package frozen chopped spinach, thawed and drained
4 Roma tomatoes, skinned, seeded, and chopped

¼ teaspoon salt
¼ teaspoon freshly ground black pepper
1 teaspoon Northwest Italy Ethmix
   (see page 287)
¼ cup freshly grated Parmesan cheese

Cook the pasta according to package directions and set aside.

Heat the oil in a high-sided skillet over medium. Add the garlic and cook 30 seconds. Toss in the artichoke hearts and mushrooms. Cook about 3 minutes until they begin to brown. Stir in the spinach, tomatoes, salt, black pepper, spice mix, and reserved pasta. Cook until heated through.

Serve on hot plates. Garnish with the Parmesan cheese.

Per serving: 318 calories, 6 g fat, 1 g saturated fat (6% calories from saturated fat), 54 g carbohydrate, 13 g protein, 7 g dietary fiber, 151 mg sodium. Exchanges: 3 Starch, 2 Vegetable, 1 Fat

Arugula

Eruca vesicaria sativa (domestic)

I grew up with watercress salads; therefore, the slightly more peppery taste/texture of arugula was acceptable if not competitive until, like Lawrence of Arabia, I wound up in Akaba. (Surely you must remember Peter O'Toole as Lawrence sitting on a camel and shouting out to his army, "To Akaba"?)

Akaba, a port city of Jordan on the Gulf of Akaba, was amazingly full of arugula on our February visit. I had great local lamb, broiled over branches of dried fennel and served on a plate filled with just-blanched arugula tossed in a goat cheese and yogurt dressing. Wonderful food, and from that somewhat exotic moment onward, watercress dropped into second place.

As it turned out, arugula became one of my first plantings in the new garden, and judging by the speed at which it grew, the old Italian word *rochetta*, which had been morphed into *rocket* (arugula's other common name), became an appropriate description!

As soon as the soil reached 55°F, I planted the seeds in a 4-inch-wide band, using about 60 seeds for each 12 inches. This was for an early crop to be used in salads (usually when 3 inches tall). When you harvest the greens, leave several plants behind with 4 inches of clear space to grow taller for more spicy leaves to use as a garnish or as a lightly steamed vegetable.

Providing that you stay with smaller portions, as in mixed-green salads, you'll avoid the oxalate that can be bothersome for people with a history of kidney stones. (I've had only one of these, so that's not regarded as a "history" and hasn't put me off arugula!)

The Numbers

Per 100 g raw (3.5 oz; 1 cup): 25 calories, 0.66 g fat, 0 g saturated fat, 3.7 g carbohydrate, 2.6 g protein, 1.6 g dietary fiber, 27 mg sodium

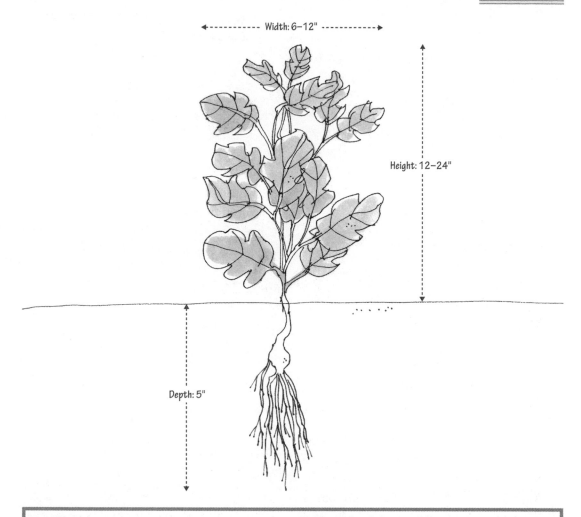

Width: 6–12"

Height: 12–24"

Depth: 5"

Annual
Water: Light
Sun: Moderate to partial shade
Companion Planting:
PRO: Everything
CON: Nothing
Pests: Flea beetles
Diseases: Very rare
Soil: Humus-rich, moist; compost down to 3 inches below surface
Fertilizer: Single application per growing season

pH: 6.0–7.0
Varieties: Rocket, Italian Wild Rustic, Astro, Runway (early)
Zones: 3–6
Planting: Early spring, seed ¼ inch deep; when seedlings are 3 inches, thin to 6 inches apart
Germinate: 5–7 days
Maturity: 40 days
Harvest: June through December
Rotation: Avoid following cabbage family
Edible: Leaves and flowers

ARUGULA WRAP

A fine side dish for richer Mexican food, such as refried beans.

SERVES 4

FOR TREENA'S VINAIGRETTE
1 garlic clove, bashed and chopped
2 tablespoons extra-virgin olive oil
¼ cup rice vinegar
½ teaspoon dry mustard
1 teaspoon packed dark brown sugar
Pinch cayenne (optional)

FOR THE WRAPS
4 (6-inch) corn tortillas
1 large bunch arugula

Whiz the garlic, oil, vinegar, mustard, brown sugar, and cayenne in a blender until slightly thickened.

Wrap the tortillas in waxed paper and heat in the microwave on high for 2 minutes or wrap in foil and heat at 350°F in a conventional oven for 5 minutes.

Wash the arugula in cold water and spin or pat dry. Choose 2–3 stems per serving, dip into the vinaigrette, and lay on each of the tortillas. Roll and serve alongside soup or salads.

The remaining arugula will be great as part of a green salad that can be dressed with the remaining vinaigrette.

Per serving: 152 calories, 8 g fat, 1 g saturated fat (6% calories from saturated fat), 17 g carbohydrate, 3 g protein, 2 g dietary fiber, 50 mg sodium. Exchanges: 1 Starch

ARUGULA SALAD WITH YOGURT GOAT CHEESE DRESSING

Utter simplicity. Once tasted, you will never need to add one other ingredient! (Although pine nuts are nice.)

SERVES 4

4 cups washed and trimmed tender, new-growth arugula
8 ounces low-fat plain yogurt
1 ounce soft goat cheese

Mound 1 cup arugula on each of 4 salad plates. Combine the yogurt and goat cheese. Divide the dressing among the arugula salads.

Per serving: 60 calories, 3 g fat, 2 g saturated fat (30% calories from saturated fat), 5 g carbohydrate, 5 g protein, 0 g dietary fiber, 71 mg sodium. Exchanges: ½ Fat, ½ Carbohydrate

GRILLED FISH ON A BED OF BITTER GREENS

This was such a good use for the abundant growth I got this year. It helped stop it from bolting during the unusual sunny days!

SERVES 4

4 cups arugula (or radicchio, endive, escarole, romaine, or a mixture of these)

4 teaspoons Treena's Vinaigrette (see page 74)
4 (4-ounce) halibut fillets (tilapia does just as
  well)
¼ teaspoon salt
¼ teaspoon freshly ground black pepper
2 tablespoons freshly squeezed lemon juice

Wash the greens and spin dry. Tear into bite-size pieces and toss with the vinaigrette. Divide among 4 dinner plates.

Season the fish with salt and black pepper. Grill, skin side up, over medium heat, uncovered, 3–5 minutes. Turn and grill 3–5 minutes more. (You can gauge the time by measuring the thickness of the fish and cooking 8 minutes per inch.)

Remove the skin as you take the halibut off the grill. Set the fillets on the greens and sprinkle with lemon juice. Tiny new red potatoes go wonderfully with this dish.

Per serving: 147 calories, 2 g fat, 1 g saturated fat (6% calories from saturated fat), 2 g carbohydrate, 30 g protein, 0 g dietary fiber, 238 mg sodium. Exchanges: 4 Very Lean Meat

Asparagus

Asparagus officinalis

Here is another reason why I intend to have gardening as an ongoing passionate *pastime*. Nothing about growing asparagus is instant. In fact, don't expect to get any results for two years' time!

I've used the acronym FABIS (fresh and best in season) throughout the book because it highlights the rites of passage for gardeners who love to eat. It draws attention to the prime season for each plant, and it is very useful as a guide to regional cuisines that use plants that complement one another and are harvested at the same time.

Asparagus is a great early-spring favorite. In fact, it can almost lead the field once it's established. It is a plant that requires your patience, since even a newly purchased 2-year-old root can take 3 years to provide the tender young spears.

In that it only needs about 4+ hours of sun, it is a fine crop to grow in a partially shaded corner of the garden—a little out of the way with perhaps a comfortable planting of parsley alongside it?

Once established—and well fed—it can keep on going for at least 12 years. All you have to do is cut it back when the plant browns, re-move all the old leaves (and their beetles), dig in good manured compost, mulch it thickly with straw, and . . . wait for spring

I prefer my spears to be very small. (The big varieties like Jersey Giant seem to me to have lost that fine delicate flavor.) I truly dislike using a Hollandaise (butter, eggs, and lemon) sauce because it overwhelms the flavor. Better a little salt and white pepper and a spritz of extra-virgin olive oil.

Note: To go the extra mile in understanding how to grow asparagus, please see Stephen Albert's *Kitchen Garden Grower's Guide*. And for an excellent booklet on the subject, nobody has done it better than Michael Higgins in *Grow the Best Asparagus*, which is available from Territorial Seed Company (see References and Resources).

The Numbers

Asparagus has moderate amounts of purines that may be troublesome for people with gout. It is, however, a good source of niacin and iron.

Per 100 g steamed (3.5 oz): 20 calories, 0.12 g fat, 0 g saturated fat, 4 g carbohydrate, 2 g protein, 2 g dietary fiber, 2 mg sodium

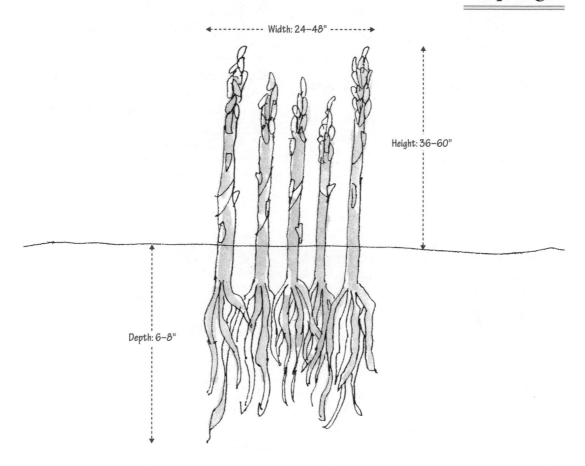

Width: 24–48"

Height: 36–60"

Depth: 6–8"

Perennial
Water: Heavy but not waterlogged
Sun: 4 hours minimum
Companion Planting:
PRO: Tomato, parsley, basil
CON: Carrots, onions, chives, garlic, leeks, potatoes
Pests/Diseases: Aphids, asparagus beetles, slugs, snails, spider mites, asparagus rust
Soil: Deep, loose, well-drained soil in raised beds—well composted

Fertilizer: Heavy feeder, fish emulsion
pH: 6.5–7.0
Varieties: Jersey Knight (smaller), Jersey Giant, Greenwich, Mild Winter UC 157
Zones: 3–6
Planting: Seed ¼ inch deep, 3 weeks before last frost
Germinate: 14–18 days
Harvest: Early spring in second year
Rotation: Avoid following onion plants
Edible: Young tender shoots (spears)

CHILLED STEAMED ASPARAGUS

This basic preparation method features three alternative endings. It's your choice!

SERVES 4

1 pound (or more) fresh asparagus

TOPPINGS
1 tablespoon freshly grated Parmesan cheese
or
2 teaspoons freshly squeezed lemon juice and
    a sprinkling of fresh dill or tarragon
or
2 tablespoons Treena's Vinaigrette (see
    page 74) or other low-fat salad dressing

Pop the bottom ends off the asparagus stems. They will snap at the point the stalk gets tough, so you won't have any stringy ends. Place in a steamer over boiling water and steam 3–5 minutes or until crisp tender and still beautifully green.

Place in a bowl of cold water to stop the cooking. Drain and chill.

Dust with Parmesan cheese and eat whole as finger food; cut on the diagonal into 2-inch pieces and toss with lemon juice and fresh herbs; or cut on the diagonal into 2-inch pieces, toss with the vinaigrette, and serve as a side salad on a leaf of butter lettuce garnished with a couple of cherry tomatoes.

With Parmesan cheese: Per serving: 31 calories, 1 g fat, 0 g saturated fat, 4 g carbohydrate, 0.5 g protein, 0 g dietary fiber, 35 mg sodium. Exchanges: 1 Vegetable

With lemon and fresh herbs: Per serving: 26 calories, 0 g fat, 0 g saturated fat, 5 g carbohydrate, 0 g protein, 0 g dietary fiber, 12 mg sodium. Exchanges: 1 Vegetable

With vinaigrette: Per serving: 48 calories, 3 g fat, 0 g saturated fat, 5 g carbohydrate, 0 g protein, 0 g dietary fiber, 60 mg sodium. Exchanges: 1 Vegetable, ½ Fat

SESAME GRILLED ASPARAGUS

For very little bother you can get a truly different vegetable.

SERVES 4

32 stalks fresh asparagus
1 tablespoon low-sodium soy sauce
1 tablespoon rice vinegar
1 teaspoon sugar
½ teaspoon toasted sesame oil
Pinch dried crushed chiles or Shanghai
    Coastline Ethmix (see page 288)
1 teaspoon toasted sesame seeds

Preheat the broiler to about 400°F.

Wash the asparagus and snap off the tough ends.

Combine the soy sauce, vinegar, sugar, sesame oil, and chiles. Brush the mixture on the asparagus and let marinate at least 15 minutes. Lay the spears under the broiler and cook, turning once, until tender (up to 8 minutes depending on size).

Serve sprinkled lightly with the sesame seeds.

Per serving: 46 calories, 1 g fat, 0 g saturated fat, 5 g carbohydrate, 4 g protein, 3 g dietary fiber, 350 mg sodium. Exchanges: 1 Vegetable

COLD ASPARAGUS SALAD

A fine side dish for cold poached salmon.
SERVES 4

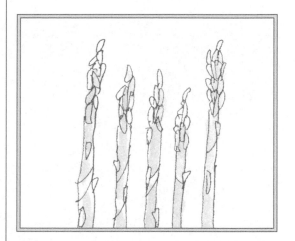

2 pounds fresh asparagus
1 teaspoon extra-virgin olive oil
1 tablespoon red wine vinegar
¼ teaspoon salt
¼ teaspoon freshly ground black pepper
2 tablespoons chopped fresh dill

Wash and snap the ends off the asparagus. Cut on the diagonal into 1-inch pieces. Steam in a basket over boiling water 3–5 minutes or until crisp tender. Plunge into cold water to stop cooking. Drain and lay on a platter.

Drizzle with oil and vinegar, and scatter salt, black pepper, and dill over the top. Toss gently and let sit for ½ hour. Serve at room temperature or chilled.

Per serving: 32 calories, 1 g fat, 0 g saturated fat, 4 g carbohydrate, 5 g protein, 1 g dietary fiber, 150 mg sodium. Exchanges: 1 Vegetable

Beans

Phaseolus spp.

Where *in* the earth shall we begin with a vegetable that boasts more than 13,000 species? To start, beans come in two types: in the pod and horticultural, or shell, beans.

In the pod describes beans such as bush and pole green beans, snap, French, wax, Romano, and stringless. They are mostly green but can be yellow or purple and are always eaten fresh *in their pod.*

Horticultural beans include flageolet, borlotti, and cranberry. Usually all are dried, but some are eaten fresh, directly from the pod, such as fava and lima. Almost all of these came from southern Mexico and Central America and Peru, where they have been cultivated for more than 7,000 years, but they didn't make an appearance in Europe until the 15th century.

I planted both types: an in-the-pod runner called Blue Lake and a fava. They both did well, with the fava coming in at a close second. I think it could have won if I'd known to harvest the beans earlier than I did. I waited until midsummer, when the pods had swollen magnificently, but the beans inside had developed a typical blue-gray leathery jacket, which can be cut at the flecked end and squeezed out (to reveal a bean looking like a large lima). But this is really too much fuss by far, so it is better to take them young and tender (see "Fava Beans" on page 144.)

You can plant a new crop every 10 days for a continual harvest, and you can plant in autumn for a winter crop.

Very thin, green in-the-pod beans need only enough steaming time to enhance their color (2–3 minutes).

If you let the shell beans alone, they'll grow and eventually yellow, easily opening to spill out their white good-size beans. These can be sun-dried and stored away from light and moisture in fabric bags, not in glass or plastic. I always rinse and pick over and discard any broken, moldy, or discolored shell beans, and then soak them overnight before cooking.

The Numbers

Red kidney beans per 100 g raw (3.5 oz; ½ cup): 127 calories, 0.5 g fat, 0 g saturated fat, 23 g carbohydrate, 9 g protein, 7 g dietary fiber, 1 mg sodium

Green beans per 100 g raw (3.5 oz; ½ cup): 31 calories, 0 g fat, 0 g saturated fat, 7 g carbohydrate, 2 g protein, 3 g dietary fiber, 6 mg sodium

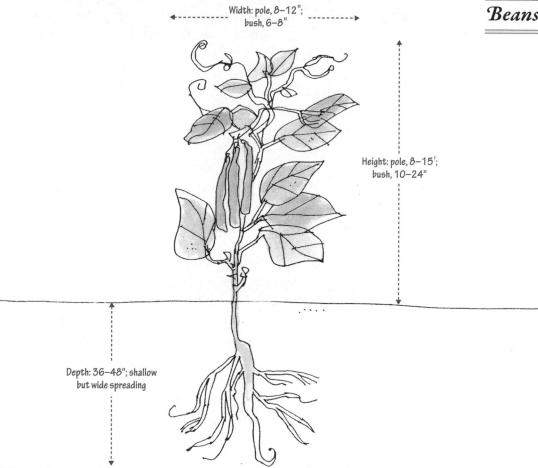

Width: pole, 8–12";
bush, 6–8"

Height: pole, 8–15';
bush, 10–24"

Depth: 36–48"; shallow
but wide spreading

Annual
Water: Light; more after blooms but try to keep the foliage dry to avoid disease
Sun: Full
Companion Planting:
PRO: Bush/pole beans, carrots, celery, chard
CON: Beets, cabbage, onions
Pests: Aphids, bean leaf beetles, cabbage loopers, slugs, whiteflies
Diseases: Anthracnose, blight, mildew, crown rot
Soil: Humus-rich, loose, well-drained; add nitrogen-fixing bacteria in new garden
Fertilizer: Low nitrogen, moderate phosphorus, potassium
pH: 6.0–6.8

Varieties:
IN THE POD: Blue Lake (bushy pole), Venture (extra early bush)
HORTICULTURAL/SHELL: Borlotti (red/cream), Great Northern White, King of the Garden (lima), fava
Zones: 3–11
Planting: Spring, seed 1-inch deep when soil is 65°F and above, from then on every 10 days; also in fall for a winter crop
Germinate: 4–10 days
Blooms: Summer
Harvest: Bush variety, 45–60 days; pole variety, 60–85 days
Rotation: Alternate with leafy greens like chard; leave bed for 3 years before reseeding with beans
Edible: Seeds and, in some cases, pods

BEAN DIP WITH A KICK

Bean dips are always popular at a party. This one can deliver quite a punch, depending on how you handle a ¼ teaspoon measure of spices.

SERVES 4

1 (15-ounce) can low-sodium Great Northern beans, rinsed and drained
¼ cup low-fat salad dressing, any variety
¼ teaspoon hot pepper flakes or to taste
1 tablespoon chopped fresh parsley
1 pound carrots cut into sticks or ready-peeled small carrots, or other cut-up veggies

In a blender, combine beans with salad dressing until smooth and creamy. Add hot pepper flakes according to your taste or split the mixture into mild and lethal heat. Sprinkle with the parsley and serve as a dip for carrots or other cut-up vegetables.

Per serving: 176 calories, 2 g fat, 0 g saturated fat, 33 g carbohydrate, 8 g protein, 7 g dietary fiber, 172 mg sodium. Exchanges: 1½ Starch, 2 Vegetable

SENATE BEAN SOUP

This is the famous soup served in the Senate in Washington, DC, and especially welcome on raw ice-bound winter days. Although it's normally made with ham hocks (more pork barrel for you), this variation is purely vegetarian to meet our focus on vegetables. The smoked paprika is used to replace the color and flavor taken out when the classic ham hock is removed.

SERVES 6

6 cups water
1 bay leaf
3 whole cloves
1 pound dried navy beans, rinsed, picked over, and soaked overnight
½ teaspoon nonaromatic olive oil
1½ cups chopped sweet onion
4 garlic cloves, bashed and chopped
2 carrots, peeled and cut into ¼-inch dice (yield 1½ cups)
2 ribs celery, cut into ¼-inch dice (yield 1 cup)
1 medium russet potato, peeled and chopped (yield 1½ cups)
½ teaspoon ground cumin
¼ teaspoon dried summer savory
2 tablespoons chopped fresh parsley plus more for garnish
½ teaspoon salt
¼ teaspoon freshly ground pepper
1 tablespoon smoked paprika or to taste

Pour water into a medium saucepan with the bay leaf and cloves. Add the beans, bring to a boil, reduce the heat to medium-low, and simmer 1½ hours or until the beans are tender but not mushy. (You can cut cooking time by using a pressure cooker; check the manufacturer's instructions. You can also use canned beans.)

When the beans are cooked, heat the oil in a chef's pan or skillet over medium-high. Sauté the onions for 2 minutes and then add the garlic, carrots, celery, and potato. Cook for 3 more minutes before adding to the cooked beans and their cooking liquid. Stir in the cumin and summer savory, and simmer 20 minutes or until the vegetables are tender.

Pour about a third of the bean mixture into a blender and whiz until smooth. Return it to the rest of the beans and stir in the parsley, salt, and pepper. Add the smoked paprika. Serve with more chopped parsley.

Per serving: 344 calories, 2 g fat, 0 g saturated fat, 64 g carbohydrate, 16 g protein, 15 g dietary fiber, 322 mg sodium. Exchanges: 3½ Starch, 1 Very Lean Meat, 2 Vegetable

STRING WING BEAN SALAD

An extremely low-fat salad with tons of flavor.
SERVES 4

FOR THE SALAD
1 pound green beans or wing beans, tipped, tailed, and cut in half
¼ teaspoon salt
¼ teaspoon freshly ground black pepper
⅛ teaspoon ground allspice
4 fresh Italian plum tomatoes, such as Roma, cut lengthwise into eighths
¼ cup roughly chopped stuffed green olives
6 fresh basil leaves, finely sliced (yield 1 tablespoon)
2 green onions, sliced into ¼-inch pieces (yield ¼ cup)

FOR THE GLAZE
¼ teaspoon arrowroot
½ teaspoon water
¼ cup balsamic or red wine vinegar

To prepare the salad, place the beans in a large vegetable steamer and sprinkle with the salt, black pepper, and allspice. Cover and steam for 6 minutes.

Combine the tomatoes, olives, basil, and onions in a large serving bowl and set aside.

Prepare the glaze: Combine the arrowroot with the water to make a slurry. Pour the vinegar into a small saucepan and add the slurry. Stir over medium heat until clear, glossy, and slightly thickened.

Add the cooked beans to the tomato mixture in the serving bowl and toss with the warm vinegar glaze.

Per serving: 49 calories, 1 g fat, 0 g saturated fat, 9 g carbohydrate, 1 g protein, 4 g dietary fiber, 360 mg sodium. Exchanges: 2 Vegetables

Beets and Beet Greens

Beta vulgaris esculenta

Red beets have such a grand color and flavor, especially when they wind up in the classic Polish borscht, along with its inevitable velvety sour cream finish . . . Now that would be reason enough to plant the root were it not for the added benefit of the equally delicious young beet leaves, which actually have better nutritional value than the root.

Our beets grew rapidly in the only semi-shaded part of our garden, but they still got a good 6–7 hours of sun each day. I thinned them to a 2-inch clear space several times. (I steamed the early 6-inch-high greens with their immature roots and served them with nonfat vegetarian canned baked beans—delicious!)

I love the idea that this wild North African native was first cultivated by the Egyptians; somehow it has added a layer of the exotic that Poland—no matter how great its cuisine—doesn't evoke.

My earliest memories of beets revolve around the thin pickled slices served with salads and the way my grandmother used to dice beets and stir them into clouds of amazingly light and fluffy mashed potatoes, along with a handful of parsley. There was no need for cream, milk, or butter; the sweet/sour of the pickled beet and its smooth light purple companion were enough!

In early spring into summer, I have also used the leaves in small pieces in salad mixes.

I found out, too late for my first year, about the Chioggia—a classic heirloom beet with a candy striped interior that doesn't bleed like the deep red varieties. They lose their distinct red and white rings when boiled or steamed, but do better when wrapped in foil and roasted. So next year I'll plant the yellow Goldens and the curiously striped Chioggias.

The Numbers

Beets contain high levels of oxalate, which could be of concern for kidney stones.

Roots for each 100 g boiled (3.5 oz; ½ cup): 43 calories, 0 g fat, 0 g saturated fat, 10 g carbohydrate, 2 g protein, 3 g dietary fiber, 77 mg sodium

Leaves for each 100 g raw (3.5 oz; 1 cup firmly packed): 22 calories, 0 g fat, 0 g saturated fat, 4 g carbohydrate, 2 g protein, 4 g dietary fiber, 226 mg sodium

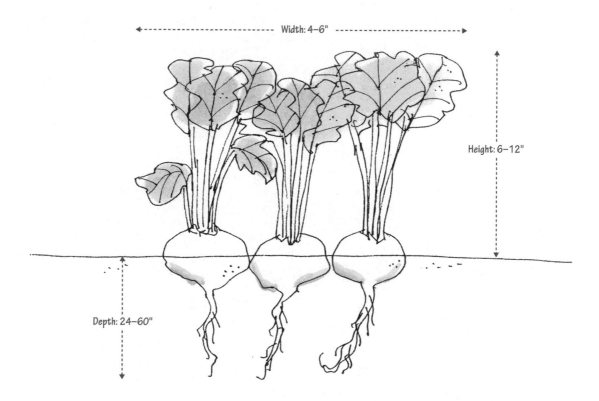

Width: 4–6"

Height: 6–12"

Depth: 24–60"

Annual/Cool Season
Water: Overhead, regular; to keep leaves crisp
Sun: Partial shade
Companion Planting:
PRO: Bush beans, cabbage, leeks, lettuce, onions, radishes
CON: Mustard, pole beans
Pests: Beet leafhoppers, webworms, weevils, flea beetles
Diseases: Leaf spot, scab
Soil: Light loam, well drained, free of stones
Fertilizer: Ample manure/compost, 9 inches down; fish emulsion when leaves are 6 inches high

pH: 6.5–7.5
Varieties: Red Ace, Chioggia (candy striped), Golden (yellow), Crosby Egyptian
Zones: 5–10
Planting: Seed ¼–½ inch deep, 2–4 weeks before last frost; thin seedlings 4–6 inches apart
Germinate: 4–10 days, then every 2–3 weeks for successive planting until midsummer
Blooms: 2nd year
Harvest: 49–91 days
Rotation: Avoid following spinach or chard
Edible: Roots and leaf greens

BEETS

Basic Preparation

Wash the beet roots and the leaves well. Cut the greens off the beets, leaving an inch of stem. Leave the long root intact.

Cut the greens into ¼-inch pieces. Set aside.

Cover the beets with water in a saucepan and cook whole until tender, 30–45 minutes, depending on their size. Drain and run under cold water to cool. Peel and cut into quarters or slice.

Alternatively, roast the raw beet root, wrapped in foil, at 350°F for 40 minutes.

BEET AND POTATO PUREE

This takes me right back to my boyhood. How I loved this side dish! Recently I've added fresh basil leaves, which provide a splendid color and flavor contrast.

SERVES 4

2 medium russet potatoes
3 medium beets, boiled or roasted, sliced
  (see Basic Preparation)
¼ teaspoon salt
¼ teaspoon freshly ground black pepper
8 fresh whole basil leaves

Peel the potatoes and cut in eighths. Cook for 15 minutes in boiling water. Add the sliced cooked beets and cook until the potatoes are tender, about 5 minutes more. Drain.

Mash the potatoes and beets together, and stir in the salt and black pepper. I like a rather lumpy mash for its interesting texture, but if you want it completely smooth, you can whiz it in a food processor. Add the basil just before serving.

Per serving: 75 calories, 0 g fat, 0 g saturated fat, 17 g carbohydrate, 3 g protein, 2 g dietary fiber, 178 mg sodium. Exchanges: 1 Starch

BEET SALAD

A truly different salad to take along to a potluck in midsummer, it could steal the show!

SERVES 6

1 pound boiled or roasted beets, cut into
  ½-inch dice
⅓ cup cider vinegar
1 teaspoon chopped fresh chives
½ cup yogurt cheese (see page 290)
1 tablespoon chopped fresh parsley
Large bunch watercress or whole arugula
  leaves, chilled

In a large bowl, mix the beets, vinegar, and chives, and cover and let marinate for 30 minutes at room temperature.

Strain, discarding the marinade. Place the

beets back into the bowl and stir in the yogurt cheese and parsley.

Toss the beets with the chilled greens and serve.

Per serving: 53 calories, 0 g fat, 0 g saturated fat, 11 g carbohydrate, 3 g protein, 2 g dietary fiber, 83 mg sodium

BEETS AND GREENS WITH AN ORANGE REDUCTION

For beet lovers, this use of the whole plant at one time is a great joy. The orange juice combines well with the beets' natural sweetness.

SERVES 4

1 bunch (4 large or 8 small) beet roots, boiled or roasted (see Basic Preparation), cut into quarters with greens
½ cup freshly squeezed orange juice
¼ teaspoon salt

Place the beet greens in a large skillet with the orange juice, cover, and bring to a boil. Reduce the heat to a slow boil and cook 3–4 minutes until nearly tender. Toss in the quartered beets and continue cooking, uncovered, until they are heated through and the liquid is almost gone. Season with salt and serve.

Per serving: 72 calories, 0 g fat, 0 g saturated fat, 16 g carbohydrate, 2 g protein, 4 g dietary fiber, 345 mg sodium. Exchanges: 3 Vegetable

ROASTED CHIOGGIA BEETS

Peeling the beets before you cook them can be messy, so wear an apron and disposable kitchen gloves.

SERVES 4

4 medium Chioggia beets (about 2 inches in diameter)
2 tablespoons freshly squeezed lime juice
¼ teaspoon ground cardamom
1 tablespoon honey
1 teaspoon nonaromatic olive oil

Preheat the oven to 400°F.

Peel the beets and cut into 1-inch chunks.

Combine the lime juice, cardamom, honey, and oil in a small bowl. Place the beets in a 9-inch baking dish and toss with the lime juice mixture.

Lay a sheet of aluminum foil over the top and bake 30 minutes. Remove the foil and bake 20 minutes longer or until the beets are glazed and tender.

Per serving: 82 calories, 1 g fat, 0 g saturated fat, 17 g carbohydrate, 2 g protein, 4 g dietary fiber, 89 mg sodium. Exchanges: 2 Vegetable

Bok Choy

Brassica rapa var. *chinesis*

Until I began the garden, I had only a nodding (but still affectionate) relationship with the large-leaf, heavy, white-stalked bok choy and its miniature variety mei qing choy, which I've always called baby bok choy.

I had understood that bok choy, related to the Napa cabbage (see page 188), has another close relative called pe-tsai (*Brassica rapa* var. *pekinensis*), which is a small dessert-spoon-size variety, with dark green leaves that you can "cut and come again" leaf by leaf throughout the growing season.

The term *cut and come again* refers to leafy plants, like lettuce, chard, and mustard, that can be harvested as young leaves without pulling up the entire plant. Cuts are usually made about 2 inches above the soil level. I use a pair of scissors that I keep in a plastic box with a few antiseptic cloths to wipe the blades just in case there are any diseases that could be spread.

Bok choy and its family members did really well in my new raised beds when temperatures were relatively cool. Then suddenly (and surprisingly to many of us) it got quite hot—in the upper 80s and 90s—for a week or so, and my happy plants bolted rapidly. (So harvest the outer leaves when young for best flavor and to help avoid bolting as the days lengthen.)

I'd read that they gather up their best flavor as the days get shorter. Mine never got that chance because I'd planted them in full sun. Next time, I'll wait until autumn to plant, and pray for a mild winter.

I especially like to use the white, tender stalk of the larger variety as a stir-fry base, since it adds a refreshing keynote that is slightly sweet. And because pe-tsai cooks so quickly, it is a splendid last-minute addition to stir-fries.

The Numbers

Bok choy has remarkable anticancer properties, including glucosinolates and vitamins C and A.

For every 100 g raw (3.5 oz; 1 cup): 13 calories, 0 g fat, 0 g saturated fat, 2 g carbohydrate, 2 g protein, 1 g dietary fiber, 65 mg sodium

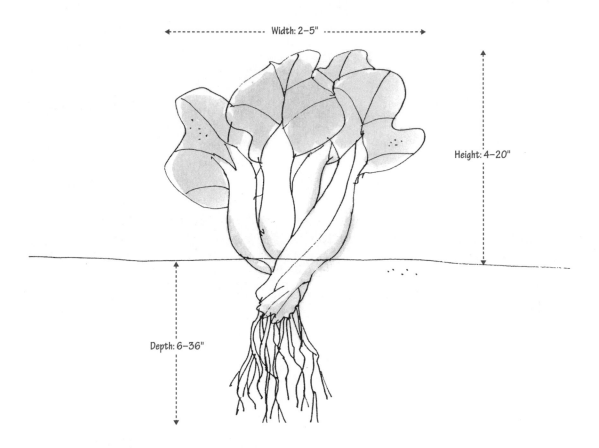

Width: 2–5"

Height: 4–20"

Depth: 6–36"

Annual/Cool Season
Water: Moderate and often
Sun: Part shade; 6 hours per day
Companion Planting:
PRO: Beets, lettuce, onions, radishes, spinach
CON: Tomatoes, potatoes, peppers
Pests: Aphids, slugs, cabbage worm
Diseases: Yellows, black rot
Soil: Rich humus, good drainage, fertile clay loam
Fertilizer: Use good compost in autumn
pH: 6.5–7.5

Varieties: Bok choy (not cold tolerant); mei qing choy (baby size); Napa (see page 188)
Zones: 3–6
Planting: Seed ¼-inch deep, 10–12 days before first frost
Germinate: 4–10 days
Harvest: From seed, 65–70 days; from transplant, 45–50 days
Rotation: Don't follow cabbage family
Edible: Leaves and stalks

STEAMED BABY BOK CHOY

Truly elegant in appearance, all bok choy needs is a swift spray of olive oil and absolute-last-minute cooking.

SERVES 4

4 baby bok choy (up to 5 inches long)
¼ teaspoon salt
¼ teaspoon freshly ground black pepper
Extra-virgin olive oil cooking spray

Cut the bok choy in half lengthwise. Lay them in a large steamer and season with salt and black pepper. Steam covered for 3 minutes. Spritz with olive oil. Serve hot immediately.

Per serving: 9 calories, 0 g fat, 0 g saturated fat, 1 g carbohydrate, 1 g protein, 1 g dietary fiber, 106 mg sodium. Exchanges: Free Food

STEAMED MATURE BOK CHOY

As with many vegetables of this type, including Swiss chard, bok choy is best cooked in two stages, since the stalk takes longer than the tender leaf.

SERVES 4

1 large bok choy
¼ teaspoon salt

¼ teaspoon freshly ground black pepper
1 tablespoon freshly squeezed lemon juice

Cut off the bottom of the stalk to separate the stems. Cut the thick white stems from the green leaves. Wash and trim as needed.

Steam the white parts in a steamer basket for 3 minutes, stir, season with half the salt and black pepper, and steam 3 more minutes. Divide among four hot plates and keep warm.

Lay the leaves in the steamer, season with the remaining salt and black pepper, and steam 2 minutes. Lay on the plates with the stems, sprinkle with lemon juice, and serve.

Per serving: 9 calories, 0 g fat, 0 g saturated fat, 1 g carbohydrate, 1 g dietary fiber, 106 mg sodium, 4 g protein. Exchanges: Free Food

STIR FRIED BOK CHOY

This can be a warm salad or a side dish for a colorful entrée.

SERVES 4

1 head mature bok choy
1 teaspoon nonaromatic olive oil
2 garlic cloves, crushed
1 tablespoon chopped gingerroot
1 green onion, chopped
1 tablespoon Chinese hoisin or low-sodium soy sauce

Cut 2 inches off the bottom of the bunch of bok choy and discard. Separate the leaves and stems, and wash carefully. Drain and dry on paper towels. Cut the stems from the leaves. Cut the stems across into ¼-inch slices and the leaves into ¼-inch strips. Keep separate.

Heat the oil in a large skillet over medium-high. Drop in the garlic, ginger, and onion, and cook 30 seconds. Add the bok choy stems and stir-fry 3–5 minutes. Toss in the leaves and cook 1 minute longer. Add the hoisin or soy sauce and stir to coat the bok choy. Serve immediately.

Per serving: 33 calories, 2 g fat, 0 g saturated fat, 4 g carbohydrate, 3 g protein, 2 g dietary fiber, 235 mg sodium. Exchanges: 1 Vegetable

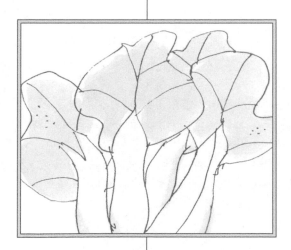

Broccoli

Brassica oleracea var. *italica*

Many of us remember the fuss when President George H. W. Bush admitted to a dislike of broccoli, which only goes to prove that our understanding of what's important in politics is possibly flawed. I must admit, however, that my wife, Treena, is on his side, taking (for about the first time) a contrary point of view to my preference.

This remarkable plant is an early example of human intervention. According to several sources, the ancient Romans tinkered with a local wild cabbage, native to the eastern coastline of Italy, and came up with the plant we know today.

You'll find that broccoli seeds are described as early, midseason, and late. It's a good idea to do two plantings by starting indoors from seed some 8 weeks before the last frost and then transplanting them to flats 2 inches apart when 5 inches tall (about 5 weeks from seed). Then gradually harden them off outside for a week or so before you put them in the raised beds. Repeat the process in late summer for a winter crop. Plants bolt in hot temperatures, so plant in shade if possible or plant for a fall crop.

I'm a great fan of broccoli's tiny family members, spring raab and broccolini (a cross between broccoli and kai lan, Chinese broccoli), which have very thin stalks and equally small flowering heads. Everything is edible, requiring only 2–4 minutes of steaming time. They have little of the familiar sulfurous aroma and are wonderfully nutritious—well worth the effort to grow, especially as these varieties are somewhat pricey to buy at the supermarket.

The Numbers

The sulforaphame, a key anticancer ingredient, is 30–50 times stronger in spring raab than in broccoli. Both plants also have the other well-proven cancer fighter, indole-3-carbinol.

For each 100 g cooked (3.5 oz; ½ cup): 35 calories, 0 g fat, 0 g saturated fat, 7 g carbohydrate, 2 g protein, 3 g dietary fiber, 41 mg sodium

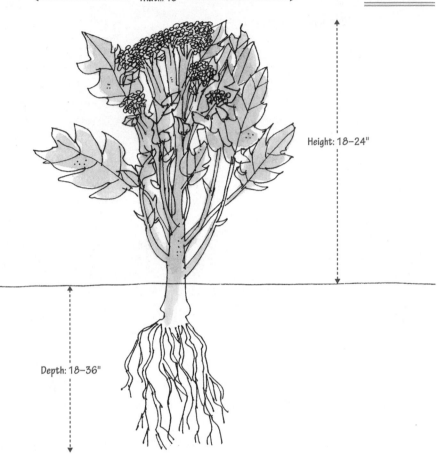

Width: 15"

Height: 18–24"

Depth: 18–36"

Annual/Hardy/Cool Season
Water: Ground level irrigation only
Sun: Partial shade is okay; may need extra shade in hot weather, over 80°F
Companion Planting:
PRO: Bush beans, beets, carrots, celery, chard, cucumbers, lettuce, tomatoes
CON: Pole beans, strawberries
Pests: Aphids, cabbage loopers, cutworms, slugs, weevils, whiteflies
Diseases: Black rot, mildew, clubroot
Soil: Humus-rich, moist, well-drained, sandy loam
Fertilizer: Fish emulsion every 2–3 weeks after buds form

pH: 6.0–7.0
Varieties: Early Dividend (spring), Green Comet (spring), spring raab
Zones: 3–11
Planting: Spring and autumn, seed ½ inch deep; change planting beds annually; indoors, start 6–10 weeks before last frost, then transplant when 5 inches tall, harden off 10 days, and move to raised beds 14–21 inches apart
Germinate: 7–10 days
Harvest: 78–98 days
Rotation: Avoid following cabbage family
Edible: Heads and stalks

BROCCOLI

Basic Preparation

I really like broccoli, especially when it's perfectly cooked—the stem just tender and the heads radiantly green. At the last moment, I add fresh basil leaves sliced fine as a garnish, with a spritz of extra-virgin olive oil. Just a touch of sea salt, and I couldn't be happier. Well, perhaps when I've steamed some small heads for just 1–2 minutes, let them cool, then used them as a dipper for hummus lightened up with my yogurt cheese (see page 290) to create a delicious flavor combination!

STEAMED BROCCOLI

It's been my experience that dislike is usually based on a childhood rebellion and can, as we mature, be easily changed, but when you prepare this dish, be sure that the stalks are softened even though the green darkens. The basil and lemon add a special taste treat to convince the unbeliever.

SERVES 4

1½ pounds broccoli
¼ teaspoon salt
½ teaspoon dried basil
1 teaspoon freshly squeezed lemon juice

Remove the tough bottom of each stalk and discard. Cut off the stalks where they meet the florets. Peel the stalks, cut into ¼-inch diagonal slices, and place in a steamer, or save them and use in a stir-fry or soup if you would rather.

Cut apart the florets and lay them on top of the stems. Season with salt, scatter the basil over top, and sprinkle with lemon juice. Steam 5–7 minutes and serve immediately. I find that 5 minutes will usually be enough time to cook the florets without the stems.

Per serving: 35 calories, 0 g fat, 0 g saturated fat, 7 g carbohydrate, 3 g protein, 3 g dietary fiber, 180 mg sodium. Exchanges: 2 Vegetable

GREEN ON GREENS WITH GINGER GREEN SAUCE

Here we have an unusual combination of greens with different textures accented by the remarkable ginger sauce.

SERVES 4

FOR THE GREEN SAUCE
2 cups tightly packed fresh spinach leaves
½ cup low-sodium vegetable stock
  (see page 288)
¼ teaspoon low-sodium soy sauce
½ teaspoon sesame oil
2 teaspoons rice wine vinegar or white vinegar
2 teaspoons grated gingerroot

FOR THE VEGETABLES

2 cups sliced green beans (bite-size pieces)
2 cups cut broccoli florets (bite-size pieces)
Extra-virgin olive oil cooking spray

Puree the green sauce ingredients in a blender until the sauce is a vivid green and very smooth.

Steam the green beans and broccoli in a basket about 5 minutes or just until each is bright green and crisp tender.

To serve, drizzle some green sauce on each plate and top with ½ cup each hot green beans and hot broccoli. Spray lightly with the olive oil.

Per serving: 54 calories, 2 g fat, 0 g saturated fat, 8 g carbohydrate, 3 g protein, 2 g dietary fiber, 133 mg sodium. Exchanges: 2 Vegetable

BROCCOLI ENDIVE SALAD

This is a good example of a composed salad, one in which each ingredient is carefully placed and not simply tossed together.

SERVES 6

1 pound broccoli florets
¾ cup low-fat French or Italian salad dressing, divided into ¼ cups (or Treena's Vinaigrette, page 74)
1 pound Belgium endive
2 red bell peppers, cut into strips, or 2 cups tiny tomatoes
1 tablespoon toasted pine nuts

Tip the broccoli into a pot of boiling water to blanch for 1 minute. Turn into a colander in the sink and briefly run under cold water to stop the cooking. Drain thoroughly in the colander, transfer to a bowl, and toss with ¼ cup of the salad dressing.

Cut the cone-shaped core out of the bottom of each endive. The leaves should separate. In a separate bowl, toss gently with another ¼ cup of dressing.

To compose the salad on a platter or on individual plates, lay the endive leaves around the sides. Set the pepper strips (or tomatoes) on the leaves. Place the marinated broccoli in the middle and top with the pine nuts. Drizzle the remaining ¼ cup dressing over all.

Per serving: 96 calories, 3 g fat, 0 g saturated fat, 17 g carbohydrate, 4 g protein, 5 g dietary fiber, 272 mg sodium. Exchanges: 2 Vegetable, ½ Fat, ½ Carbohydrate

Brussels Sprouts

Brassica oleracea var. *gemmifera*

The Brussels sprout is another much misunderstood vegetable that often heads the list of most avoided foods, along with tofu and liver!

This is possibly due to the best—or worst—efforts of Anglo-Saxon cooks. As a child, I recall these tight little cabbages being boiled to death (literally!) at my boarding school. They lay there, very pale green and soggy in their salted water, smelling strongly of sulfur. While sprouts can be steamed (never boiled!), I have found that a slow roast will allow for both tenderness and sweetness to be developed to such a degree that it even won over one of our grandchildren, who now actually puts in a request for them.

Remember to pinch off the stem when it reaches 20 inches in height. Then heap soil around the stem (2–3 inches) to hold it up as the sprouts grow. They will mature from the ground up; pick off the leaves first when the sprouts form. Harvest the sprouts when ½ inch in diameter, when they are the sweetest. Brussels sprouts' bad rep may also be due to missteps when harvesting. The mildest and sweetest flavor is developed after a light frost, which allows plant strength to flow to the buds. Cover with bird netting and avoid handling when the plants are wet and most prone to disease.

The Numbers

Brussels sprouts pack a good measure of vitamin B_6, thiamine, and potassium, along with cancer-fighting glucosinolates.

For each 100 g cooked (3.5 oz; ¾ cup): 42 calories, 0 g fat, 0 g saturated fat, 8 g carbohydrate, 4 g protein, 4 g dietary fiber, 15 mg sodium

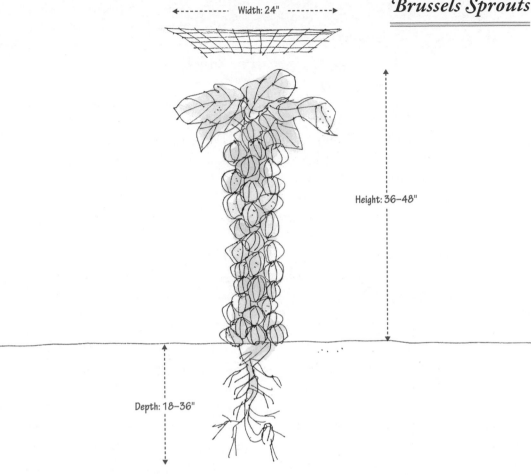

Width: 24"

Height: 36–48"

Depth: 18–36"

Annual/Cool Season
Water: Regular, moist
Sun: Full
Companion Planting:
PRO: Artichokes, beets, celery, peas, spinach
CON: Kohlrabi, pole beans, strawberries, tomatoes
Pests: Aphids, cabbage, loppers, butterflies, flea beetles, slugs, whiteflies. Use a net to avoid losing buds to small birds.
Diseases: Black rot, mildew, yellows
Soil: Moist, humus-rich, fertile soil, rich sandy loam, or silt loam
Fertilizer: Fish emulsion every 2–3 weeks; avoid excess nitrogen, which causes rapid leaf growth that robs sprout formation

pH: 5.5–6.8
Varieties: Jade Cross hybrid, Valiant (for sweeter, nuttier flavor), Catskill (small size, good autumn harvest)
Zones: 4–7
Planting: Seed ¼–½ inch deep in early summer
Germinate: 3–10 days
Harvest: From seed, 100–110 days; from transplant, 80–90 days
Rotation: Avoid following members of the cabbage family. Don't plant in same bed for 4 years—just move them around!
Edible: Sprouts (small buds)

BRUSSELS SPROUTS

Basic Preparation

No matter which cooking method you choose, prepare the spouts by first stripping off the outer (usually faded) leaves, trim the dried-out stalk flat, and cut a cross (an X) deeply into the stalk (especially for the larger ones). They can be steamed for 8–10 minutes—but never boil them in plain water because they tend to become waterlogged and insipid!

cross into the stalk ends. Combine the oil, garlic, salt, and black pepper, and toss with the prepared sprouts. Place in a small baking dish in a single layer.

Lay the rosemary sprigs on top (or sprinkle with dried rosemary) and roast 20 minutes or until tender. A quick shake halfway through will help them cook more evenly.

Per serving: 55 calories, 2 g fat, 0 g saturated fat, 8 g carbohydrate, 2 g protein, 3 g dietary fiber, 162 mg sodium. Exchanges: 2 Vegetable

ROASTED BRUSSELS SPROUTS

Slow roasting tends to concentrate sweetness and can convert nonbelievers with just one taste.

SERVES 4

32 small Brussels sprouts
1 tablespoon olive oil
2 garlic cloves, crushed
¼ teaspoon salt
¼ teaspoon freshly ground black pepper
2 3-inch sprigs rosemary or ½ teaspoon dried, finely chopped

Preheat the oven to 350°F.

Peel away any discolored leaves from the Brussels sprouts and trim the stalks. Cut a deep

ROSEMARY BRAISED BRUSSELS SPROUTS

This could be the ultimate Brussels sprouts recipe. If you can't win them over with this, then perhaps you need to move on until some-one grows up!

SERVES 4

1 pound smallest possible Brussels sprouts
1 cup low-sodium vegetable stock
   (see page 288)
1 teaspoon dried or a 4-inch branch of fresh rosemary
¼ teaspoon salt
1 teaspoon arrowroot or cornstarch mixed with 1 tablespoon stock or water (slurry)

Preheat the oven to 400°F.

Strip the outer leaves off the Brussels sprouts.

If they are very small, cook whole. Cut in half if they're larger than ¾ inch in diameter.

Bring the stock to a boil in a medium saucepan. Add the rosemary, salt, and prepared sprouts. Bring back to a boil and cook for 3 minutes, then turn everything into a small ovenproof dish and braise for 10 minutes or until just tender.

Stir in the slurry and heat over medium until the sauce is glossy and slightly thickened. Serve with a little sauce spooned over to glisten.

Per serving: 54 calories, 1 g fat, 0 g saturated fat, 12 g carbohydrate, 2 g dietary fiber, 187 mg sodium. Exchanges: 2 Vegetable

Trim the sprouts and cut in half; steam in a basket until tender, about 5 minutes.

Warm the oil in a medium skillet over medium heat. Add the thyme, caraway seeds, and vinegar. Drop in the steamed sprouts, season with salt and black pepper, and toss to coat well with the sauce, cooking about 2 minutes. Serve immediately while they are still bright green.

Per serving: 61 calories, 2 g fat, 0 g saturated fat, 10 g carbohydrate, 2 g dietary fiber, 169 mg sodium. Exchanges: 2 Vegetable, ½ Fat

WARM BRUSSELS SPROUT SALAD

There are times when a warm salad is preferred, such as in the late fall. This is a good example, but it really does need good (expensive) balsamic to be a true success.

SERVES 4

1 (12-ounce) package frozen Brussels sprouts or 1 pound fresh
1 teaspoon olive oil
½ teaspoon dried thyme or 2 teaspoons fresh
¼ teaspoon caraway seeds
2 tablespoons balsamic vinegar
¼ teaspoon salt
¼ teaspoon freshly ground black pepper

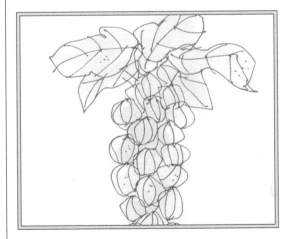

Cabbage

Brassica oleracea var. *capitata*

I thoroughly enjoy a number of German dishes, and I count as one of my very best friends the great Bavarian master chef Karl Guggennoss, dean of Culinary Studies at Johnson and Wales University, one of the largest chef-training schools in the world.

Chef Guggennoss loves red cabbage, and so do I. But, as I have discovered, I do have my limits. I devoted an entire row of my fledgling garden to red cabbage—one after the other after the other . . . Ah, for an occasional green-leafed Savoy cabbage!

To add further complications, a combination of my not-so-well-regulated overhead irrigation and a particularly hot, sunny period caused the heads to split!

If you are an experienced gardener, you will, at this point, be wagging your head back and forth and muttering, "Didn't he know better?" The answer is, of course, "No. I didn't." That's the kind of thing you learn by mistake during your first year ever!

Apparently their rapid early summer growth (sun plus water) caused the splitting. The water should be on the roots, as *in bed* irrigation. And should the sun blaze forth next year, then I shall grasp the cabbage, like my chiropractor grabs my head, and give it a gentle half turn to the left (or right) to detach some of the shallow roots and thus slow the growth. If the sun persists, then I'll create some shade for them.

Whether it is red or green or nearly white, I love the succulent, smooth sweetness of cabbage, especially when paired with sweet onions sautéed with a little olive oil and perhaps a few dill or coriander seeds.

The Numbers

For each 100 g cooked (3.5 oz; 1 cup): 23 calories, 0 g fat, 0 g saturated fat, 6 carbohydrate, 1 g protein, 2 g dietary fiber, 8 mg sodium.

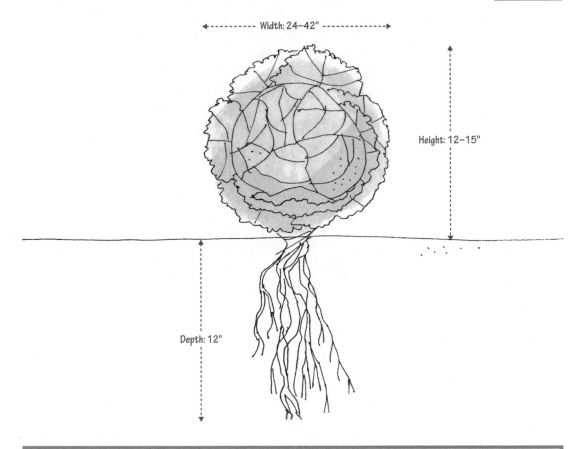

Width: 24–42"

Height: 12–15"

Depth: 12"

Annual/Cool Season

Water: Heavy, then moderate when head is formed; use drip irrigation and avoid overhead watering, especially in hot weather

Sun: Full, shade if hot

Companion Planting:

PRO: Beets, bush beans, carrots, celery, spinach, onions

CON: Pole beans, tomatoes, strawberries

Pests: Aphids, flea beetles, birds

Diseases: Yellow, mildew

Soil: Medium light, fertile, well-drained soil; spring plants do well in sandier soil; autumn plants do well with more clay

Fertilizer: Manure before planting; fertilize with heavy nitrogen, phosphorus, and potassium, then high nitrogen, as they grow; fish emulsion every 3–4 weeks

pH: 6.5–7.5

Varieties: Both Savoy King and Savoy Chieftain have sweeter/milder flavors than the round-head variety. Charmant is a good early season choice.

Zones: 3–11

Planting: Seed ¼ inch deep, 10–12 weeks before first frost for autumn harvest, 8–10 inches apart

Germinate: 5–10 days

Harvest: From seed, 70–120 days; from transplant, 49–56 days

Rotation: Avoid following cabbage family for 3 years to avoid soil-borne diseases and pests.

Edible: Leafy heads

CABBAGE ROLLS

This main dish takes time the first time you attempt it. But no doubt it will become a family favorite, and the labor involved is worth the reward. While I have endeavored to keep the recipes in this book all vegetarian, this is one that I have failed to convert—even trying to use nuts and grains as a substitute. I welcome your suggestions for a non-meat recipe; feel free to contact me via my website, listed at the back of the book.

MAKES 12 ROLLS

FOR THE ROLLS

1 large head green Savoy-type cabbage (9–10 inches in diameter)

1 teaspoon nonaromatic olive oil

2 cups finely chopped sweet onions

4 garlic cloves, bashed and chopped

6 ounces leanest ground beef (9% fat)

6 ounces ground white meat turkey

¼ cup raw long-grain white rice

2 tablespoons tomato puree

¼ cup beef broth

¼ teaspoon dried dill

¼ teaspoon salt

¼ teaspoon freshly ground black pepper

2 tablespoons chopped fresh parsley

FOR THE SAUCE

1½ cups tomato puree

1½ cups beef broth

¼ cup packed dark brown sugar

½ cup cider vinegar

¼ teaspoon freshly ground black pepper

¼ teaspoon dried dill

¼ teaspoon caraway seeds

3 bay leaves

2 teaspoons arrowroot mixed with 2 tablespoons water (slurry)

Preheat the oven to 350°F. Spray a 9×13-inch baking pan with cooking spray. Fill a large pot with water, cover, and bring to a boil.

To make the rolls, carve the core out of the cabbage and discard. Place the head in the boiling water and cook, covered, for 10 minutes. Take out of the boiling water and plunge into a bowl of cold water to cool.

Heat the oil in a chef's pan over medium-high. Drop the onions into the pan and cook 3 minutes or until they begin to turn translucent. Add the garlic and cook 1 more minute. Place half the onion mixture in a large bowl. Leave the rest in the pan to make the sauce and remove from the heat. Combine the beef and turkey, rice, tomato puree, broth, dill, salt, black pepper, and parsley with the onion mixture in the bowl.

To make the sauce, pour the tomato puree, broth, brown sugar, vinegar, black pepper, dill, caraway seeds, and bay leaves into the chef's pan with the reserved onion and garlic and bring to a simmer on medium-low while you make the rolls, about 15 minutes.

Drain the cabbage and separate 12 of the largest cabbage leaves without tearing them. Cut out the center heavy rib from each leaf, leaving a shallow V shape. Spread out on a clean work surface. Divide the filling among the leaves (a heaping tablespoon is about right). Overlap the sides where you removed the stems, fold over the sides first, and then roll to completely enclose the filling.

Set the rolls side by side in the prepared pan and pour half the sauce over all. Lay a piece of foil on top. Bake 30 minutes. Remove the foil and bake 30 minutes longer until the internal temperature is 150°F.

Divide the cabbage rolls among six warm plates. Pour the remaining sauce into a saucepan with the arrowroot slurry and cook over medium-high until thickened and glossy. Spoon over the waiting rolls.

Per 2 rolls: 249 calories, 7 g fat, 2 g saturated fat (7% calories from saturated fat), 32 g carbohydrate, 12 g protein, 6 g dietary fiber, 291 mg sodium. Exchanges: 1 Starch, 1 Lean Meat, 3 Vegetable, 1 Fat

CABBAGE SAUTÉ WITH CARAWAY

This is one of Treena's favorites, although she's recently gone cool on caraway, so we switched to dill and my Germany Ethmix spice mix.

SERVES 4

1 teaspoon nonaromatic olive oil
1 large onion, sliced
1 pound (1 small) cabbage, shredded
¼ teaspoon salt
¼ teaspoon freshly ground black pepper
1 teaspoon caraway seeds or ½ teaspoon each of dill seeds and Germany Ethmix (see page 287)

Heat the oil in a high-sided skillet over medium-high. Add the onion and cook, stirring occasionally, 8 minutes or until golden.

Stir in the cabbage, salt, black pepper, and caraway seeds. Cook, stirring, for about 12 minutes or until tender. Serve with a broiled beef steak tomato and a few boiled red potatoes.

Per serving: 64 calories, 1 g fat, 0 g saturated fat, 12 g carbohydrate, 2 g protein, 4 g dietary fiber, 168 mg sodium. Exchanges: 3 Vegetable

PLUM AND RED CABBAGE SALAD

This fruit and vegetable combination is dramatically different—and quite delicious. And yes, this dish does use my overplanted red cabbage.

SERVES 8

1 small head red cabbage, shredded to about 4 cups
8 yellow, purple, or green sweet plums, pitted and sliced
¼ cup chopped fresh parsley

FOR THE DRESSING
1 tablespoon extra-virgin olive oil
3 tablespoons balsamic or rice vinegar
¼ teaspoon salt
¼ teaspoon freshly ground black pepper

In a large bowl, combine the shredded cabbage, plums, and parsley. In a small bowl, whisk the dressing ingredients together and toss with the prepared fruit and vegetables.

Per serving: 49 calories, 2 g fat, 0 g saturated fat, 9 g carbohydrate, 1 g protein, 1 g dietary fiber, 78 mg sodium. Exchanges: ½ Fruit, ½ Fat

Carrots

Daucus carota var. *sativus*

I found it odd that the familiar orange color of the carrot wasn't its original shade; it didn't get that color until it was introduced into Europe. Much earlier, at least 300 BCE, when it was part of a family called Umbelliferae, it was mostly purple and black. So if you've recently seen the deep-colored carrots among the trendy heirloom vegetables at your specialty grocer, they are actually reverting to type.

When planting from seed, add sand to seeds to help early spacing. Mulch after thinning to retain moisture and prevent greening. Thin to 2 inches apart when tops are 4 inches tall, and keep surface moist during germination.

I planted a Nantes carrot that promised a medium-size cylindrical variety rather than the narrow tapered ones. During my thinning of the crop, I tried the tiny ones and found them tasteless. Later as baby carrots, they had developed some sweetness, but it wasn't until late August that the sweetness kept on getting better and better all the way up to Christmas (we had a warmer than usual fall), when I cleaned the beds.

Carrots have been my constant measure of success and enjoyment—they really are so much better than store bought, which seem to be largely made up of already peeled baby carrots in plastic bags (proving that convenience is king or that scraping a carrot is now considered hard labor!) or huge, woody, and split or fashion-model slender carrots, complete with greens. To my experience, these are almost always tasteless.

The Numbers

Just two carrots provide roughly four times the recommended daily allowance (RDA) of vitamin A. They also boast very good levels of vitamin K, biotin, and fiber.

For every 100 g raw (3.5 oz; ½ cup): 41 calories, 0 g fat, 0 g saturated fat, 10 g carbohydrate, 1 g protein, 3 g dietary fiber, 69 mg sodium

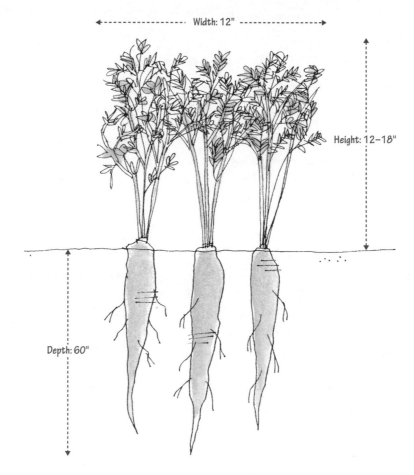

Width: 12"

Height: 12–18"

Depth: 60"

Annual/Cool Season
Water: Moderate
Sun: Full
Companion Planting:
PRO: Beans, Brussels sprouts, cabbage, chives, lettuce, radishes
CON: Celery, dill, parsnips
Pests: Aphids, nematodes, caterpillars, slugs, snails, weevils
Diseases: Blights, soft rot, yellows
Soil: Deep, loose, light sandy loam free of all lumps and stones; must also hold moisture well
Fertilizer: Avoid fresh manure or high-nitrogen fertilizer; fish emulsion 3 weeks after germination and when tops are 6–8 inches tall

pH: 5.5–6.8
Varieties: Nantes (moderate-size cylinders), Chantenay (best in shallow, clay soil), Danvers Half Long (sweet, stocky)
Zones: 3–12
Planting: Seed ¼–½ inch deep in early spring or about 2 weeks after last frost, 2 inches apart
Germinate: 6 days
Harvest: Baby carrots, 30–40 days; mature carrots, 50–80 days
Rotation: Avoid following celery, dill, fennel, parsley, parsnip
Edible: Roots

CARROTS

Basic Preparation

When freshly dug, carrots don't need to be peeled—just scrub and rinse well to eliminate the grit. Fresh carrots are perfect steamed whole or in chunks for about 14 minutes. I use a light dusting of nutmeg with a spritz of olive oil—perfection!

CARROT AND PARSNIP PUREE

This is one of our all item favorites, a splendid fall dish when the parsnips are perfect and the carrots sweetest.

SERVES 4

1 pound carrots, peeled and thinly sliced
1 pound small parsnips, peeled and thinly sliced
¼ teaspoon salt
¼ teaspoon freshly ground black pepper
3 tablespoons sesame seeds

Preheat the oven to 350°F.

Steam the carrots and parsnips 15 minutes or until very soft. Mash roughly and stir in the salt and black pepper.

Place in a small ungreased baking dish and scatter the sesame seeds over the top. Bake 20 minutes or until good and hot and the sesame seeds are nicely browned.

Per serving: 168 calories, 3 g fat, 1 g saturated fat (5% calories from saturated fat), 31 g carbohydrate, 4 g protein, 8 g dietary fiber, 221 mg sodium. Exchanges: 1½ Starch, 1 Vegetable, ½ Fat

CARROT SALAD

With its brilliant colors and a fresh real taste, this is a great side dish for a potluck or picnic.

SERVES 4

1 pound carrots, well scrubbed or peeled and coarsely grated
1 orange, peeled, seeded, and chopped
½ cup raisins
1 tablespoon chopped fresh mint
2 tablespoons freshly squeezed lime juice
Freshly grated zest of 1 lime

Combine the carrots, chopped orange, raisins, mint, lime juice, and zest. Chill for an hour or two to let the flavors mingle.

Per serving: 127 calories, 0 g fat, 0 g saturated fat, 32 g carbohydrate, 2 g protein, 6 g dietary fiber, 71 mg sodium. Exchanges: 2 Vegetable, 1½ Fruit

SAUTÉED SHREDDED CARROTS WITH DILL

The addition of nutmeg and dill lift this simple carrot dish to a new aromatic height.

SERVES 4

1 teaspoon nonaromatic olive oil
4 cups shredded carrots
1 teaspoon dried dill
¼ teaspoon salt
1 tablespoon chopped fresh dill (optional)
1 teaspoon grated nutmeg

Heat the oil in a high-sided skillet over medium-high. Add the carrots and dried dill, and sauté about 6 minutes, stirring often until tender.

Stir in the salt, fresh dill, and nutmeg, and serve.

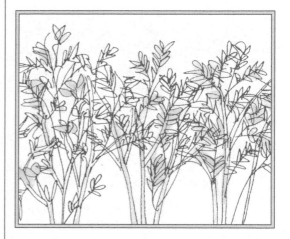

Per serving: 58 calories, 1 g fat, 0 g saturated fat, 11 g carbohydrate, 1 g protein, 3 g dietary fiber, 221 mg sodium. Exchanges: 2 Vegetable

Cauliflower

Brassica oleracea var. *botrytis*

Cauliflower, a somewhat tender (heat- and cold-sensitive) vegetable, made its way from Asia to Turkey around 600 BCE and hung around there for nearly 2,000 years—and still does. Northern Europe finally got a taste for it, or an ability to grow it, in the 1500s.

It is advisable to plant early to protect the vegetable from too much hot sun, or set up a screen to shield it. Try fall planting to avoid the early hot summer sun, since above 68°F the florets lose their quality. When individual florets are 2–3 inches wide, tie the leaves over the head to shade it and to keep the head (curd) white; harvest 4–10 days later. This technique is called *blanching* (not to be confused with the culinary method of plunging into boiling water for a few moments).

There are a number of colored varieties of cauliflower; the usual white curds come in a broccoli green or a very odd purple; all varieties grow the same way as the white variety. I think the choice is almost purely aesthetic, because although the pure white vegetable can be a welcome relief with darker dishes, it appears bland alongside boiled potatoes, plain pasta, and poached fish. Even so, I tried the purple, and it looked gross!

In my youth, it was often prepared by steaming the whole head, bathing it with a rich cheddar cheese sauce, and placing it in a very hot oven (450°F–500°F) to reach a lovely dappled aromatic brown. But you can also add a less-rich dusting of smoked paprika and a spritz of olive oil and finish with 2–3 minutes in the oven just before serving.

The Numbers

It you have a thyroid condition, you may want to limit your consumption somewhat because cauliflower contains goitrogens, which can cause the thyroid to enlarge.

For every 100 g raw (3.5 oz; ½ cup): 25 calories, 0 g fat, 0 g saturated fat, 5 g carbohydrate, 2 g protein, 3 g dietary fiber, 30 mg sodium

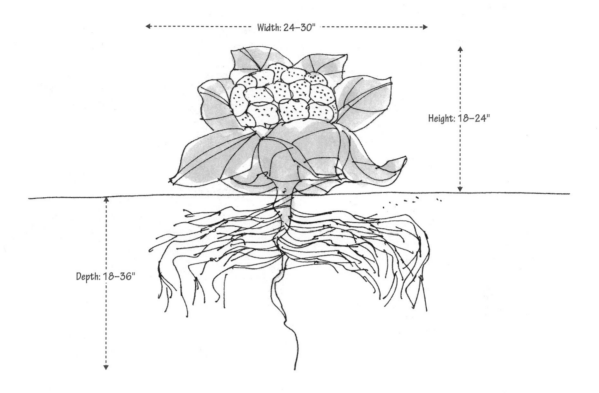

Width: 24–30"

Height: 18–24"

Depth: 18–36"

Annual/Cool Season
Water: Moderate/even, drip irrigation
Sun: Avoid intense heat; plant in partial shade
Companion Planting:
PRO: Beets, carrots, celery, lettuce, spinach
CON: Strawberries, tomatoes
Pests: Cepheid, cabbage worms, fleas, beetles, cutworms
Diseases: Downy mildew, fusarium wilt
Soil: Light, humus-rich, moist, well-drained soil
Fertilizer: Heavy feeder, every 3–4 weeks, fish emulsion compost tea
pH: 6.4–7.4

Varieties: Snowball, Fremont (self-blanching in that it keeps itself white), Chartreuse (green head), purple head
Zones: 3–11
Planting: Seed ¼–½ inch deep, 15 inches apart, after last frost to early spring
Germination: 4–10 days
Harvest: From seed, 70–120 days; from transplant, 55–80 days, when heads are 4–8 inches
Rotation: Precede with hydrogen fixing plants; avoid cabbage family beds
Edible: White (or colored) curds (florets)

CAULIFLOWER

Basic Preparation

When cooking cauliflower, you need to watch the cooking time carefully: too long and it becomes a watery mush; too short and it develops a strong sulfur aroma and an odd chewy texture. It does well when used as a *raw* vegetable with dips.

CAULIFLOWER AND CARROTS WITH FENNEL SEEDS

I like to offset the pure white of the florets with the bright orange carrots. The fennel is just enough to spark interest with its anise flavor.

SERVES 6

2 small heads cauliflower, broken or cut into florets (yield 6 cups)
1 teaspoon fennel seeds
¼ teaspoon salt
6 medium carrots, peeled and cut on the diagonal into ¼-inch slices (yield 2 cups)
2 tablespoons chopped fresh parsley

Place the cauliflower florets on the bottom platform of a two-tiered steamer. Sprinkle the fennel seeds and salt over the top. Place the carrots in the second platform and stack it on

top.* Place both over boiling water, cover, and steam 12 minutes until vegetables are crisp tender or 18 minutes for softer vegetables.

Combine the cauliflower and carrots and serve with a good dusting of parsley.

If you do not have a two-tiered steamer, steam the vegetables in two batches, keeping the cauliflower warm while the carrots cook.

Per serving: 50 calories, 0 g fat, 0 g saturated fat, 11 g carbohydrate, 3 g protein, 4 g dietary fiber, 169 mg sodium. Exchanges: 3 Vegetable

CAULIFLOWER EAST INDIAN STYLE

If you enjoy a mild curry taste, I think you'll love this golden cauliflower.

SERVES 4

1 small head cauliflower
1 teaspoon nonaromatic olive oil
½ cup chopped sweet onion
1 tablespoon grated gingerroot
1 tablespoon mild curry powder
½ cup low-sodium chicken or vegetable stock (see page 288)
¼ teaspoon salt
1 teaspoon cornstarch mixed with
    1 tablespoon stock (slurry)
2 tablespoons freshly squeezed lemon juice
1 tablespoon chopped fresh parsley

Prepare the cauliflower by cutting from the bottom into small florets. Discard large pieces of stem. Rinse and allow to drain in a colander.

Heat the oil in a high-sided skillet over medium-high. Sauté the onion, ginger, and curry powder for 2 minutes. Stir in the stock, then add the drained cauliflower and salt. Cook, covered, about 10 minutes or until tender.

Push the cauliflower aside and stir in the slurry. Heat over medium heat and stir until thickened and glossy. Mix the cauliflower back into the sauce. Sprinkle with lemon juice and serve, garnished with parsley for nice color.

Per serving: 66 calories, 1 g fat, 0 g saturated fat, 10 g carbohydrate, 3 g protein, 3 g dietary fiber, 190 mg sodium. Exchanges: 2 Vegetable, ½ Fat

CAULIFLOWER WITH CARROT "CHEESE" SAUCE

This recipe may seem like a fiddle but the results are well worth the effort.

SERVES 4

4 cups cauliflower florets
3 carrots, peeled and sliced into ½-inch
    rounds (yield 1½ cups)
½ cup evaporated skim milk
¼ cup water
1 teaspoon Dijon mustard
½ teaspoon Worcestershire sauce
1 tablespoon freshly squeezed lemon juice
¼ teaspoon salt

Pinch cayenne
Pinch cumin
¼ cup freshly grated Parmesan cheese
Dusting of smoked paprika

Steam cauliflower 18 minutes or until tender but not mushy. Set aside.

Cook the carrots in the evaporated milk and water, covered, in a medium saucepan, 10–15 minutes or until very soft. Place the carrots and cooking liquid, mustard, Worcestershire sauce, and lemon juice in a blender, and whiz for 2–3 minutes or until smooth and glossy. Add the salt, cayenne, and cumin, and whiz to mix.

Place the cauliflower in a small baking dish. Spoon the carrot sauce over the cauliflower and scatter the Parmesan cheese over the top. Brown under a preheated broiler 4 inches from heat and serve, garnished with a dusting of smoked paprika.

Per serving: 92 calories, 2 g fat, 1 g saturated fat (9% calories from saturated fat), 13 g carbohydrate, 6 g protein, 3 g dietary fiber, 356 mg sodium. Exchanges: 3 Vegetable, ½ Fat

Celery

Apium graveolens var. *dulce*

As long ago as 900 BCE, celery was at home in the marshlands of southern Europe. In fact, it wasn't plucked out of its stick-in-the-mud behavior until the 16th century, when the Italians began its cultivation.

I really like its flavor in both salads and stews. What I don't like is when the strings are tight and hard, and the flavor harsh and chalky. I've had several such encounters with store bought, and it's made me decide to grow my own and try to avoid these disappointments. This will be a year-two project because I ran out of time and space.

I got lots of advice from my expert friends that left me with some choices.

I had to decide to go for self-blanching varieties or undergo the hard work of blanching the plants myself. In gardening terms, *blanching* means to shield the stalk with either paper or boards to lighten its color and, in this case, reduce stringiness. Since I don't have much space for celery, I decided to go with the extra work to get the maximum benefit.

This entailed another decision: to grow the plants in a trench or pop a 1-liter plastic milk bottle over each plant. I've decided on the trench. In midseason, I'll tie the stalks together, wrap waxed paper around the bunch, and heap soil all the way up to the leaves, where it will stay as the plant grows.

Having given you all the troublesome details of intervention, it remains for me to provide some possible good news. Self-blanching varieties spontaneously lose the chlorophyll and don't need paper or trenches, but there are strings attached, so to speak, since the self-blanching varieties are not completely stringless!

The Numbers

The leaves have more nutritional value than the stalks. So use the whole plant for maximum nutritional benefit.

For each 100 g raw (3.5 oz; ½ cup): 16 calories, 0.14 g fat, 0 g saturated fat, 4 g carbohydrate, 1 g protein, 2 g dietary fiber, 87 mg sodium

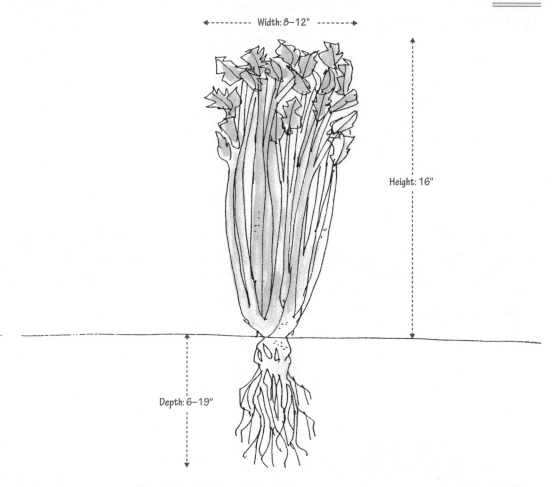

Width: 8–12"

Height: 16"

Depth: 6–19"

Biennial/Annual

Water: Heavy

Sun: Part shade, avoid direct long days of direct sun. Will bolt at temperatures above 60°F for a week or so, but shading will help.

Companion Planting:

PRO: Beans, cabbage, tomatoes, lettuce, peas

CON: Carrots, pumpkin squash

Pests: Aphids, cabbage loopers, whiteflies, nematodes

Diseases: Blight, leaf spot

Soil: Humus-rich soil with good drainage

Fertilizer: Dig in compost to 12 inches before planting; fish emulsion every 2–3 weeks

pH: 5.8–6.8

Varieties: Golden Self-Blanching, Tendercrisp

Zones: 5–10

Planting: Sow indoors 10 weeks before last frost; sow outdoors 19 weeks before first frost; plant ⅛ inch deep, 6–8 inches apart

Germinate: 10 days

Harvest: 120–180 days before first frost in autumn

Rotation: Don't follow lettuce, cabbage

Edible: Leaves, stalks, seeds, roots (celeriac)

BRAISED CELERY HEARTS

This is a delicious way to enjoy celery hearts as a side to any main dish.

SERVES 4

1 teaspoon olive oil
2 cups chopped sweet onions
3 tablespoons tomato paste
½ teaspoon dried oregano
2 cups low-sodium vegetable stock
    (see page 288)
¼ teaspoon salt
¼ teaspoon freshly ground black pepper
2 heads celery or 4 celery hearts
1 tablespoon chopped fresh parsley

Preheat the oven to 350°F.

Heat the oil in a skillet over medium-high. Sauté the onion until golden, then add the tomato paste. Continue cooking until the tomato paste darkens. Remove from heat, add the oregano, stock, salt, and black pepper. Return to low heat and let it simmer while you prepare the celery.

Cut the bottom 6 inches off the base of each head of celery. Cut in half lengthwise. Remove the outer ribs until you get to the tender, lighter-colored heart. Save the tops and trim for salads and stocks.

Lay the hearts in a small ungreased baking dish in one layer, and pour the tomato-onion sauce over them until half covered. Cover the dish and bake 35–40 minutes or until tender. Serve the hearts whole on each of 4 hot din-ner plates, and spoon the remaining sauce over them. Sprinkle with the parsley and serve.

Per serving: 93 calories, 1 g fat, 0 g saturated fat, 20 g carbohydrate, 3 g protein, 3 g dietary fiber, 446 mg sodium. Exchanges: 3 Vegetable

CELERIAC APPLE SALAD

You can use the heart of the celery without the need to cook it as you would the root, which has a more complex flavor and texture; well worth a try.

SERVES 4

1 small celeriac (celery root), peeled and sliced
    (yield 1½ cups)
2 small (or 1 large) red apples, cored and
    chopped (yield 1½ cups)
4 leaves butter lettuce

FOR THE DRESSING
2 tablespoons rice vinegar
1 tablespoon nonaromatic olive oil
1 teaspoon Dijon mustard
½ teaspoon dried tarragon or 2 teaspoons
    chopped fresh
¼ teaspoon salt
¼ teaspoon freshly ground black pepper

Drop the celeriac slices into boiling water in a medium saucepan. Bring back to a boil and cook 3 minutes. Drain and run the celeriac under cold water to cool. Cut the slices into strips and place in a large bowl. Add the apples and mix.

Combine the vinegar, oil, mustard, tarragon, salt, and black pepper in a small bowl. Pour over the celeriac and apples, and toss to coat.

Arrange the lettuce leaves on a platter and spoon the salad on top.

Per serving: 84 calories, 4 g fat, 0.5 g saturated fat (5% calories from saturated fat), 13 g carbohydrate, 2 g dietary fiber, 234 mg sodium. Exchanges: 1 Vegetable, ½ Fruit, 1 Fat

CELERIAC AND POTATO PURÉE

This could become the Rolls Royce of mashed potatoes if you enjoy the flavor of celery.
SERVES 6

1 small celeriac (celery root), about 1 pound
    unpeeled
2 large russet potatoes
¼ teaspoon salt
2 cups water
¼ cup yogurt cheese (see page 290)
¼ teaspoon white pepper
3 tablespoons finely sliced fresh celery leaves

Scrub the celeriac with a vegetable brush. Cut off the top and bottom and discard. Peel the celery root with a knife, making sure to cut out all the brown spots and any woody parts near

the center. Slice thickly and then cut into 1-inch pieces.

Peel the potatoes and cut into 1-inch slices. Put the celery root, potatoes, salt, and water in a medium saucepan. Cover and bring to a boil, then simmer on medium-low for 25 minutes or until very soft.

Strain the vegetables and mash well in the saucepan. Stir in the yogurt cheese, white pepper, and celery leaves. Cover until ready to serve, or serve immediately.

Per serving: 63 calories, 1 g fat, 0 g saturated fat, 12 g carbohydrate, 2 g protein, 2 g dietary fiber, 173 mg sodium. Exchanges: 2 Vegetable

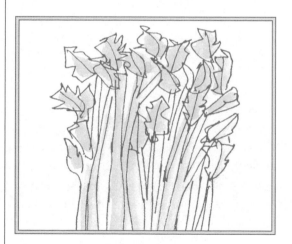

Chard

Beta vulgaris var. *cicla*

Whenever I cook spinach, I have this sinking feeling that seems to be influenced by the rapid loss of bulk. Such lovely leaves simply darken and disappear! While this rapid shrinking can be lessened, it can be avoided completely by switching to chard, also known as Swiss chard.

You can start your chard by sowing indoors (a fiber-based egg carton filled with potting soil will fit perfectly on a sunny kitchen window ledge). Sow 1–2 weeks before your last frost. Plant out in raised beds 8–12 inches apart in all directions.

When the plants are 6 inches tall, move down the row and snip off the outer leaves. Later you can cut the whole plant down to just 2 inches, and it will regrow for a winter crop. In midsummer (if left uncut), it can rapidly go to seed.

Chard has deep green, robust textured ruffled leaves that stand up perfectly to steaming—or a swift sauté or stir-fry. As well, there are its designer stalks, which come in a variety of colors, from white to scarlet. The variety Bright Lights has both orange and yellow stalks.

All this color is wonderful in the garden, but it does pale down in cooking. The stalks must be detached and cooked separately because they take at least twice the time as the leaves.

I'm also fond of chard as a finely sliced garnish to soups and stews. I roll several destalked leaves like a cigar and then cut across in what is called a chiffonade and then again across each bundle to reduce the length to pieces no more than 1 inch by, say, ¼ inch or less. This heap of raw greens with red, yellow, and white flecks can then be added at the last moment to a soup or stew or even an omelet—all delicious!

The Numbers

Chard is rich in vitamin K_1 and osteocalcin, which promote bone growth.

For each 100 g cooked (3.5 oz): 19 calories, 0 g fat, 0 g saturated fat, 4 g carbohydrate, 2 g protein, 2 g dietary fiber, 213 mg sodium

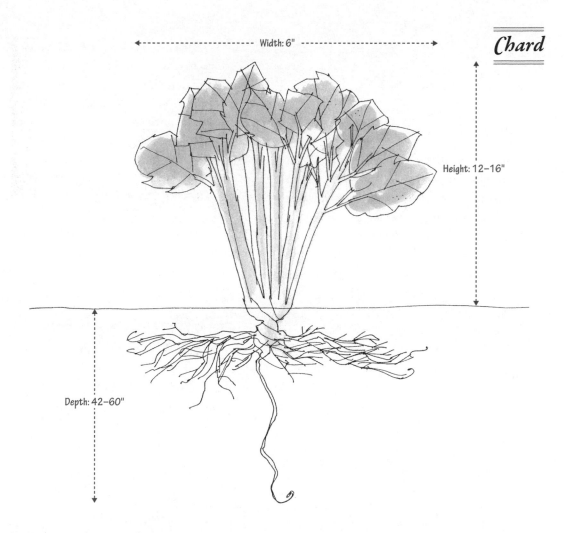

Width: 6"

Height: 12–16"

Depth: 42–60"

Biennial/Annual/Cool Season
Water: Moderate
Sun: Full
Companion Planting:
PRO: Cabbage, garlic, leeks, onions, mustard
CON: Beets, spinach
Pests: Aphids, flea beetles, nematodes
Diseases: Leaf spot, mildew
Soil: Good drainage; keep cool with mulch
Fertilizer: Low-nitrogen fish emulsion every 4–6 weeks
pH: 6.0–6.8 (+7.5)

Varieties: Scarlet Charlotte (red), Bright Lights (multicolored), Fordhook Giant
Zones: 2–10
Planting: Seed ½–¾ inch deep, 2 weeks after last frost. Plant 1–2 inches apart and then thin to 8–12 inches.
Germinate: 7 days
Harvest: 45–55 days
Rotation: Don't follow beets or spinach; okay to follow legumes
Edible: Leaves, stalks

CHARD

Basic Preparation

Wash leaves and stocks very well, as the somewhat crinkled leaf can harbor soil. Then strip off the greens from the stalk using a sharp knife, just as you might sharpen a pencil.

I keep the stalks for a day or two in the refrigerator, where they begin to go limp, and then chop them up and steam them for 8 minutes. This cooking method will help retain the color but still make the stalks tender. The greens can also be steamed.

STEAMED SWISS CHARD

Swiss chard has tons of flavor and great eye appeal, with its rainbow-colored stems that also add wonderful texture. It's a great alternative to spinach and loses less of its bulk during cooking.

SERVES 4

2 bunches (about 14 ounces) Swiss chard
1 tablespoon balsamic vinegar or freshly squeezed lemon juice
1 teaspoon extra-virgin olive oil

Wash the chard leaves in a sink full of cold water. Cut the stems off and slice them cross-wise into ½-inch pieces. Cut the leaves crosswise into ½-inch strips.

Toss the stems into a steamer and steam, covered, for 8 minutes. Add the leaves and cook 4 minutes more until just tender. Toss with the vinegar and oil, and serve.

Per serving: 30 calories, 1 g fat, 0 g saturated fat, 4 g carbohydrate, 2 g protein, 2 g dietary fiber, 157 mg sodium. Exchanges: 1 Vegetable

SOUTHWEST SWISS CHARD AND BEAN SOUP

This is an excellent soup, with robust Tex-Mex flavors. Serve with a nice piece of cornbread and dream of the Grand Canyon.

SERVES 4

1 bunch (about 7 ounces) Swiss chard
1 teaspoon olive oil
1½ cups chopped onion
2 garlic cloves, bashed and chopped
1 tablespoon mild chili powder
1 teaspoon ground cumin
3 cups low-sodium vegetable stock (see page 288)
1 (15-ounce) can pinto beans, rinsed and drained, or fresh from the pod
1 medium tomato, skinned and diced
¼ teaspoon salt

Wash the chard and remove the stems. Trim any discolored ends and cut the stems into

½-inch pieces. Stack the leaves and cut across into ½-inch strips; then cut them in the other direction to keep the length to 2 inches.

Heat the oil in a high-sided skillet or large saucepan over medium-high. Sauté the onion 4 or 5 minutes until it starts to soften. Add the garlic, chard stems, chili powder, and cumin, and cook 1 minute more.

Pour in the stock, add the beans and tomatoes, and bring to a boil. Reduce the heat and simmer 5 minutes or until the chard stems and beans are tender. Season with salt. Add leaves to heat through.

Per serving: 160 calories, 3 g fat, 0 g saturated fat, 26 g carbohydrate, 7 g protein, 8 g dietary fiber, 472 mg sodium. Exchanges: 1 Starch, 1 Vegetable, ½ Fat

WILTED WINTER SALAD

Just when you thought the time for salads was over, here's a late-season warm salad that uses the last of the produce before winter strikes.

SERVES 4

1 bunch Swiss chard
1 teaspoon olive oil
½ cup sliced roasted red peppers
½ cup quartered water chestnuts
2 tablespoons balsamic vinegar

Wash the chard and remove the stems. Chop the stems into ½-inch pieces. Cut the leaves into bite-size pieces. Heat the oil in a large pan

over medium-high. Sauté the stems about 3 minutes or until crisp tender. Add the leaves and cook 2–3 minutes or until just wilted.

Toss with the red peppers, water chestnuts, and vinegar. Serve warm.

Per serving: 54 calories, 1 g fat, 0 g saturated fat, 11 g carbohydrate, 2 g protein, 2 g dietary fiber, 211 mg sodium. Exchanges: 2 Vegetable

Chickpeas

Cicer arietinum

The chickpea, aka the garbanzo bean, is a remarkably nutritious pea that began its life in Turkey and got to us via India in the 1600s. The word *garbanzo* means "little ram," which describes the somewhat crumpled head shape of the bean.

I'm devoted to it because of its smooth texture and mellow, rich taste. It is, of course, the basis for hummus, the North African bean paste, but it's also used in stews and casseroles from the same region. It provides good protein and excellent fiber, which reduces the immediate absorption of the carbohydrates.

Until last year, I had heard of only one color other than the standard cream, and that was an unappetizing black (Black Kabuli). Then I got some fresh frozen immature beans in the post from Clearwater Country Foods in Genesee, Idaho, that were bright green and behaved perfectly in a green hummus and wherever I'd added lima beans in the past (see Brunswick Stew, page 146). Fortunately, I got some planting peas, but it was too late for my first year, so I've set aside a special patch to see how they grow in year two. The bed in which I've chosen to plant the peas held bush beans in year one, which should help with the chickpeas' ability to fix nitrogen in the soil.

Nitrogen fixation is a splendid example of the awesome ability of nature to provide a metaphor for great neighbors who look out for each other's needs. Let's assume that you've planted lettuce or cabbage (lots of green leaves). These are called *heavy feeders*, especially of nitrogen, which stimulates their leaf and stem growth. These plants draw on the soil nitrogen supply and can seriously deplete it. Now we can add blood meal, guano, hoof and horn meal, soybean meal, and cottonseed meal, as well as compost—all natural nitrogen.

Along come the good neighbor plants: beans, peas, and soybeans. As they grow, they interact with soil-borne bacteria and take nitrogen from the air (most other plants can't do this). This is called *nitrogen fixation*. The bean plant stores this nitrogen in its roots in the form of nodules and uses the nitrogen for its *initial* growth. The root-stored growth bacteria, called *Rhizobia*, multiply and absorb nitrogen in excess of the plants' needs and then use this surplus to enrich the soil.

Now you can see the reason to switch beds and plant leafy greens where beans and peas have boldly gone before.

The Numbers

Chickpeas are an excellent source of molybdenum, which recent reports suggest is useful in the natural detoxification of the body. Some folks have an allergic reaction, so test with a small portion.

Per serving: 100 calories, 2 g fat, 0 g saturated fat, 16 g carbohydrate, 4 g protein, 5 g dietary fiber, 25 mg sodium

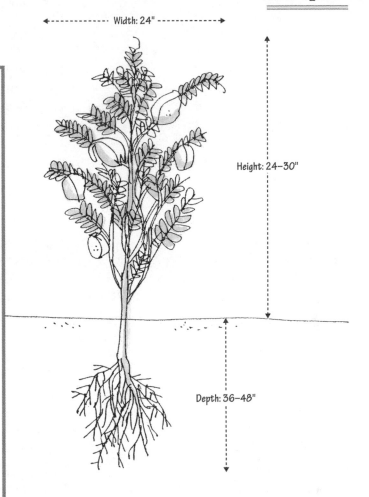

Width: 24"

Height: 24–30"

Depth: 36–48"

Annual/Cool Season

Water: Evenly moist until chickpeas have pushed through the soil; regularly during flowering and pod formation. Avoid overhead watering.

Sun: Full, but will grow in partial shade

Companion Planting:

PRO: Potatoes, cucumbers, corn, strawberries, celery, summer savory

CON: Garlic

Pests: Aphids, bean beetles, flea beetles, leafhoppers, mites

Diseases: Blight, mosaic, anthracnose (Note: there are disease-resistant varieties)

Soil: Loose, well-drained soil, rich in organic matter

Fertilizer: Add aged compost to planting beds in advance of planting, and potassium and phosphorus during growing time

pH: 6.0–6.8

Varieties: Chickpea (garbanzo), gram, Black Kabuli, Garden Green

Plant Care: Avoid handling chickpeas when wet or with heavy dew, as this may promote the spread of fungus spores

Zones: 3–11

Planting: Indoors, start in a peat or paper pot several weeks before transplanting out. Outside, sow 1½–2 inches deep, 3–6 inches apart, as early as 2–3 weeks before the average last frost in spring. Thin out to 12–24 inches apart.

Germinate: 4–10 days

Harvest: About 100 days

Rotation: Rotate chickpeas and other legumes to add nitrogen to the soil

Edible: Immature seed

HUMMUS

I really couldn't leave out a basic recipe for hummus. I've used the green variety both as an experiment and for St. Patrick's Day. You can also use the standard cream color.

SERVES 4

1 pound fresh green chickpeas or
    1 (15.5-ounce) can low-sodium chickpeas,
    rinsed and drained
1 tablespoon tahini
2 tablespoons freshly squeezed lemon juice
2 garlic cloves, chopped
¼ teaspoon salt
¼–½ cup water*
Pinch cayenne
¼ cup chopped fresh parsley

*Don't use more than ½ cup of water—you want a thick texture.

If using fresh chickpeas, steam them for 10 minutes until tender.

Place the chickpeas in a food processor or blender. Add the tahini, lemon juice, garlic, salt, water, and cayenne. Whiz until smooth. Scrape into a bowl and stir in the parsley. Serve with fresh cut-up vegetables or as a sandwich spread.

Per serving: 103 calories, 3 g fat, 0 g saturated fat, 14 g carbohydrate, 5 g protein, 3 g dietary fiber, 404 mg sodium. Exchanges: 1 Starch, 1 Fat

ROASTED CHICKPEA SNACK

Quite the eye-catching and healthful snack, especially with green garbanzos, but you can always use the regular cream-colored variety.

SERVES 4

2 teaspoons olive oil
Pinch ground turmeric
Pinch cayenne
1 tablespoon freshly squeezed lime juice
½ teaspoon ground cumin
¼ teaspoon salt
1 pound fresh green chickpeas or 1 (15.5-
    ounce) can low-sodium chickpeas, rinsed
    and drained

Preheat the oven to 350°F.

Combine the olive oil, turmeric, cayenne, lime juice, cumin, and salt in a bowl. Add the chickpeas and toss to coat.

Spread in a single layer on a baking sheet and bake 30 minutes for fresh and 15 minutes for canned or until chickpeas are slightly crunchy. Cool and serve.

Per serving: 148 calories, 4 g fat, 0 g saturated fat, 24 g carbohydrate, 4 g protein, 5 g dietary fiber, 456 mg sodium. Exchanges: 1½ Starch, ½ Fat

UPSIDE-DOWN CHICKPEA PIE

Let's assume for a moment that you have taken the plunge and decided for a season to eat in a vegan or vegetarian manner. You want to try a relatively elaborate concoction, just to see what it entails and if it's worth the effort. This could be your experiment.

SERVES 4

¹⁄₁₆ teaspoon saffron powder

¼ cup water

1 cup long-grain white rice

1 teaspoon nonaromatic olive oil

1 onion, finely chopped (yield 1 cup)

2 garlic cloves, bashed and chopped

1 small (2–3 inches) eggplant, peeled and cut into ¾-inch pieces

¾ teaspoon ground cumin

½ teaspoon ground allspice

1 teaspoon ground cardamom

¹⁄₁₆ teaspoon ground cinnamon

¹⁄₁₆ teaspoon ground cloves

¾ teaspoon salt

½ teaspoon freshly ground black pepper

½ teaspoon almond extract

1 pound fresh chickpeas

2 tablespoons freshly squeezed lemon juice

4 ounces toasted almonds

2 cups low-sodium vegetable stock (see page 288)

1 tablespoon chopped fresh parsley

1 tablespoon chopped fresh spearmint

Stir the saffron into the water to dissolve. Add the rice, mix well, and set aside.

Heat ½ teaspoon of the oil in a high-sided skillet over medium-high. Sauté the onion for 5 minutes, then stir in the garlic and eggplant. Add the cumin, allspice, cardamom, cinnamon, cloves, salt, black pepper, and almond extract. Continue cooking for 3 more minutes, then remove to a plate to keep warm.

Heat the remaining oil in the same pan without washing it. When it's nice and hot, add the chickpeas and toss well for 2 minutes. When browned, return the eggplant mixture to the pan, add the lemon juice, and cook for 5 minutes. Stir in the toasted almonds.

Spread the mixture evenly in a greased 10-inch nonstick skillet. Cover with the rice mixture and pour 1½ cups of the stock over the top. Bring to a boil, reduce the heat to low, cover, and cook 10 minutes. Remove the cover and shake the pan to make sure the vegetables are not sticking Press the uncooked rice down into the liquid, adding more stock as you need it. Place the lid back on and cook 15 more minutes or until the rice is tender and the liquid has been absorbed.

Cover the pan with a serving plate and turn it over carefully. The pie should slip right out. Combine the parsley and mint and scatter over the top. Cut into 4 wedges and serve on hot plates.

Per serving: 397 calories, 4 g fat, 1 g saturated fat (3% calories from saturated fat), 78 g carbohydrate, 15 g protein, 13 g dietary fiber, 449 mg sodium. Exchanges: 3 ½ Starch, 2 Vegetable, 1 Fat

Chiles

Capsicumfrutescens

My wife, Treena, is known for her almost asbestos palate that can withstand a vindaloo (Indian curry) of equal heat to that enjoyed by the late king of Norway, who, like us, frequented Veeraswamy in Swallow Street just off Piccadilly Circus in London.

It's because of the difference between my pallid palate and her robust one that I'm grateful to good old Wilbur Scoville, who recruited a gallant band of volunteers to rub cut chiles on the soft inside of their lips and use numbers to describe what can only be called *pain*.

Recent research suggests that nerve endings gradually adjust to this P Factor (the initial used to denote *pain*), allowing the consumer to slowly ascend the Scoville Scale as their nerve endings become deadened—or should I say *killed off*?

Curiously, there are more recorded benefits to human health than ills. Chiles actually seem to assist digestion in some people, but not all. It is best to seek advice on its use before you endure the cure!

Hot peppers will need an indoor start, usually 2 months before the last frost. They grow well in fiber-constructed egg cartons set in a shallow tray, which allows the bottoms to stay wet.

It's important to transfer the young seedlings to 2-inch square pots, where their roots have the space to develop. I left mine indoors until about 5 inches tall. I then set them out next to my tomatoes and gave them 15 inches of clear space around. I was given a couple of apparently good tips. Since peppers love magnesium, just sprinkle 1 teaspoonful around the base of each plant. And, before harvesting, stop the water, because dry conditions will boost the spiciness.

The soil temperature needs to be above 60°F before you transplant. It's a *great* idea to invest a few dollars in a garden probe thermometer to ensure that you don't jump the gun!

You'll find that the plants will thrive at daytime temperatures above 70°F and nights at 60°F. Should it get any lower, you may need to use a lightweight fabric row cover held above the plants by wire hoops, as cold weather causes the blooms to drop off. No bloom, no peppers!

When harvesting, use disposable gloves, as the capsaicin can get in your eyes, and it's painful!

The Numbers

For each 100 g raw (3.5 oz; ½ cup): 40 calories, 0 g fat, 0 g saturated fat, 9 g carbohydrate, 2 g protein, 2 g dietary fiber, 7 mg sodium

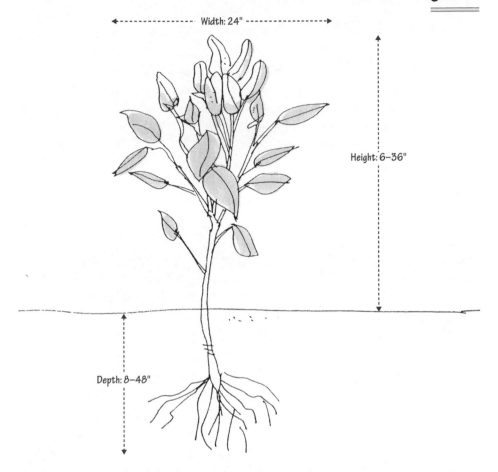

Width: 24"

Height: 6–36"

Depth: 8–48"

Annual/Perennial (in tropical climates)
Water: Moderate, but less when fruited; by restricting water, you can increase spice/heat
Sun: Full
Companion Planting:
PRO: Basil, eggplant, onions, tomatoes
CON: Fennel, kohlrabi
Pests: Aphids, snails, slugs, weevils
Diseases: Rot, mildew, leaf spot
Soil: Light, well-drained soil
Fertilizer: Magnesium needed (1 teaspoon Epsom salts around each plant base); medium to heavy feeder; fish emulsion at flowering and 2–3 times during the plant's life

pH: 5.5–6.8
Varieties: Anaheim (green to read, very mild), cayenne, sweet cayenne, Jimmy Nardello (hot: 10,000 SU), chiltepin, chile piquin (very hot: 50,000+ SU), jalapeño, Mucho Nacho (green to red, 5,000–10,000 SU), habanero, Jamaican Hot Chocolate (extremely hot: 100,000–500,000 SU)
Planting: Indoors, seed ¼–½ inch deep, 8 weeks before last frost; outdoors, transplant when soil is 55°F, space 15 inches apart
Germination: 7–10 days
Harvest: From seed, 60–90 days
Rotation: Do not follow eggplant, tomato, or potato
Edible: Pod and seeds

STUFFED MILD CHILES

A really unusual appetizer, these peppers are just enough to whet the appetite and start a conversation. If they look a bit lonely on the plate, garnish with some fresh arugula.

SERVES 4

2 mild chile peppers, such as Anaheim
½ teaspoon olive oil
½ cup chopped onion
¼ teaspoon ground cumin
1 garlic clove, chopped
½ cup fresh or frozen corn kernels
2 cups chopped Swiss chard or spinach
½ cup low-sodium salsa
⅓ cup grated reduced-fat Monterey jack
    cheese
1 tablespoon freshly grated Parmesan cheese
2 tablespoons bread crumbs, fresh or panko
1 teaspoon smoked paprika
1 bunch arugula (optional garnish)

Preheat the oven to 375°F. Grease a small baking sheet.

Cut the chiles in half lengthwise and remove the seeds and ribs.

Heat the oil in a medium skillet and sauté the onions with the cumin 5 minutes until soft and translucent but not brown. Add the garlic and cook 1 minute more. Stir in the corn, Swiss chard, and salsa. Remove from the heat and stir in the Monterey jack cheese.

Combine the Parmesan cheese and bread crumbs in a small bowl.

Divide the vegetable mixture among the halved peppers, top with the Parmesan mixture, and dust with paprika. Place the chiles in the prepared baking sheet and bake 20 minutes or until the vegetables are tender and the top is golden. Garnish the serving plates with the arugula if desired.

Per serving (½ chile): 136 calories, 3 g fat, 2 g saturated fat (13% calories from saturated fat), 21 g carbohydrate, 7 g protein, 2 g dietary fiber, 340 mg sodium. Exchanges: ½ Starch, 1 Lean Meat, 1½ Vegetable

CHILIQUILES

This is a good way to immerse yourself in an all-in-one feast from the garden. Caution: Since the carbohydrates are perhaps on the high side, if you have a special need, simply reduce the amount of tortillas by half and keep the extra sauce for another meal.

I've used canned chipotle chiles (smoked jalapeños) for their added flavor, but you can use fresh Anaheim for a milder, crisper finish.

SERVES 4

10 (8-inch) corn tortillas
1 (28-ounce) can diced tomatoes in juice
2 pounds Roma tomatoes, peeled, skinned,
    seeded, and diced
2 canned chipotle chiles, rinsed and seeded
    (if you like it blistering hot, leave the seeds)
½ teaspoon nonaromatic olive oil
1 large sweet onion, cut into ¼-inch dice
3 garlic cloves, bashed and chopped

2 cups low-sodium vegetable stock (see page 288)

¼ teaspoon salt

FOR THE GARNISH

½ cup low-fat plain yogurt

1½ cups shredded cooked chicken

¼ cup freshly grated Parmesan cheese

½ cup chopped fresh cilantro

To make tortilla chips, preheat the oven to 350°F. Spray two baking sheets with cooking spray.

Stack the tortillas and cut into eighths. Lay out the tortilla wedges in one layer in the prepared baking sheets. Lightly spray the tops with cooking spray and bake 15–20 minutes or until crisp. Set aside.

Drain the tomatoes, reserving the liquid. Place all the tomatoes in a blender with the chipotles and whiz until pureed but with some texture.

Heat the oil in a large high-sided chef's pan or skillet over medium. Sauté half the onions about 7 minutes until golden. Stir in the garlic and cook another minute. Raise to medium-high heat and pour in the tomato mixture. Cook, stirring often, 5 minutes until the sauce thickens and starts to spatter. Pour the reserved tomato juice into a measuring cup and add stock to make 2½ cups. Add to the skillet along with the salt and bring to a boil. You should have 4½ cups sauce. Stir in the tortilla chips, making sure each one is coated with sauce. Bring back to a boil and then remove from the heat. Cover and let stand 5 minutes—no more!

Divide among 4 hot plates and top with the remaining onions, yogurt, chicken, Parmesan cheese, and cilantro. The dish can also be served directly from the skillet, topped attractively with the garnish.

Per serving: 432 calories, 9 g fat, 3 g saturated fat (7% calories from saturated fat), 64 g carbohydrate, 28 g protein, 9 g dietary fiber, 933 mg sodium. Exchanges: 3 Starch, 2 Lean Meat, 2 Vegetable, ½ Fat

Collards

Brassica oleracea var. *acephala*

About the time that Robin Hood was living rough in Sherwood Forest, the local villagers who sustained him and his merry men may well have grown *coleworts* as part of his supply chain!

Coleworts are really collards, or perhaps that's backward? They are the same loose-leafed cabbage—all dark green leaves with no head formation.

Much like cabbages, collards are always sown outdoors when the soil reaches 60°F. Be careful to sow lightly; you can mix the seeds with sand to spread them out more easily. As they grow, keep thinning them out. Eventually, the really sturdy ones will need 18 inches of clearance all around. Keep harvesting the larger outer leaves before they get over 20 inches long by pruning them off carefully, leaving the central bud untouched. You can plant as late as autumn for a winter crop because they like a light frosting, but use a row cover if it gets seriously cold.

Unfortunately, these greens have been subjected to overcooking for generations in the South, where they accompany such all-time greats as black-eyed peas and hoppin' John.

I suspect that the idea may have started with the intention of softening the very tough (in the matured plant) stalks, but by the time that happens, the leaf is rendered into a kind of succulent, highly flavored fibrous custard that looks as though a squad of Marines had washed out their fatigues in the pot.

I love the texture and flavor that can be achieved when the stalks are fully removed before the leaves hit the pot, and the brilliant green is retained by less cooking time.

The Southern custom of adding lemon juice and cayenne is a fine idea and makes the adventure a real triumph.

The Numbers

There is a moderate to high supply of oxalate, which may promote kidney stones, and goitrogens, which affect the thyroid. The concentration of both is reduced by cooking.

For each 100 g raw (3.5 oz; 1 cup): 30 calories, 0 g fat, 0 g saturated fat, 6 g carbohydrate, 2 g protein, 4 g dietary fiber, 20 mg sodium

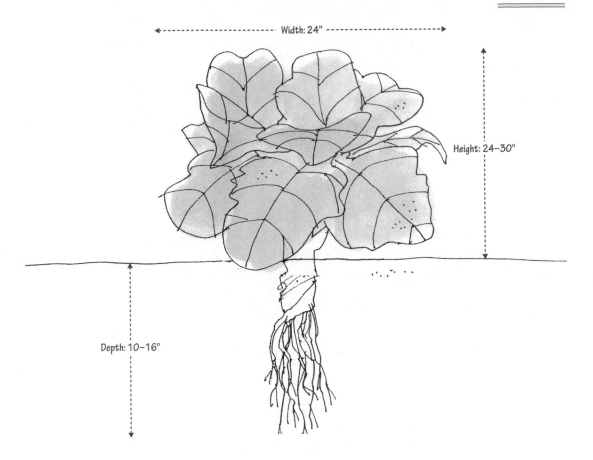

Width: 24"

Height: 24–30"

Depth: 10–16"

Biennial/Annual/Hardy/Cool Season
Water: Moderate
Sun: Full
Companion Planting:
PRO: tomatoes, peppers
CON: Celery, potatoes, cabbages
Pests: Aphids, loopers, worms, flea beetles
Diseases: Rotate beds to avoid common diseases
Soil: Medium-light soil, well dug in before planting
Fertilizer: Compost well; fish emulsion every 3–4 weeks
pH: 5.5–6.8
Varieties: Champion, Vates

Zones: 3 and warmer
Planting: Seed ¼–½ inch deep, 4 weeks before last frost; plant out 2 inches and thin progressively to 16 inches
Germinate: 10 days
Harvest: 60–90 days
Rotation: Don't follow cabbage family, as diseases can easily follow
Edible: Leaves

STEAMED COLLARDS

Just in case you missed it, I really must repeat the absolute need to strip the leaves from the very tough stalks. You can mature the stalks in the refrigerator for 3–4 days to tenderize them for faster steaming and use in a later dish.

SERVES 4

1 pound collards
¼ teaspoon dried basil
¼ teaspoon freshly ground black pepper or
    ¼ teaspoon cayenne
1 tablespoon freshly squeezed lemon juice
¼ teaspoon salt

Wash the collards and remove the heavy stems. Pile a few of the leaves on top of each other, roll into a cylinder, and cut across into strips. Repeat with the rest.

Place the leaves in a steamer; add the basil, black pepper, lemon juice, and salt. Steam 4–6 minutes or until tender but still nice and green.

Per serving: 28 calories, 0 g fat, 0 g saturated fat, 6 g carbohydrate, 3 g protein, 4 g dietary fiber, 161 mg sodium. Exchanges: 1 Vegetable

COLLARDS WITH A SPICY TWIST

Collards are a grand staple in Southern cooking, but this recipe recommends a much shorter cooking time than what's traditionally done, to retain more color.

SERVES 4

1 pound collard greens
½ teaspoon nonaromatic olive oil
2 ounces Canadian bacon, chopped
    (optional)*
½ teaspoon dried thyme
Pinch cayenne
1 teaspoon freshly squeezed lemon juice

Add smoked paprika to taste if you don't add the bacon.

Wash the collards and remove the heavy stems. Stack a third of the leaves on top of each other and roll into a cigar. Cut into ¼-inch ribbons. Repeat with the rest of the greens. Set aside.

Heat the oil in a large skillet over medium-high. Fry the bacon until it starts to color. Add the collards, thyme, and cayenne, and stir to mix well. Cover and cook, stirring occasionally, 7 minutes or until the leaves are tender but still green.

Sprinkle on the lemon juice and serve.

Per serving: 49 calories, 1 g fat, 0 g saturated fat, 6 g carbohydrate, 5 g protein, 4 g dietary fiber, 207 mg sodium. Exchanges: 1 Very Lean Meat, 1 Vegetable

SOUTHERN JAPANESE MISO AND SWEET POTATO SOUP

If you haven't yet tried miso, this could be your best chance at success. It's wonderfully aromatic, and the bright shiny threads of collard greens do wonders for its looks.

Miso is a soybean paste obtained from the fermenting process used to make tamari. In its golden variation, it can be found in the refrigerator sections at health food stores and good supermarkets. It is delicious and can be added to many vegetable soups or casseroles to great effect for both taste and nutrition.

SERVES 4

8 ounces soba (Japanese buckwheat) noodles or whole wheat spaghetti

6 cups low-sodium vegetable stock (see page 288)

3 dried shiitake mushrooms, stems removed and discarded

6 green onions, white parts cut on the diagonal into ½-inch slices, greens cut into ¼-inch rings

2 carrots, cut on the diagonal into ½-inch slices

1 medium sweet potato, cut into ½-inch pieces (yield 1½ cups)

1 medium turnip, cut into ½×1-inch strips

¼ cup white miso

¼ teaspoon cayenne

1 pound collard greens, stems removed, cut into ⅛-inch strips

Place the noodles in a large pot of vigorously boiling water and cook for 10 minutes or until tender but not soft. Drain, rinse in cold water to stop the cooking, and set the colander over a pot of hot water to reheat.

While the noodles are cooking, bring the stock to a boil in a large saucepan. Add the shiitakes, remove the pan from the heat, and let soak for 10 minutes. Remove the mushrooms, reserving the stock, and cut in thin strips; set aside.

Bring the stock back to a simmer over medium heat. Add the white parts of the onion and the carrots, and cook gently for 5 minutes. Add the sweet potato, turnip, and mushroom strips, and simmer 10 more minutes or until the vegetables are tender but still firm.

Dissolve the miso paste in a bit of the hot stock, add cayenne, and stir the mixture into the soup. Scatter the collards onto the surface, stirring until well mixed. Simmer 3 minutes.

Divide the noodles among four heated bowls and ladle the soup on top. Scatter the green onion over all. Please serve everything very hot—the rising cloud of aroma is a treat in itself.

Per serving: 195 calories, 0 g fat, 0 g saturated fat, 40 g carbohydrate, 5 g protein, 3 g dietary fiber, 943 mg sodium. Exchanges: 2 Starch, 1 Vegetable, ½ Fat

Corn

Zea mays var. *rugosa*

Once again the designers have had their way, and the golden yellow corn of my youth (and yours?) has morphed into red, blue, black, white, and all kinds of mottled split personalities.

They all share a common sweetness that is profoundly more delicious on the day they are picked. Along with the sweetness, however, come the inevitable calories from carbohydrates. But when served on the cob, their sheer visual size can help limit their effect on those with diabetes. Corn does come complete with quite a high fiber content, and each gram of fiber can be deducted from the overall carbohydrate total.

I've always enjoyed the way the kernels can be used in sauces, soups, and casseroles; as fritters; in pancakes; and even in waffles! They supply little sunbursts of color along with the sweetness, but they also introduce a texture that can be wonderful when set against a smooth, mild background, as in my Corn Chowder (page 134).

There is a pretty obvious cultural preference for buttering corn, which can sometimes be overdone—so much so that the *treat* of the season can become a potential *threat*. I've suggested a saffron- (or turmeric-) colored sauce as a visual alternative. It obviously doesn't taste like butter, but it is, in its own right, very pleasing.

I really don't have the space for corn, and I live almost next door to some of the finest corn in the world!

Having said that, I'm still keen to see how it works. My pals recommend Golden Midget for a smaller garden, since it grows only 36 inches high. The soil needs to be just above 70°F. Corn needs moderate water until the plant flowers and then heavier watering for the growing season. The soil must be kept moist without flooding the plant's shallow root system until the tassels appear. At this point, the water needs to go deep until the silks form. This is when the male flower tassel releases pollen, which drops on the female flower silk. The plant may need a gentle shaking to help the pollination take place.

You can test when the ear is ready by pinching a corn kernel; it should be milky.

The Numbers

Quantities on the cob vary to such a degree as to defy measurement, so the reference used here is to kernels that can be easily measured.

For each 100 g kernels (3.5 oz; ½ cup): 108 calories, 1 g fat, 0 g saturated fat, 25 g carbohydrate, 3 g protein, 3 g dietary fiber, 0 mg sodium

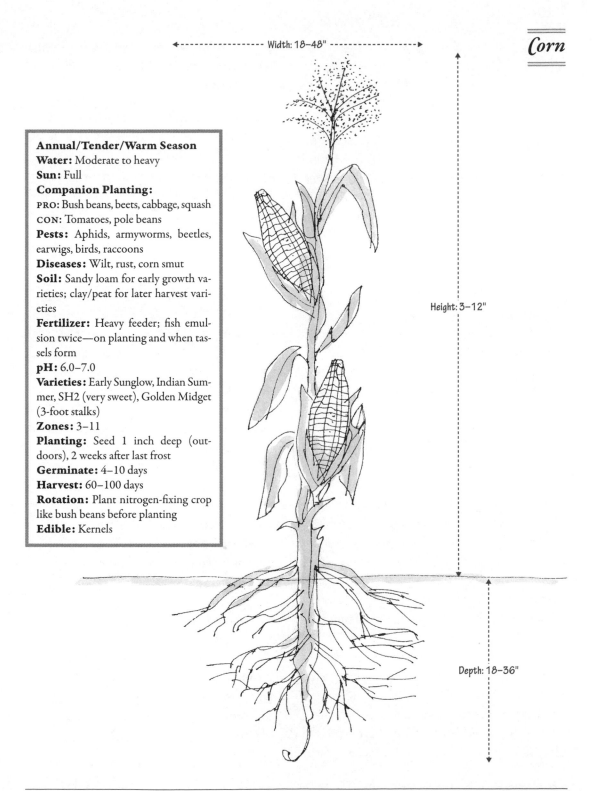

Width: 18–48"

Height: 3–12'

Depth: 18–36"

Annual/Tender/Warm Season

Water: Moderate to heavy

Sun: Full

Companion Planting:

PRO: Bush beans, beets, cabbage, squash

CON: Tomatoes, pole beans

Pests: Aphids, armyworms, beetles, earwigs, birds, raccoons

Diseases: Wilt, rust, corn smut

Soil: Sandy loam for early growth varieties; clay/peat for later harvest varieties

Fertilizer: Heavy feeder; fish emulsion twice—on planting and when tassels form

pH: 6.0–7.0

Varieties: Early Sunglow, Indian Summer, SH2 (very sweet), Golden Midget (3-foot stalks)

Zones: 3–11

Planting: Seed 1 inch deep (outdoors), 2 weeks after last frost

Germinate: 4–10 days

Harvest: 60–100 days

Rotation: Plant nitrogen-fixing crop like bush beans before planting

Edible: Kernels

CORN ON THE COB IN THE HUSK

Warmth speeds the conversion of sugars to starch, which results in a less sweet ear of corn. Corn should be stored in the refrigerator but not more than one day. It's best eaten the day it's picked.

SERVES 4

4 ears corn with husks
½ cup low-sodium vegetable stock (see page 288)
1½ teaspoons arrowroot or cornstarch
Touch of powdered saffron (optional)

Gently pull back the husks around the corn without pulling them clear off. Remove and discard the silk. Pull the husks back up around the corn and tie at the top with kitchen string or a piece of wire if you're going to grill them.

Steam in a single layer over boiling water in a large flat steamer for 15 minutes; microwave in a single layer on high 9–12 minutes (fewer ears will take less time); or grill.

To grill over hot coals, first soak in cold water for 15 minutes then grill, turning once—15 minutes for small ears and up to 30 minutes for very large ones.

Allow to cool a little before removing the husks. If possible, run each ear under cold water to cool the husks enough to handle.

Combine the stock and arrowroot or cornstarch (you can add saffron for a butter color). Heat and stir until it clears and thickens. Brush

on the corn in place of butter before serving. Then if you can't do without it, by all means add your butter!

Per serving: 94 calories, 3 g fat, 0 g saturated fat, 19 g carbohydrate, 4 g protein, 2 g dietary fiber, 68 mg sodium. Exchanges: 2 Starch

CORN CHOWDER

Most chowders find their appeal in what I call mouth round fullness, *a texture that comes from butter, heavy cream, and starch. I set out to keep the texture and lose the possible risk from too much fat. Try adding good bread and a crisp salad to make this a lunch worthy of celebrating the season.*

SERVES 6

FOR THE CHOWDER
½ teaspoon light olive oil
2 cups finely chopped onion
6 ears corn, kernels shaved off the cob (yield 3½ cups)
½ teaspoon dried thyme
1 teaspoon finely diced parsley stalks
¼ teaspoon salt
⅛ teaspoon freshly ground black pepper
1 (12-ounce) can evaporated skim milk
2 cups soy milk
2 tablespoons cornstarch
4 tablespoons dry white wine (I prefer dealcoholized Chardonnay)

FOR THE GARNISH

½ teaspoon canned chipotle pepper (smoked jalapeño) or ¼ teaspoon ground, if dried
⅓ cup finely diced red bell pepper
1 tablespoon chopped fresh parsley

Per serving: 213 calories, 3 g fat, 0 g saturated fat, 40 g carbohydrate, 16 g protein, 3 g dietary fiber, 9 mg sodium. Exchanges: 1½ Starch, 1 Vegetable, 1 Fat-Free Milk

To make the chowder, warm the oil in a large saucepan over medium-low. Sauté the onion and ½ cup of the corn kernels 12–15 minutes until very soft. Stir occasionally so the onion doesn't brown. Add the thyme, parsley stalks, salt, and black pepper.

Transfer the onion mixture to a blender and add ½ cup of the evaporated milk. Purée the mixture for about 2 minutes. Add the remaining evaporated milk and blend for another 3 minutes or until silky smooth. Return to the saucepan along with the remaining corn.

Pour the soy milk into the blender to pick up any flavorful bits left behind, and pour into the saucepan with the corn. Bring to a boil, then reduce the heat and simmer for 10 minutes.

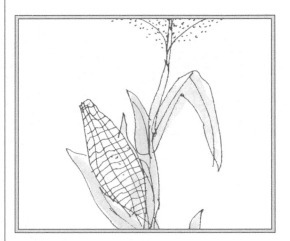

Combine the cornstarch with the wine to make a slurry. Remove the soup from the heat and stir in the slurry. If you will not be serving the soup right away, set it aside and allow it to cool. A few minutes before you are ready to serve, return the soup to the heat and stir occasionally until warm and slightly thickened.

To prepare the garnish, warm a small frying pan over medium-high. Sauté the chipotle, bell pepper, and parsley for 3 minutes. Remove from the heat and set aside.

Serve the chowder in warmed bowls and top each serving with 1 heaping tablespoon of the garnish.

Cucumber

Cucumis sativus

My first crop of cucumbers was anything but cool. Since cukes are actually well known as heat lovers, I planted a full row that allowed them to creep out over our concrete and fine-pebble driveway. I expected them to spread out, but they stayed close to the fence, where, despite their being crowded, they blossomed vigorously.

I made an apparently classic mistake in leaving them too long to harvest. So one day they were nicely green and relatively small at 5–6 inches; the next day, a number of them turned a pale green, and then—bingo!—they went yellow! And bitter! And bloated!

In the midst of this failure, a straggly little plant that I'd been given by a friend, who described it as a pickling gherkin (Diamant), went into overdrive against the sheltered sunny wall of our new greenhouse, delivering a bountiful supply of tiny 1½-inch footballs.

My plan for next year is to grow the English style—I promise you that this has nothing to do with bias! I shall grow them on a trellis and see if they'll make it in the space vacated by the gherkins.

The good thing about the trellis is that it provides good air circulation, which in my judgment clearly trumps a hot driveway!

The Numbers

Cucumbers of any variety are pretty cool if you're following a weight-loss program. They are also among the lowest sodium foods available and promote the healing of tendon tissue with their high silica content.

For 100 g raw (3.5 oz; ½ cup): 13 calories, 0 g fat, 3 g carbohydrate, 1 g protein, 1 g dietary fiber, 0 mg sodium

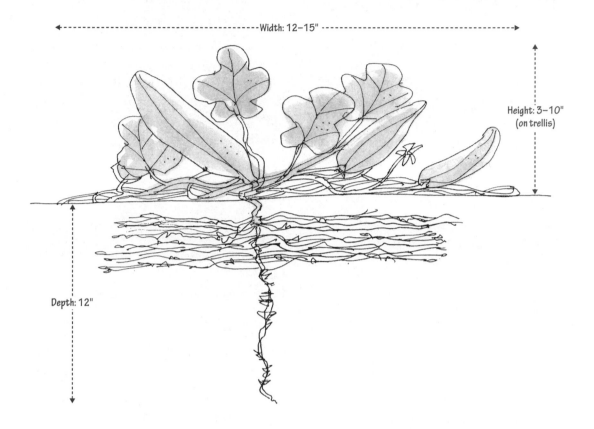

Width: 12–15"

Height: 3–10"
(on trellis)

Depth: 12"

Annual
Water: Moderate to heavy (watch leaves going yellow to judge amount needed)
Sun: Full (3 hours minimum)
Companion Planting:
PRO: Bush bean, cabbage family, lettuce, squash
CON: Potatoes, herbs
Pests: Aphids, cucumber beetles, flea beetles, mites
Diseases: Anthracnose, mildew
Soil: Sandy loam with good drainage
Fertilizer: Compost well; fish emulsion 1–2 times per month; fertilize with plenty of phosphorus and potassium, moderate nitrogen

pH: 6.5–7.5
Varieties: General Lee, Northern Pickling (small pickles), Armenian (greenhouse English style), Diamant (an early gherkin)
Zones: 4–7
Planting: Seed ¾–1 inch deep outside when soil temperature above 68°F, 12 inches apart
Germinate: 5–7 days
Harvest: 55–65 days when uniformly green and smaller size (5–6 inches); don't allow to yellow
Rotation: Don't follow other cucumber plants
Edible: Fruit

CUCUMBER RAITA SALAD

This is a classic cooling side dish for curries.
SERVES 4

1 English cucumber or young slicing
    cucumber
3 green onions, finely chopped
1 tablespoon chopped fresh cilantro
1 tablespoon chopped spearmint
½ cup low-fat plain yogurt
1 tablespoon freshly squeezed
    lime juice
½ teaspoon ground cumin
½ teaspoon ground coriander
¼ teaspoon salt
¼ teaspoon freshly ground black pepper

Wash the cucumber and partially peel in long strips, leaving alternating stripes of green skin and white flesh. Cut lengthwise into long thin slices, then across into matchsticks. Combine with the onion, cilantro, and spearmint in a large bowl.

Whisk the yogurt, lime juice, cumin, coriander, salt, and black pepper together to make the dressing. Toss with the vegetables and let sit for 10 minutes to marinate. Serve with any hot dish to cool your burning mouth!

Per serving: 27 calories, 0 g fat, 0 g saturated fat, 6 g carbohydrate, 2 g protein, 1 g dietary fiber, 166 mg sodium. Exchanges: 1 Vegetable

CUCUMBER SALAD WITH TOMATOES

As an appetizer, this is hard to beat. It almost makes taste buds sit up and beg! Sometimes I like to peel the cucumbers in strips, showing 1-inch tracks of green and white. It adds both color and texture.
SERVES 4

2 cups diced cucumber, partially peeled
1 cup seeded and diced tomatoes
¼ cup chopped sweet onion
2 teaspoons chopped fresh dill or ½ teaspoon
    dried
½ cup Treena's Vinaigrette (see page 74)

Toss together the cucumbers, tomatoes, onion, dill, and vinaigrette. Chill 1 hour and serve.

Per serving: 43 calories, 2 g fat, 0 g saturated fat, 1 g protein, 11 g carbohydrate, 1 g dietary fiber, 372 mg sodium. Exchanges: 1 Vegetable, 1 Fat

SALMON WITH CUCUMBER SAUCE

In the Skagit Valley, this is about as close to home as it gets to a perfect example of FABIS (fresh and best in season).
SERVES 4

2 cups peeled, seeded, and diced cucumbers

1 tablespoon chopped fresh dill

1 teaspoon chopped fresh mint

⅛ teaspoon freshly ground white pepper

⅛ teaspoon sea salt

½ cup dealcoholized white wine

1 tablespoon cornstarch mixed with
   2 tablespoons dealcoholized white
   wine (slurry)

1 cup yogurt cheese (see page 290)

FOR THE SALMON

2 (12-ounce) skinless, boneless King salmon
   fillets

1 teaspoon light olive oil

Dash toasted sesame oil

⅛ teaspoon freshly ground white pepper

⅛ teaspoon salt

In a medium saucepan, combine the cucumbers, dill, mint, white pepper, and salt, and cook over low heat for 10 minutes. Add the wine and slurry, and stir until the sauce is thickened, about 30 seconds. Remove from the heat and let cool. Stir in the yogurt cheese very gently.

To make the salmon, preheat the broiler. Place a rack in a broiler pan and cover with foil.

Pour the oils onto a plate and sprinkle with the white pepper and salt. Season both sides of the salmon fillets by wiping them through the oil on the plate. Place the salmon on the prepared broiler rack and broil 3–4 inches from heat, 5 minutes on each side. Transfer the salmon to a cutting board.

To serve, cut each salmon fillet in half. Spoon a bed of sauce onto each dinner plate and place one piece of salmon in the middle. Drizzle

more sauce in a narrow band down the center of the salmon.

Per serving: 375 calories, 19 g fat, 6 g saturated fat (14% calories from saturated fat), 9 g carbohydrate, 39 g protein, 0 g dietary fiber, 272 mg sodium

SZECHUAN CUCUMBER SALAD

SERVES 4

1 pound cucumbers, peeled, seeded, and cut
   into 2-inch strips

3 green onions, sliced

1 teaspoon chopped garlic

1½ tablespoons low-sodium soy sauce

½ teaspoon toasted sesame oil

1 teaspoon rice vinegar

¼ teaspoon sugar

⅛ teaspoon ground allspice

¼ teaspoon hot red pepper flakes

Combine the cucumbers, onions, and garlic in a glass bowl.

Whisk together the soy sauce, oil, vinegar, sugar, allspice, and red pepper flakes.

Pour the dressing over the vegetables, toss, and let sit for 10 minutes before serving.

Per serving: 28 calories, 1 g fat, 0 g saturated fat, 5 g carbohydrate, 2 g protein, 1 g dietary fiber, 227 mg sodium. Exchanges: 1 Vegetable

Eggplant

Solanum melongena

For some people, like my wife, Treena, eggplant is an acquired taste, which perhaps has as much to do with its texture as anything However, it's possible to reduce its bitterness and, to some degree, its slippery texture.

My planting went in too late to bear fruit. It really pays to get a good start and plant it the moment a patch of soil reaches 70°F. If the nights drop to 55°F or below, you'll need row covers, and you may also need to cover the soil with black plastic or plastic mulch to retain soil warmth.

To get larger fruit, you can carefully prune 2–3 branches on each plant. Large fruit can make it in higher daytime temperatures. Small fruit are better suited to cool-weather areas like mine.

I often use eggplant when I'm changing a meat-centered dish to a vegetarian (or, more accurately, meatless) one. When pressed, eggplant changes from a slippery sponge to a more tooth-resistant texture—almost like that of a thin slice of meat. And because eggplant absorbs the flavors you add, such as garlic, herbs, and tomatoes, I am able to bypass Treena's resistance.

The Numbers

Because of its family relationship to the nightshade family, it *may* in rare cases pose a problem for arthritis sufferers, although the science remains unproven. Still, I like to use it for the benefits drawn from its firm texture, which can satisfy the meat eaters among us who need some coaxing to cross over the meat-and-two-vegetables line to the three-or-more-vegetables-on-the-plate club.

For 100 g cooked (3.5 oz; ½ cup): 35 calories, 0 g fat, 0 g saturated fat, 9 g carbohydrate, 1 g protein, 2.5 g dietary fiber, 1 mg sodium

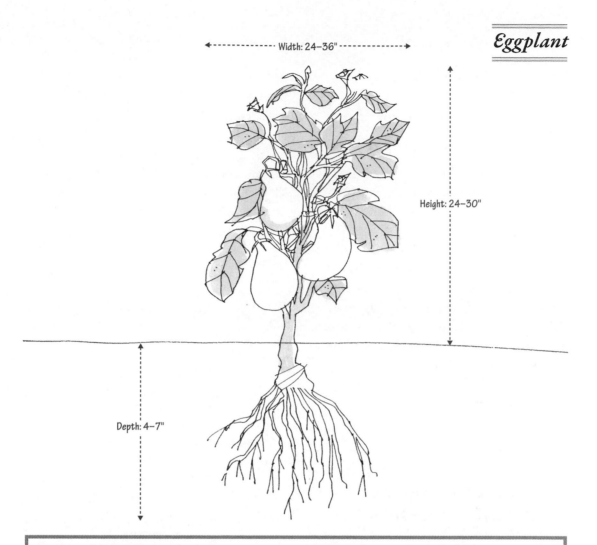

Width: 24–36"

Height: 24–30"

Depth: 4–7"

Perennial (Zone 10)/Annual in other zones
Water: Heavy, drip irrigation
Sun: Full; shade if over 100°F
Companion Planting:
PRO: Peas, beans, peppers
CON: Corn, fennel, tomatoes
Pests: Lace bugs, aphids, cutworms, whiteflies
Diseases: Root rot, anthracnose
Soil: Well-drained soil in warm locations, preferably in raised beds; light, sandy loam
Fertilizer: Fish emulsion every 3–4 weeks
pH: 5.5–6.8
Varieties: Black Beauty (deep purple), Ichiban (long, easier to grow in hot weather)

Plant Care: Pinch off branch tips when plant is 6 feet tall; keep fruit one to a branch for larger size
Zones: 5–12 (perennial in Zone 10, where the plants can survive the winter)
Planting: Seed ¼–½ inch deep (indoors), 4–6 weeks before last frost; put transplants out when temperature exceeds 70°F, 3–5 inches apart, and then thin to 18–24 inches
Germinate: 10–15 days
Harvest: From seed, 100–140 days; from transplant, 50–75 days
Rotation: Should follow beans or peas if possible
Edible: Fruit

EGGPLANT

Basic Preparation

To overcome Treena's dislike of this splendid plant, I cut ½-inch-thick slices across the girth and dust with salt (about ¼ teaspoon per slice, which will be rinsed off later). Then I press the pieces between two plates (or trays), weigh it down with a 2- to 3-pound weight and leave it for 1 hour. The salt leaches out the somewhat bitter juices. Then I rinse and dry the pressed slices with paper towels. If the eggplant is to be broiled or pan-fried, drench lightly in a little flour mixed with smoked paprika and a spritz of olive oil to give it a deeper flavor and color.

MEDITERRANEAN ROASTED EGGPLANT

This recipe makes an excellent entrée, as a centerpiece for your meal instead of meat. It also works great as a side dish. (Just cut the serving size in half to make eight servings instead of four.)

SERVES 4

2 small eggplants, about 4-inches in diameter
1 cup low-sodium pizza sauce
¼ cup low-fat plain yogurt
1 garlic clove, finely chopped

Preheat the oven to 350°F. Spray a 12-inch baking pan with olive oil.

Remove the stem ends and slice the eggplant into ¾-inch slices. Lay the eggplant in the prepared pan in a single layer. Spoon pizza sauce on each slice. Bake 30 minutes.

Stir the yogurt and garlic together. Drizzle the sauce in thin lines on each of the eggplant slices before serving (you can do this easily by putting the sauce in a plastic squirt bottle).

Per serving: 95 calories, 2 g fat, 0 g saturated fat, 18 g carbohydrate, 4 g protein, 9 g dietary fiber, 275 mg sodium. Exchanges: 3 Vegetable

RATATOUILLE

This was the classic way to serve zucchini and eggplant even before the movie! This is our all-time-favorite summer vegetable combination, made hugely better because the main ingredients come straight from the garden!

SERVES 6

2 medium (1-pound) eggplants, cut into
    2-inch cubes
3 teaspoons olive oil, divided
1 sweet onion, cut into 1-inch chunks
4 garlic cloves, bashed and chopped
1 red bell pepper, seeded and cut into ½-inch
    strips
1 green bell pepper, seeded and cut into
    ½-inch strips
3 medium zucchini, cut into 1-inch chunks

3 cups peeled, seeded, and diced fresh
   tomatoes
1 tablespoon chopped fresh oregano
¼ teaspoon salt
¼ teaspoon freshly ground black pepper
¼ cup chopped fresh parsley
¼ cup chopped fresh basil

Preheat oven to 400°F.

Place the eggplant cubes in a baking dish, spray lightly with olive oil cooking spray and bake 20 minutes or until tender. Set aside.

Heat 1 teaspoon of the oil in a high-sided skillet over medium-high. Sauté the onions 2 minutes, add the garlic, and cook 1 minute more. Stir in the bell peppers and zucchini, and cook about 10 minutes until wilted. Add the tomatoes, oregano, salt, and black pepper, and cook 10 minutes.

Stir in the eggplant and simmer 10 minutes more or until everything is tender. Add the remaining 2 teaspoons olive oil, parsley, and basil, and stir.

Serve hot or at room temperature as a side dish. For a main dish, spoon over toasted Italian bread, polenta, pasta, or rice.

Per serving: 127 calories, 3 g fat, 0 g saturated fat, 24 g carbohydrate, 1 g protein, 3 g dietary fiber, 332 mg sodium. Exchanges: 5 Vegetable

ROASTED EGGPLANT AND RED PEPPER SANDWICH

This is my all-time-favorite sandwich, but Treena truly hates it, so I indulge only occasionally and to compensate for her absence in my life when she is away with friends.

If you have a hinged compression (panini) grill, then please use it to toast the filling and the bread.

SERVES 4

8 small slices French or Italian bread, toasted
Extra-virgin olive oil cooking spray
2 garlic cloves, cut in half
1 medium eggplant, cut into ½-inch slices
¼ teaspoon salt
¼ teaspoon freshly ground black pepper
1 cup sliced roasted red peppers

Preheat the broiler. Lay the bread on the broiler pan, coat lightly with extra-virgin olive oil cooking spray, and toast lightly on both sides. Rub the top of each with the garlic and set aside.

Set the oven to 450°F. Grease a baking sheet.

Arrange the eggplant slices in the prepared sheet and coat lightly with the cooking spray. Season with salt and black pepper. Roast 20 minutes or until tender and caramelized.

Cover each slice of bread with the roasted eggplant and lay the roasted red pepper strips over the top. Give each one a quick spritz of the cooking spray and serve.

Per serving: 250 calories, 2 g fat, 0 g saturated fat, 49 g carbohydrate, 10 g protein, 8 g dietary fiber, 779 mg sodium. Exchanges: 2 Starch, 1 Vegetable

Fava Bean

Vicia faba

Growing my own fava beans took what I thought about them to a whole new level.

In Britain, they are well known as *broad beans*, which indeed they are! They are a better buy when grown in the garden than bought in the store because the pods are huge and inedible, which makes the eventual bean quite costly.

In England, we would cook the relatively young bean in a white sauce—the outer jacket on the inner bean was still tender, and they were quite a treat.

But it was in Greece that fava made their mark as a traditional rite of passage in the early spring. Everyone served them with garlic, peppers, and heaps of oregano and feta cheese. What a wonderful thing seasons are!

My favas grew very rapidly in a warm, sunny patch. The pods began to emerge as the blossoms dropped, leaving a black furry blob that looked suspiciously like mold, but it wasn't! I let my pods grow and grow until supersize, 8–10 inches. The problem was that they developed an extra greenish gray skin on each bean that was quite tough. Next year I'll harvest them earlier.

It's important not to overwater favas. Water just before the soil dries out. Keep the soil moist during flowering and pod formation.

The Numbers

If your relatives came from the Mediterranean, check on their allergic reaction to favas, called *favism*. It is rare but genetically transmitted.

For each 100 g boiled (3.5 oz; ½ cup) mature beans: 110 calories, 0 g fat, 0 g saturated fat, 20 g carbohydrate, 8 g protein, 5 g dietary fiber, 5 mg sodium

For each 100 g boiled (3.5 oz; ½ cup) immature beans: 62 calories, 0.5 g fat, 0 g saturated fat, 10 g carbohydrate, 5 g protein, 4 g dietary fiber, 41 mg sodium

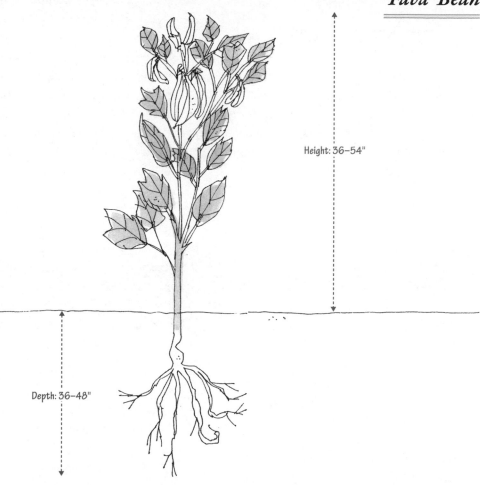

Width: 12–18"

Height: 36–54"

Depth: 36–48"

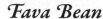

Water: Don't overwater
Sun: Full
Companion Planting:
PRO: Potatoes, cucumbers, corn, strawberries, celery, summer savory
CON: Onions, garlic
Pests: Aphids, bean beetles, flea beetles, leafhoppers, mites
Diseases: Susceptible to blight, mosaic, anthracnose
Soil: Loose, well-drained, good organic content
Fertilizer: Low nitrogen, moderate phosphorus, potassium; top-dress with bonemeal when they bloom
pH: 6.0–6.8

Varieties: Broad Windsor, Aquadulce, Con Amore, Loretta, Sweet Lorane, Windsor Long-Pod
Zones: 3–11
Planting: Early spring, as soon as the ground can be worked, from February to March, depending on climate zone; plant seeds 1–2 inches deep; sow 4–5 inches apart in rows 18–30 inches apart
Germination: 4–10 days
Harvest: 80–100 days
Rotation: Follow bean crops with a high-nitrogen-requiring crop, such as lettuce, squash, broccoli, Brussels sprouts, cabbage, cauliflower, collards
Edible: Immature beans

BRUNSWICK STEW

To my taste, the very early part of North American culinary history (fur trappers' food!) just isn't correct without either lima or fava beans. While this dish may traditionally be prepared with chicken, it's a grand kitchen-garden feast when you substitute butternut squash.

SERVES 6

1 pound butternut squash, cut into 6 segments

1 teaspoon nonaromatic olive oil

Salt and freshly ground black pepper to taste

1 large sweet onion, cut into 1-inch dice (yield 2 cups)

3 stalks celery, cut into ¼-inch slices (yield 1½ cups)

1 teaspoon diced canned chipotle or ½ teaspoon ground smoked jalapeño chile

1 red bell pepper, cut into ¼-inch slices

2 cups skinned, seeded, and chopped tomatoes

1 cup low-sodium vegetable stock (see page 288)

1 tablespoon Worcestershire sauce

¼ teaspoon cayenne

1 cup fresh baby fava beans or lima beans

1 cup fresh or frozen corn kernels

1 tablespoon arrowroot mixed with 2 tablespoons stock or water (slurry)

¼ cup chopped fresh parsley

¼ cup chopped fresh basil

Preheat the oven to 375°F.

Spray the butternut squash pieces with cooking spray, season with salt and black pepper, and roast in a small ovenproof baking dish for 40 minutes, until a thin knife comes out clean.

Heat ½ teaspoon of the oil in a 10½-inch chef's pan over medium-high. Sauté the onions 3 minutes or until they start to turn translucent. Add the celery, chipotle, and red bell pepper, and cook 3 more minutes. Remove to a plate, and without washing the pan, add the remaining ½ teaspoon oil and heat.

Pour in the tomatoes and sauté for 3 minutes to just brown, then add the stock and Worcestershire sauce. Add the cooked vegetables and the cayenne. Bring to a boil, reduce the heat, cover, and simmer 10 minutes. Add the beans and corn, and cook 12 minutes more or until the beans are tender. Stir in the slurry and heat to thicken. Spoon over the butternut squash pieces. Sprinkle with the parsley and basil and serve.

Per serving: 155 calories, 1 g fat, 0 g saturated fat, 34 g carbohydrate, 5 g protein, 8 g dietary fiber, 141 mg sodium. Exchanges: 1 Starch, 4 Vegetable

FAVA BEAN SOUP WITH CARROTS

I've always enjoyed fava beans, but they must be harvested early to save all the trouble of removing the tough inner bean skins. Paired with very new carrots, this is a perfect example of a FABIS (fresh and best in season) dish

for the Skagit Valley in the Pacific Northwest, where both mature at the same time.

SERVES 4

1 teaspoon nonaromatic olive oil
1 cup chopped onions
1 cup sliced carrots
2 cups fresh baby fava beans
3 cups low-sodium vegetable stock
   (see page 288)
2 cups chopped fresh spinach
¼ teaspoon salt
¼ teaspoon freshly ground black pepper

Heat the oil in a large saucepan over medium-high. Sauté the onions 2 minutes. Stir in the carrots and beans. Pour in the stock, bring to a boil, reduce the heat, and simmer 20 minutes, until the carrots are tender.

Add the spinach, salt, and black pepper, and simmer 5 minutes longer.

Per serving: 120 calories, 2 g fat, 0 g saturated fat, 31 g carbohydrate, 6 g protein, 6 g dietary fiber, 327 mg sodium. Exchanges: 1½ Starch, 1 Lean Meat, 2 Vegetable

FAVA BEAN SOUP

When the fava beans are full and ready, this is the perfect way to celebrate their arrival. It's an early-summer gardener's celebration! If the beans are young, they can be cooked as is. Later on, their pale leathery jackets will need

to be removed; just pinch at the "bar" end to remove the tender green beans.

SERVES 6

1 teaspoon nonaromatic olive oil
½ pound sweet onions, chopped
2 garlic cloves, bashed and sliced
1 cup chopped fennel bulb or celery
1 (10.75-ounce) can tomato puree
1 quart water
Bouquet garni (recipe follows)
1 pound shucked fresh fava beans or 1
   (19-ounce) can, drained
2 cups finely chopped tightly packed stemmed
   mustard greens
1 pound plum tomatoes, peeled, seeded, and
   chopped
¼ teaspoon freshly ground black pepper
½ teaspoon salt

Heat the oil in a high-sided skillet over medium-high. Sauté the onions and garlic 3 minutes. Add the fennel or celery, tomato puree, and water. Bring to a boil, drop in the bouquet garni and beans, and simmer 5 minutes.

Add the mustard greens and tomatoes, black pepper, and salt. Simmer 4 more minutes. Remove the bouquet garni. If using fennel, chop 1 tablespoon of the tender fennel tops ("feathers") and scatter over the top; if using celery, finely chop some leaves as a garnish.

Bouquet Garni
2 bay leaves
6 sprigs parsley
1 teaspoon dried thyme
1 teaspoon dried oregano
3-inch rib of celery

Wrap all the ingredients in cheesecloth and tie off.

Per serving: 114 calories, 2 g fat, 0 g saturated fat, 21 g carbohydrate, 6 g protein, 6 g dietary fiber, 252 mg sodium. Exchanges: 1 Starch, 3 Vegetable, ½ Fat

GREEK PIE

I grant you that this looks tricky, and certainly phyllo pastry isn't easy, but my handling tips help. As a gracious treat to vegetarian (lacto-ovo) guests, it's hard to beat. I have used fresh baby fava beans, but should you be off season and wanting to experience this recipe, you can use canned favas or, in a pinch, lima beans.

Working with Phyllo
Phyllo pastry is generally found in the frozen food section of the supermarket. The package should be thawed overnight in the refrigerator. As you assemble the pie, cover any unused phyllo with a damp cloth to keep it from drying out. If you have long fingernails, be especially careful not to tear holes in the phyllo. Wrap leftover phyllo in wax paper and plastic wrap for storage in either the freezer or the refrigerator.

SERVES 4

1 teaspoon olive oil
1 bunch (about 8) green onions, sliced into
    ½-inch rounds
½ pound mushrooms, quartered (yield 2 cups)

1 teaspoon freshly squeezed lemon juice
1 medium zucchini, cut into chunks
⅛ teaspoon white pepper
¼ teaspoon salt
1 teaspoon dried oregano
1 cup low-sodium vegetable stock (see
    page 288) or ½ cup stock plus ½ cup
    dealcoholized dry white wine
1 pound fresh baby fava beans
2 tablespoons freshly grated Parmesan cheese
1 tablespoon arrowroot
1 cup egg substitute
8 sheets phyllo dough
1 (10-ounce) package frozen, chopped
    spinach, thawed and pressed dry

Preheat the oven to 350°F. Spray an 8-inch square baking dish with cooking spray.

Heat the oil in a high-sided skillet over medium-high. Cook the onions for 1 minute, then toss in the mushrooms and lemon juice, and cook 3 minutes more. Stir in the zucchini, white pepper, salt, and oregano, and cook, stirring, for 1 minute more.

Pour in the stock and bring to a vigorous boil to reduce by half. Pull the skillet off the heat and stir in the beans and Parmesan cheese. Combine the arrowroot with the egg substitute and pour over the mixture in the pan. Stir and let cool while you work on the crust.

Lay the stack of phyllo sheets on a clean work surface. Spray the top sheet with cooking spray, peel it off, and lay it (sprayed side up) in the prepared dish, allowing it to overlap the edges. (Don't overwork the sheets; let gravity settle them to the bottom of the dish.) Spray the second sheet and set it squarely on top of the first one. Do the same thing to the third and fourth sheets, but lay them at a 90-degree angle to the first two. Cover the remaining phyllo sheets with plastic while you fill the pie.

Scatter half the spinach over the first layers of phyllo and spread half the mushroom mixture over it evenly. Make another layer of spinach and of mushroom mixture and fold in the over-lapping phyllo sheets. (They will not cover the spinach and mushroom mixtures completely.)

From the remaining phyllo, spray another sheet and lay it on top. Spray and stack 3 more sheets as before. Trim the edges, cut through the top layer of phyllo so that it is marked out into its final four serving portions, and bake 35–40 minutes or until golden on top. To serve, cut all the way through the bottom of the pie and place on hot plates.

Per serving: 287 calories, 5 g fat, 1 g saturated fat (3% calories from saturated fat), 41 g carbohydrate, 19 g 9protein, 8 g dietary fiber, 618 mg sodium. Ex-changes: 2 Starch, 3 Vegetable, 2 Fat

Fennel

Foeniculum vulgare var. *azoricum*

If you enjoy a subtle flavor of licorice or fresh basil, it will be a fairly good bet that fennel can fit into your kitchen-garden plans. Technically classified as an herb, it is also used as a vegetable, eaten raw or cooked.

Fennel looks like an overweight celery but with fine feathery fronds. It's important not to let them grow any fatter in their exposed aboveground bulb than 2–3 inches; more than that and the outer stems can become tough and fibrous.

As with both celery and leeks, fennel can be treated to mulching that is heaped up the sides to keep the outer stems a very pale green to white, which also helps both taste and texture. You should start the mulch when the bulb is egg size. I found out that too vigorous weeding can damage fennel's shallow roots. If this happens, the plants will bolt, so the mulch will do double-duty in blanching and weed suppression!

If you pinch off the seed stalks, you will encourage greater bulb size.

My favorite method of cooking fennel borrows from the Italian cuisine in Venice, where we've spent some very happy and delicious days. Simply halve the bulb lengthwise (if it's 2–3 inches in diameter) and cut off the shortened top branches (to use in stews, soups, etc.). Broil the bulb under radiant heat or over barbecue coals until nicely browned and crisp tender. Use a spritz of olive oil, a little sea salt, and freshly ground white pepper to season.

When served alongside a nice piece of freshly caught fish with a few newly dug fingerling potatoes, there can be little in this world to rival the experience.

The Numbers

For each 100 g raw (3.5 oz; ½ cup): 31 calories, 0 g fat, 0 g saturated fat, 7 g carbohydrate, 1 g protein, 3 g dietary fiber, 52 mg sodium

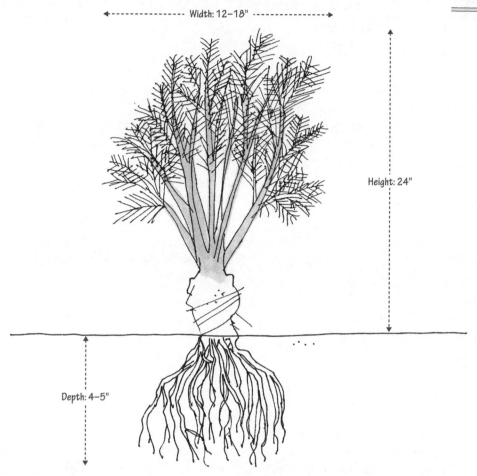

Width: 12–18"

Height: 24"

Depth: 4–5"

Perennial/Summer Annual/Hardy
Water: Light
Sun: Full
Companion Planting:
PRO: Mint family
CON: Dill, coriander
Pests: Celery worms, parsley worms
Diseases: None
Soil: Sandy loam with good humus content, good drainage
Fertilizer: Moderate fertilizing; compost tea every 4–5 weeks
pH: 6.5–7.0

Varieties: Herald (for spring planting), Rudy, Trieste (large, aromatic bulbs)
Zones: 3–10
Planting: Early spring to midsummer, when soil temperature is 65°F–75°F; seeds to ¼ inch deep; space seedlings or thin plants to 10–12 inches apart, in rows 18–24 inches apart.
Germinate: 7–14 days
Harvest: 90–115 days
Rotation: Don't follow carrot, parsnip
Edible: Swollen bulb (above the surface) and feathered leaves (fronds)

STEAMED AND BROILED FENNEL

This is a domestic problem: I love it, but Treena doesn't care for the licorice flavor, no matter how subtle it may be. If it weren't for that one fact, it would meet her need for very low calories with good visual portion size. So fennel in whatever incarnation is only an occasional solitary treat for me but could fill the plate for you!

SERVES 4

2 medium to large fennel bulbs
¼ teaspoon salt
¼ teaspoon freshly ground black pepper
2 tablespoons freshly squeezed lemon juice
Dusting of smoked paprika

Preheat the broiler.

Trim off the stems, fronds, and any discolored outside layers of the bulb. Chop and save a few of the fronds to scatter over the top of the finished dish. Cut the bulbs in half lengthwise.

Place the fennel slices in a steamer and steam over boiling water for 8–10 minutes or until crisp tender.

Season with salt and black pepper, brush lemon juice on both sides, and lay them in a single layer on a broiler pan. Spray lightly with olive oil cooking spray, and dust with paprika. Broil about 3 inches from the heat source until golden brown, about 4 minutes. Turn and brown the other side. Divide among 4 hot plates and scatter the reserved fronds over the top.

Per serving: 38 calories, 0 g fat, 0 g saturated fat, 9 g carbohydrate, 1 g protein, 4 g dietary fiber, 206 mg sodium. Exchanges: 1 Vegetable

BRAISED FENNEL IN SPICY TOMATO JUICE

For all the world this winds up looking like braised celery, and yet its flavor is quite distinctive. Accompanied with no more than 2 ounces (dry weight) of your favorite pasta, such as whole-grain angel hair, it does very well as a main dish.

SERVES 4

1 medium to large fennel bulb (about 1½ pounds)
1 teaspoon fennel seeds
1 cup spicy tomato-vegetable juice

Preheat the oven to 350°F.

Trim the fennel bulb, saving the stems to flavor soups or fish stews. Cut lengthwise into four slices.

Lay the bulb pieces in a 10-inch greased glass or ceramic baking dish. Scatter the fennel seeds over the top and pour in the juice until the fennel is half covered. Bake, covered, 45 minutes, basting with the pan juices 2–3 times, until a fine knife meets with only slight resistance.

Per serving: 65 calories, 0 g fat, 0 g saturated fat, 15 g carbohydrates, 3 g protein, 6 g dietary fiber, 243 mg sodium. Exchanges: 4 Vegetable

FENNEL AND LEEK POËLE

Many great cuisines of the world serve up a main food item (such as good fresh fish) on a poële, or bed of vegetables. This is an excellent example of a perfect bed for salmon or for several overlapping slices of broiled eggplant (see page 142) or butternut squash.

SERVES 4

1 teaspoon nonaromatic olive oil
1 cup chopped onion
1 leek, white part only, sliced
2 large fennel bulbs, trimmed of stems and
    fronds, cut in half
1 cup low-sodium vegetable stock
    (see page 288)
¼ teaspoon salt
¼ teaspoon freshly ground black pepper
4 tablespoons chopped fennel fronds

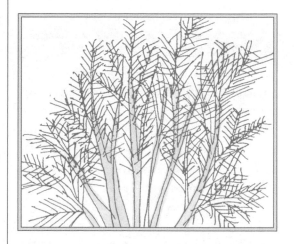

Heat the oil in a high-sided skillet over medium-high. Sauté the onion 2 minutes or until it starts to wilt. Add the leek and fennel, and stir to coat with the oil, about 1 minute. Pour in the stock, salt, and black pepper. Bring to a boil, reduce the heat, and simmer 20 minutes or until the fennel is tender. Stir in the chopped fronds and serve.

Per serving: 98 calories, 2 g fat, 0 g saturated fat, 20 g carbohydrate, 3 g protein, 6 g dietary fiber, 275 mg sodium. Exchanges: 2 Vegetable

Garlic

Allium sativum

From all my reading, it's been hard to come up with plants that have a longer history of cultivation (other than grains) than garlic. It has been cultivated since at least 3000 BCE!

Garlic loves a cool start during short days. As it grows, so should the length of the day and the temperature. It's actually best to plant in late autumn, about 6 weeks before you anticipate your first frost. Failing this, you could keep the seed bulbs in your refrigerator at about 40°F until the soil can be worked in early spring.

When the flowers form and the stems yellow, you'll need to lodge them by bending the stalk right over, pointing to the ground. Do this carefully so as not to break it.

Harvest 2–3 weeks after lodging. Brush off soil and leave on shaded screens (for air circulation) to cure until the outside is dry and the neck tightly closed.

Garlic's pronounced flavor has been enjoyed by billions and was an obvious choice for my first year in the kitchen garden—coupled, naturally, with its relative ease of farming and storage.

I grew up in the hotel business in Europe, where my parents were hoteliers. Our waitstaff was from northern Italy and Poland and thoroughly enjoyed their garlic—even to the extent of chewing whole cloves raw! This greatly troubled (nice way of saying *infuriated*) my dad, who couldn't stand its aroma on a waiter's breath. When a waiter would ask politely, "How is your meal, sir? Is everything satisfactory?" my dad would humph, "Yes—everything except your *breath*!"

The problem was solved by a stern rule: before each meal service, each garlic eater had to eat a small bunch of fresh parsley and then breathe on the maitre d', who would also inspect their teeth for large green flecks. Today's unions may not be so permissive!

For me, garlic in the right measure is an absolute essential. But it doesn't have to be used as a blunt instrument. It should have a small but important walk-on part in the drama of great food.

To become such a fan, you could try it roasted, which makes it quite mild and sweet.

The Numbers

For every 100 g raw (3.5 oz; ½ cup): 149 calories, 0.5 g fat, 0 g saturated fat, 33 g carbohydrate, 6 g protein, 2 g dietary fiber, 17 mg sodium

Note: 1 garlic clove weighs about 3 g and translates to 4 calories, 0 g fat, 1 g carbohydrate, 0 g protein, 0 g dietary fiber, 1 mg sodium

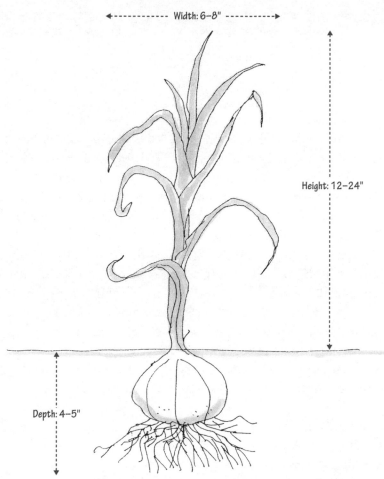

Width: 6–8"

Height: 12–24"

Depth: 4–5"

Perennial/Cool Season
Water: Low
Sun: Full
Companion Planting:
PRO: Beets, cabbage family, lettuce, tomatoes, strawberries
CON: Beans, peas
Pests: Aphids, nematodes, thrips
Diseases: Botrytis rot, white rot
Soil: Good drainage; benefits from rich composting (if possible, keep onion discards out of the compost used for garlic)
Fertilizer: Moderate

pH: 4.5–8.3
Varieties: The small clove comes from the lily family; the elephant clove is related to the leek (*Allium scorodo-prasum*) and is, in my opinion, too mild to be called garlic; silverskin (soft neck for cool regions) is my favorite to date
Zones: 5–10
Planting: Late summer, autumn; cloves, 2 inches deep, 6 weeks before last frost; 4–8 inches apart
Germinate: 7–14 days (needs 55°F for germination)
Harvest: 90–100 days
Rotation: Don't follow onion crops
Edible: Cloves and scapes

Jerusalem Artichoke

Helianthus tuberosus

This interesting vegetable has absolutely nothing to do with either Jerusalem or artichokes and therefore should more authentically be called by its other name, sunchoke, since it's part of the sunflower family that the French call *girasole*. Can you see how that might have morphed into Jerusalem?

There are, like many of today's colorful plants, a number of different shades to the little nobbly tuber: white, yellow, red, and blue. They are a great addition to the outer reaches of the garden because in midsummer, they explode into a mass display of bright yellow daisy-like blooms about 4 inches in diameter on top of a 6-foot stalk.

Well, so much for the colors—what about their habits? They are almost civic minded: Once planted, they'll go as far as you let them but will stop at a barrier (preferably bricks) set about 2 feet deep. They suffer from no severe disease and attract only mites (which can be washed off with soapy water) and gophers.

(Our underground visitors went away when we planted one of those sonar pegs).

So far, neither the deer nor the rabbits seem to be interested, so we've established a west-sloping bed for the sunchokes outside our fence.

The tuber is best eaten as a late fall treat, as they gain sweetness when the soil chills. If kept cool and moist, they can be stored up to 6 months. They can produce an alarming amount of flatulence, especially if eaten raw, so steam them briefly—they turn to mush if overcooked.

Jerusalem artichokes contain *inulin*, which allows their carbohydrates to break down to fructose, which makes them a good choice for type 2 diabetes and weight loss.

The Numbers

For each 100 g raw (3.5 oz; ½ cup): 73 calories, 10 g fat, 0 g saturated fat, 17 g carbohydrate, 2 g protein, 2 g dietary fiber, 4 mg sodium

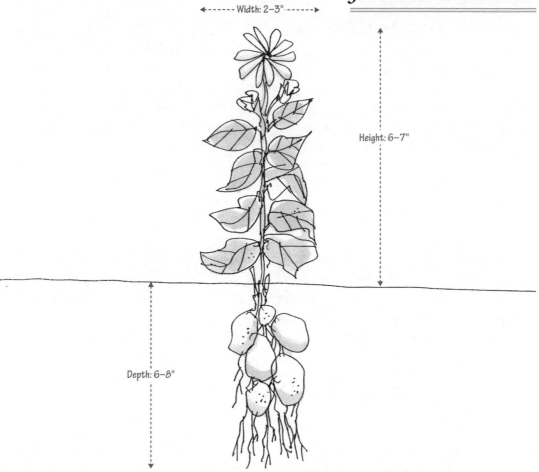

Width: 2–3"

Height: 6–7"

Depth: 6–8"

Perennial
Water: Moderate
Sun: Full
Companion Planting:
PRO: None, keep isolated
CON: None
Pests: Spray leaves in insecticidal soap for mites. Guard against gophers and voles, which love the tasty root.
Diseases: None
Soil: Humus-rich sandy loam; doesn't grow well in clay, so add sand and compost
Fertilizer: Moderate nitrogen, phosphorus, and potassium

pH: 5.8–6.2
Varieties: Mamouth, Stampede (white), Boston Red (red, as in Sox), French White (very successful for home garden)
Zones: 4–10
Planting: Tubers, 4 inches deep, 6 inches apart; 4–6 weeks after last frost for fall harvest
Germination: 7–14 days
Harvest: 110–150 days
Rotation: Don't rotate; create a permanent bed
Edible: Tuber

JERUSALEM ARTICHOKE

Basic Preparation

If this is your first encounter with a Jerusalem artichoke, know that it has an unusual texture. When used raw, its texture is not unlike the crispness of jicama or water chestnuts. When cooked, it's halfway between a potato and an eggplant.

Because its exterior is so knobby (and the skin so thin), it doesn't pay to try to peel them; just lightly scrub them, and you'll get a dark cream skin and an almost white interior.

Parboil Jerusalem artichokes in boiling salted water for about 20 minutes if medium-large (about 2 inches in diameter). Let them cool, and slice ¼-inch thick. They can be sautéed in a little olive oil well seasoned with salt and pepper. A dusting of fresh parsley or chives is a nice finishing touch.

They do not mash well, and personally, I don't enjoy their texture when boiled and served whole. They can be roasted after being cut in quarters as you would any root vegetable.

JERUSALEM ARTICHOKE AND MUSHROOM SAUTÉ

Here we have a most unusual textural recipe, with great flavors and exceptionally low glycemic numbers in what appears to be a starchy dish.

SERVES 4

1 pound Jerusalem artichokes
1 teaspoon olive oil
1 medium sweet onion, finely sliced
1 garlic clove, crushed
8 crimini brown-skinned butter mushrooms
1 tablespoon freshly squeezed lemon juice
¼ teaspoon cayenne
5 Swiss chard leaves, very finely sliced
Salt and freshly ground black pepper to taste

Scrub the outsides of the Jerusalem artichokes and place them in boiling water. Cook for 20 minutes or until just tender. Cool and cut into ¼-inch-thin round slices. Heat the olive oil in a large skillet over medium. Add the onion and sauté for 4 minutes. Add the garlic and cook for 1 minute. Add the sliced artichokes, toss well for 2 minutes, and then add the mushrooms, lemon juice, and cayenne. Toss for about 2 minutes or until mushrooms are done. Stir in the Swiss chard, season with salt and black pepper, and serve.

Per serving: 125 calories, 1 g fat, 0 g saturated fat, 26 g carbohydrate, 4 g protein, 3 g dietary fiber, 426 mg sodium

JERUSALEM ARTICHOKES WITH HOT BLACK BEAN SALSA

SERVES 4

1 (15-ounce) can reduced-sodium black
    beans, rinsed and drained
2 garlic cloves, bashed and chopped
1 cup frozen corn kernels
2 Roma tomatoes, chopped
1 jalapeño chile, chopped (retain the seeds if
    you like it hot)
⅛ teaspoon cayenne
½ teaspoon ground cumin
1 teaspoon mild chili powder
¼ cup chopped fresh cilantro
1 pound Jerusalem artichokes, boiled whole
    for 20 minutes, cooled and cut in half

Whiz half the beans with the garlic in a blender. Add a little water to get them going, if necessary.

Pour into a saucepan and add the remaining beans, corn, tomatoes, chile, cayenne, cumin, and chili powder. Heat on medium for 5 minutes, stirring occasionally to keep from sticking. Stir in half of the cilantro.

Serve the black bean salsa over the artichokes, sprinkled with the remaining cilantro.

Per serving: 212 calories, 1 g fat, 0 g saturated fat, 46 g carbohydrate, 9 g protein, 7 dietary fiber, 136 mg sodium. Exchanges: 3 Starch, 1 Vegetable

Kale

Brassica oleracea var. *acephala*

There are several important varieties of kale. Their differences are most obvious at first sight. The leaf is either tightly frilled at the edge or more open, broader, and longer, as in the Toscano variety, which I prefer.

For a late-season crop, whichever one you choose, it's really important to mark your garden calendar (you *really* need one!) to estimate the date of the first expected frost. Count back 6–8 weeks, and that is a good date to put in transplants that you can either order in advance from a local nursery or grow yourself from seed.

Kale will, of course, also grow in the spring and early summer, but frankly if you get any kind of long bright sunny days in July and August, kale's natural sweetness may be overtaken by an unacceptable bitterness.

It seems that the colder the weather, the better the flavor—especially the young, tender inside leaves, which can be cut 2 inches off the ground and will grow back for a second crop.

It seems so odd to me that kale's flavor would be so much better after a pretty good frost. If you do cut it back, do so at least 2–3 weeks before the first frost in mild fall weather, and it should grow back in time for a second harvesting.

Kale is hardy and will keep well in a plastic bag at 40°F (refrigerated) for about 1–2 weeks.

I remove the heavy stems and steam the leaves for 4–6 minutes to retain their brilliant color. I admit that the leaf is still chewy, but the sweetness of the winter crop is *so* good.

The Numbers

Kale can be extremely high in chlorophyll and carotenes, especially beta-carotene and lutein.

For each 100 g cooked (3.5 oz; 1 cup): 28 calories, 0 g fat, 0 g saturated fat, 6 g carbohydrate, 2 g protein, 2 g dietary fiber, 23 mg sodium

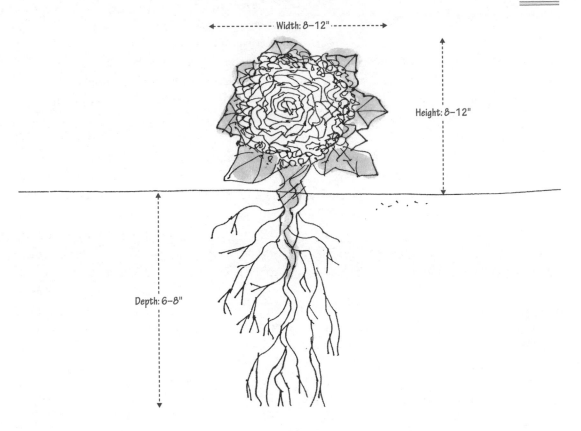

Width: 8–12"

Height: 8–12"

Depth: 6–8"

Annual/Hardy/Cool Season
Water: Heavy
Sun: Full to partial shade
Companion Planting:
PRO: Beets, bush beans, lettuce, herbs, spinach
CON: Pole beans, strawberries, tomatoes
Pests: Aphids, loopers, flea beetles, cutworms
Diseases: Black rot, clubroot
Soil: Compost well before planting in rich sandy loam with good drainage
Fertilizer: Moderate; fish emulsion every 3–4 weeks
pH: 5.5–6.8
Varieties: Dwarf Blue Curled Vates (compact, curly),

Lacinato (tall leaves), Toscano (flat, broad, sweet in the fall)
Plant Care: When leaves grow to 6–8 inches, put straw mulch around base to avoid soil contact.
Zones: 3–11
Planting: Spring, seed ½ inch deep, 6–8 weeks before last frost; autumn, seed ½ inch deep, 6 weeks before first frost; 6 inches apart
Germinate: 5–7 days
Harvest: From seed, 55–75 days; from transplant, 30–40 days
Rotation: Don't follow cabbage family.
Edible: Leaves

STEAMED KALE

This is a simple way to experience the great taste of kale. The chopped red bell pepper added to the kale before steaming lends a festive touch for a holiday dinner or for any dull winter day.

SERVES 4

1 pound kale, rinsed and heavy stems removed
2 cups chopped red bell pepper (optional)
¼ teaspoon salt
¼ teaspoon freshly ground black pepper
1 tablespoon freshly squeezed lemon juice

Place the kale in a steamer and add the red peppers. Sprinkle with the salt, black pepper, and lemon juice, and steam over boiling water for 4–6 minutes or until tender.

Per serving: 43 calories, 1 g fat, 0 g saturated fat, 8 g carbohydrate, 2 g protein, 3 g dietary fiber, 170 mg sodium. Exchanges: 1 Vegetable

KALE AND APPLE SOUP

This is a super fruit-and-vegetable combination, with a sweet, sour, and aromatic finish.

SERVES 4

2 cups low-sodium vegetable stock
   (see page 288)

1 pound kale, carefully washed and stems
   removed (yield 4 cups packed)
¼ teaspoon salt
½ teaspoon ground cumin
1 teaspoon packed dark brown sugar
1 small Granny Smith apple, cored and
   chopped into ½-inch dice (yield 1 cup)
½ cup low-fat plain yogurt

Bring the stock to a boil in a large saucepan. Add the kale, cover, turn down the heat, and simmer 8 minutes or until it is tender to the bite, with good color. In a food processor, whiz the cooked kale with a little of the liquid until smooth. Strain the processed kale and return to the pan, stirring it into the remaining liquid.

Season with the salt, cumin, and brown sugar. Stir in the apple and simmer another 8 minutes. Remove from the heat and stir in the yogurt.

Per serving: 81 calories, 1 g fat, 0 g saturated fat, 16 g carbohydrate, 4 g protein, 3 g dietary fiber, 260 mg sodium. Exchanges: 1 Carbohydrate

SOOKE SOUP

Here is an example of a soup that can provide enough interest and sustenance to become, with a side salad and great bread, an evening meal.

SERVES 6

FOR THE YOGURT SAUCE
¼ cup yogurt cheese (see page 290)
1 tablespoon dealcoholized white wine

½ teaspoon chopped fresh thyme

1 teaspoon chopped fresh chives

¼ teaspoon freshly ground black pepper

⅛ teaspoon salt

¼ teaspoon freshly ground nutmeg

FOR THE SOUP

2 Granny Smith apples, cored and peeled

1 tablespoon extra-light olive oil

Dash sesame oil

⅓ cup chopped onion

1 garlic clove, smashed and diced

6 cups low-sodium vegetable stock
   (see page 288)

½ teaspoon chopped fresh thyme

4 cups peas, blanched 4 minutes

2 cups curly kale leaves, heavy stalks
   removed

¼ cup cornstarch, mixed with ½ cup nonfat
   milk (slurry)

12 ounces smoked white fish, chopped into
   small pieces

FOR THE GARNISH

1 tablespoon chopped fresh chives

1 tablespoon chopped fresh thyme

¼ teaspoon cayenne

To prepare the yogurt sauce, combine the yogurt cheese, wine, thyme, and chives in a small bowl, stirring until all lumps have disappeared. Stir in the black pepper, salt, and nutmeg, and set aside.

To make the soup, slice one of the apples and dice the other.

In a large stew pot, heat the oils and sauté the onion and garlic for 2 minutes. Add the *sliced* apple, stirring to coat. Add the stock and thyme, bring to a boil, and simmer for 10 minutes. Add the peas.

In a steamer, cook the kale for 3–4 minutes. The kale will turn a beautiful bright green. Remove and cut into very fine strips. Keep cool for later use.

Puree the soup in a food processor or blender. Pass the pureed soup through a mesh sieve and return the sieved puree to the stew pot. Stir in the slurry and bring just to a boil, stirring constantly until thickened. Add the diced apple, fish, and kale; heat through about 3 minutes until the fish is firm.

To serve, spoon the soup into individual serving bowls and garnish with the chives, thyme, and cayenne. Dollop a spoonful of yogurt sauce on top and enjoy!

Per serving: 254 calories, 3 g fat, 1 g saturated fat (4% calories from saturated fat), 33 g carbohydrate, 21 g protein, 7 g dietary fiber, 794 mg sodium. Exchanges: 1 Starch, 1 Very Lean Meat, 1 Vegetable

Kohlrabi

Brassica oleracea var. *gongylodes*

Compare the Latin names of kohlrabi and kale and you'll see that they are almost identical. Both are *Brassica oleracea*, but there the similarity definitely ends because kohlrabi's variety name is (and I *really* love this) *gongylodes*—what a splendid description for the smooth, round, almost spaceship-like bulb that grows with kale-like smooth leaves aboveground.

Kohlrabi is actually a hybrid that looks for all the world like a pale green turnip root with blue-green leaves. In fact, the name suggests such a combination because *kohl* is German for "cabbage" and *rübi* means "turnip."

If you decide that your kitchen garden should include a few somewhat unusual plants, then by all means devote a couple of feet to kohlrabi. They are an attention grabber when you do the grand tour of your raised beds with visitors! And if you plant several in different beds, it *could* help with insect control.

Kohlrabi's flavor does best when the plant grows quickly. I would suggest that you try the cultivar called Rapid, as it can be ready in 25 days after transplanting. And the best size is like a small apple, about 2½ inches in diameter.

The leaves can be cooked as you would kale. The bulb, or gong, can be steamed whole or finely sliced and quartered as an addition to a stir-fry in much the same way you'd use water chestnuts, but with more flavor.

The Numbers

If you are prone to producing kidney stones, then you might want to stick with only smaller portions. The problem is oxalate. Some people absorb higher levels than others. If you have a family history of kidney stones, you may want to have a simple test to see if you take in more than the 3 to 8 percent that's normal. If it's high, then you might want to put a 50-milligram-per-day limit on yourself.

For each 100 g raw (3.5 oz; ½ cup): 27 calories, 0 g fat, 0 g saturated fat, 6 g carbohydrate, 1 g protein, 4 g dietary fiber, 20 mg sodium

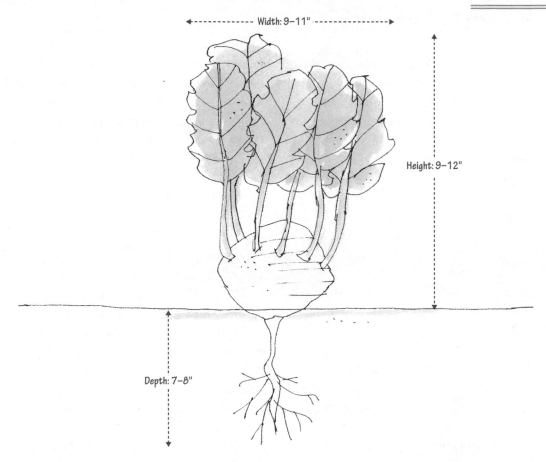

Width: 9–11"

Height: 9–12"

Depth: 7–8"

Biennial/Annual/Hardy/Cool Season
Water: Moderate
Sun: Full to partial shade
Companion Planting:
PRO: Beets, beans, celery, cucumbers, onions
CON: Pole beans, strawberries
Pests: Aphids, loopers, flea beetles, cutworms
Diseases: yellows, mildew
Soil: Lots of good compost in rich sandy loam or silt loam with good drainage
Fertilizer: When 3–4 inches tall, apply a topdressing of a moderate amount of fertilizer

pH: 5.5–6.8
Varieties: Rapid (early), Purple Danube (midseason)
Zones: 3–11
Planting: Seed ¼–½ inch deep (early season), 4 weeks before last frost; 1 inch apart; thin to 5–8 inches; the gong, or bulb, will grow above the ground; when about 2–3 inches, cut off at the roots to avoid woodiness
Germinates: 5–10 days
Harvest: From seed, 45–60 days; from transplant, 25–35 days
Rotation: Don't follow cabbage family.
Edible: Bulb stem (gong) and leaves

SAUTÉED KOHLRABI

This makes a wonderful nest for grilled fish and is a deliciously light side dish for summer barbecues and winter roasts.

SERVES 4

8 small kohlrabi bulbs, grated (yield 4 cups)
1 teaspoon olive oil
¼ teaspoon salt
¼ teaspoon freshly ground black pepper
2 tablespoons freshly squeezed lemon juice

Trim the stems and leaves from the kohlrabi. Remove the stems from the leaves, discard, and save the leaves for soups, pasta sauces, or stews. Peel the bulbs with a potato peeler and grate coarsely by hand or in a food processor.

Heat the oil in a high-sided skillet over medium-high; add the shredded kohlrabi and cook, stirring often, 3–4 minutes or until tender. Season with salt and black pepper, and toss with the lemon juice.

Per serving: 48 calories, 1 g fat, 0 g saturated fat, 9 g carbohydrate, 2 g protein, 5 g dietary fiber, 166 mg sodium. Exchanges: 2 Vegetable

NONSUCH POËLE

I named this take on the French classic after our own cottage—and Henry VIII's extravagant folly of a castle. It really is a cottage–castle combination of subtle and big flavors. A poële is initially sautéed, followed by partial poaching in a well-seasoned stock, and then steamed, which results in a grand sharing of flavors by all the ingredients.

SERVES 4

1 teaspoon olive oil
1 cup chopped sweet onion
1 tablespoon finely chopped gingerroot
2 garlic cloves, bashed and chopped
1 parsnip, cut into 1-inch dice (yield ½ cup)
1 carrot, cut into 1-inch dice (yield ½ cup)
1 kohlrabi bulb, peeled and cut into 1-inch dice (yield ½ cup)
1 turnip, peeled and cut into 1-inch dice (yield ½ cup)
2 celery ribs, sliced (yield ½ cup)
1 small orange sweet potato, peeled and cut into 1-inch dice (yield ½ cup)
1 teaspoon herbes de Provence
1 cup low-sodium vegetable stock (see page 288)
8 tiny cherry tomatoes
½ cup diagonally cut snow peas
2 teaspoons arrowroot or cornstarch mixed with 2 tablespoons water (slurry)
1 tablespoon freshly grated Parmesan cheese
1 tablespoon chopped fresh parsley

Heat the oil in a large high-sided skillet over medium-high. Sauté the onion and ginger 3 minutes or until the onion begins to turn translucent. Add the garlic and cook 1 minute more.

Add the parsnip, carrot, kohlrabi, turnip, celery, sweet potato, and herbes de Provence. Pour in the stock, cover, and bring to a boil. Reduce the heat and simmer 10 minutes or until the vegetables are tender.

Add the tomatoes and snow peas. Stir in the slurry and heat to thicken. Serve topped with Parmesan cheese and parsley.

Per serving: 90 calories, 2 g fat, 0 g saturated fat, 16 g carbohydrate, 2 g protein, 4 g dietary fiber, 95 mg sodium. Exchanges: 2 Vegetable

Leek

Allium porrum

Cultivated in ancient Egypt, the leek is a member of the onion family and has quite a history in more modern times as well. Since about 640 CE, following a Saxon battle that is commemorated as St. David's Day (March 1) in Wales, Welshmen have worn a leek in their headgear to defend against friendly fire from fellow Welshmen. These were obviously discreet enough not to attract the enemy, as would the giant leeks of today, which, if worn in the hat, would have been more of a fashion statement!

In growing leeks, the main task is to keep them white and tender. Both goals are met by planting them in a trench and gradually heaping light sandy soil (or dense mulch) up the stalk until the green leaves begin to branch outward in a V shape. You can get up to an 8-inch white stalk this way, and provided that the soil remains damp, you should have a tender shoot.

If it gets hot, the outer skin might become tough, but you can peel it away and put it into the compost. As with other members of the onion family, such as garlic, it's a good idea to keep all discarded vegetation in a separate compost that's not used to feed any other plant in the onion family. This is due to a whole raft of diseases that can inflict onions but are much less likely to cause problems with leeks.

I've always enjoyed a leek and potato soup. I had it in Paris on my first overseas trip. The soft, sweet leeks and pure white new potatoes soaked up the cream like perfect tiny sponges: rich, smooth, and delicious. Why is it that evaporated skim milk just doesn't match up to my memories! On the other hand, I think my leeks are sweeter!

The Numbers

For each 100 g boiled (3.5 oz; ½ cup): 31 calories, 0 g fat, 0 g saturated fat, 8 g carbohydrate, 1 g protein, 1 g dietary fiber, 10 mg sodium

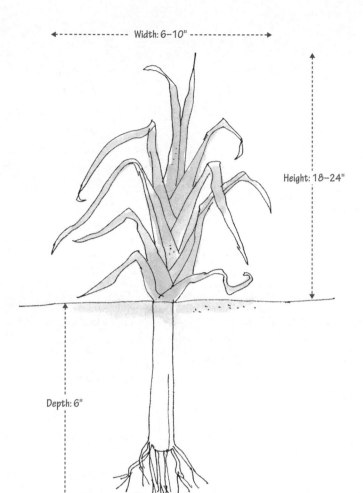

Width: 6–10"

Height: 18–24"

Depth: 6"

Biennial/Annual/Hardy/Cool Season
Water: Moderate
Sun: Full to partial shade
Companion Planting:
PRO: Beets, carrots, garlic, onions, tomatoes
CON: Beans, peas
Pests: Thrips, root maggots
Diseases: None
Soil: Fertile, loose, rich humus; well composted 3 months before transplanting
Fertilizer: Moderate nitrogen, phosphorus, potassium; side-dress every 2 weeks with fish fertilizer
pH: 6.0–6.8

Varieties: American Flag, Blue Solaise (sweet), Nebraska (cold, hardy)
Zones: 3–10
Planting: Seed ¼ inch deep (indoors), 4 weeks before last frost
Germinates: 8–16 days
Harvest: From seed, 120–170 days; from transplant, set out in the spring after last frost, 6 inches apart
Rotation: Don't follow onions, garlic, chives
Edible: White stalk and to lesser degree the lower leaves

BRAISED LEEKS

This is a very simple side dish with great flavor and texture.

SERVES 4

8 small or 4 large leeks
1 teaspoon olive oil
1 cup low-sodium vegetable stock
   (see page 288)

Cut off the curly root ends of the leeks as well as the upper green leaves. Discard the roots and save the greens for stock. Remove the two outer sheaths, which can trap dirt as the leek grows. Wash carefully, dislodging any dirt hiding in the next few sheaths. If you have to use large leeks, cut them in half lengthwise and clean carefully.

Heat the oil in a skillet over medium-high. Sauté the leeks to brown slightly. Pour in the stock until the leeks are half covered, bring to a boil, reduce the heat, cover, and simmer 30 minutes or until tender.

Per serving: 97 calories, 2 g fat, 0 g saturated fat, 20 g carbohydrate, 2 g protein, 3 g dietary fiber, 62 mg sodium. Exchanges: 3 Vegetable

LEEK, BEAN, AND SPINACH SOUP

What a splendid kitchen-garden soup for late summer, when our beans have matured in their pods!

SERVES 4

3 medium leeks
3 cups low-sodium vegetable stock
   (see page 288)
1 (15-ounce) can navy beans (or other white beans), rinsed and drained*
1 teaspoon dried thyme or 1 tablespoon chopped fresh
1 teaspoon dried basil or 1 tablespoon chopped fresh
1 cup chopped Swiss chard or New Zealand spinach
2 tablespoons toasted pine nuts

You can also use precooked fresh dried beans in their pods in late summer.

Chop the white parts of the leeks, saving the green parts for stock. Pour the stock into a large pot and add the leeks. Bring to a boil, reduce the heat, and simmer 10 minutes or until the leeks are tender.

Pour the soup through a strainer. Return the liquid to the pot and reserve ¼ cup of the leeks. Measure the beans and reserve ½ cup. Whiz the remaining leeks with the remaining beans in a blender or food processor, using enough soup liquid to make the solids go around.

Add the pureed vegetables, thyme, and basil

to the pot. Bring to a boil, and stir in the Swiss chard. Add the pine nuts and the reserved leeks and beans, reheat, and serve immediately, while the chard is still nice and green.

Per serving: 169 calories, 4 g fat, 0 g saturated fat, 28 g carbohydrate, 7 g protein, 7 g dietary fiber, 149 mg sodium. Exchanges: 1 Starch, 2 Vegetable, ½ Fat

STEAMED LEEKS AND POTATOES

This is a classic European-style dish at its finest and makes a great winter-weather first course!

SERVES 4

4 leeks, trimmed and washed well, reserving the trimmings and dark green tops
8 red new potatoes, 2 inches in diameter
1 teaspoon chopped fresh thyme
2 tablespoons crumbled soft goat cheese

FOR THE SAUCE
1 cup low-sodium vegetable stock (see page 288)
1 tablespoon cornstarch mixed with 2 tablespoons water (slurry)
½ cup yogurt cheese (see page 290)*
⅛ teaspoon salt
⅛ teaspoon freshly ground white pepper
¼ teaspoon freshly grated nutmeg

FOR THE GARNISH
Freshly ground black pepper
Finely chopped fresh parsley

Paprika
Juice of 1 lemon (¼ cup)

Handle the yogurt cheese gently to prevent it from breaking.

Pour about 1½ inches of water into a large pot, add the leek trimmings and tops, and bring to a vigorous boil. Put the potatoes and white part of the leeks into a steamer tray. Sprinkle with the thyme, place over the pot, cover, and steam about 15 minutes or until tender. Remove the steamer tray and set aside.

To prepare the sauce, heat the stock in a medium saucepan over medium heat. Pour a little hot stock into the slurry, mix well, and pour the mixture back into the saucepan. Bring to a boil, stirring constantly, for about 30 seconds until thickened. Remove the pan from the heat and set aside.

In a medium bowl, stir yogurt cheese gently until smooth. When the sauce is cool, add it to the yogurt cheese, stirring gently until well incorporated, but don't overbeat! Fold in the salt, white pepper, and nutmeg.

To serve, coarsely chop the leeks and potatoes, and mix together. Put a small mound of the mixture on each plate, and sprinkle evenly with the goat cheese. Cover with the sauce. Sprinkle with the black pepper, parsley, and paprika, and squeeze on some lemon juice. Enjoy.

Per serving: 353 calories, 2 g fat, 1 g saturated fat (3% calories from saturated fat), 72 g carbohydrate, 11 g protein, 7 g dietary fiber, 209 g sodium. Exchanges: 3 Starch, 2 Vegetable

Lemon

Citrus limon

When it comes to finding the very best ingredients to use as alternatives to those high in saturated fat, refined starch, and sodium, the list begins with citrus and then goes directly to the herb garden and on into the kitchen garden. Each of these choices is full of flavor, primary taste, and aroma, as well as texture. No wonder that recipes treated to such adjustments often wind up actually improved!

Unfortunately, the idea of TACT (taste, aroma, color, texture) replacement isn't well understood; after all, it's taken me more than 20 years to begin to fully appreciate its value!

Because of this lack of understanding, most of the efforts made to lessen risk begin and end with cutting things out, which leaves an often tasteless vacuum. What should happen is to add before you subtract!

The perfect example is to add lemon—preferably freshly squeezed—to a dish like mushrooms sautéed in butter. You will then be able to reduce the amount of butter because the lemon will provide the enhanced flavor, without the drawbacks.

I heartily recommend (and am growing) the Meyer lemon, as it is easy to grow and has a remarkable almost sweet-and-sour taste and a truly floral fragrance—well worth the effort to include in a sheltered sunny spot, or perhaps a greenhouse?

As the fruit matures (in its second year), it moves from the typically acidic to a sweeter overtone. As it sweetens, the rind gets a slightly orange blush and the flesh turns a very light orange.

I ordered my lemon as a 2-year-old dwarf bare-root tree. I received it in April and immediately transplanted it in well-drained sandy loam in a 15-inch pot, with holes drilled in the bottom to allow for drainage. I set it on a drip tray and kept it indoors in a sunny spot until the daytime temperatures went above 65°F. Then it went into a wind-sheltered sunny spot. I hope to see fruit next year.

The Numbers

For each 100 g with peel (3.5 oz; ½ cup): 20 calories, 11 g carbohydrate, 0 g fat, 0 g saturated fat, 1 g protein, 5 g dietary fiber, 3 mg sodium

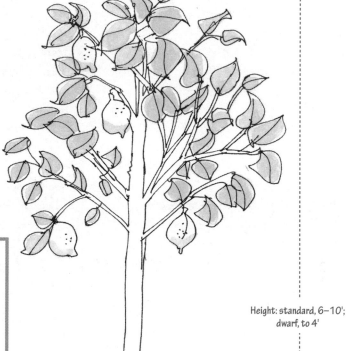

Width: standard, 6–10';
dwarf, 3–4'

Height: standard, 6–10';
dwarf, to 4'

Perennial

Water: Keep soil evenly moist but not wet

Sun: Full; light shade in afternoon where summer is very hot

Pests: Scale, whiteflies, thrips, mites (use beneficial insect traps and insecticidal soap for prevention and control of pests)

Diseases: Plant virus-free disease-resistant varieties

Soil: Moist, well-drained

Fertilizer: N-P-K ratio of 3:1:1

pH: 5.5–6.5

Varieties: Meyer, Improved Meyer (dwarf variety); both disease resistant

Zones: 8–10

Planting: In warmer climates (outdoors): spring or early autumn, space trees at least 25 feet apart or dwarf trees 10 feet apart; usually one is enough because they self-fertilize; avoid growing in areas where there is strong wind

Harvest: Begin to fruit 2–5 years after planting, then fruit year round

Edible: Flesh and skin (as zest) of fruit

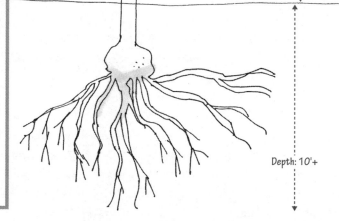

Depth: 10'+

MEYER LEMON PIE

While the classic Key Lime Pie is made with small limes from southern Florida, you can substitute your own Meyer lemons for an extraordinary difference.

SERVES 8

½ recipe Pie Crust (see page 289)
Dried beans, any variety

FOR THE FILLING
4 teaspoons freshly grated lemon zest
½ cup freshly squeezed lemon juice
4 egg yolks
1 (14-ounce) can nonfat sweetened condensed milk

FOR THE MERINGUE
2 egg whites
¼ teaspoon cream of tartar
¼ cup sugar
¼ teaspoon vanilla extract

Preheat the oven to 425°F.

Roll out the pie crust to fit an 8-inch pie tin. Lay the rolled dough in the pan without stretching it, and crimp the edge. Prick with a fork. Lay a piece of parchment or waxed paper in the pie shell and pour in enough dried beans to cover the bottom. These will act as pie weights to keep the crust from bubbling up while baking. Bake for 8 minutes or until golden brown. Reduce the heat to 350°F.

To make the filling, combine the zest, juice, egg yolks, and milk in a bowl with a whisk.

Pour into the baked crust and bake 15 minutes. When the pie is done—a thin knife will come out clean—remove it from the oven and increase the heat to 425°F.

While the pie is baking, make the meringue. Beat the egg whites until foamy. Then add the cream of tartar. When they reach the soft-peak stage, sprinkle in the sugar and continue to beat until the meringue holds stiff peaks. Beat the vanilla in at the end. Spoon the meringue around the sides of the pie and seal to prevent it from shrinking. Scoop the rest into the center and smooth it down. Pick up peaks with the back of a spoon and bake for 4 minutes or until golden brown.

Per serving: 293 calories, 7 g fat, 3 g saturated fat (9% calories from saturated fat), 49 g carbohydrate, 7 g protein, 0 g dietary fiber, 108 mg sodium. Exchanges: 1½ Fat, 2½ Carbohydrate

SAUTÉED MUSHROOMS WITH LEMON AND DILL

Lemon juice takes the place of fat, does a great job of enhancing the browning, and boosts the flavor of the mushrooms in a whole new way.

SERVES 4

1 pound 1-inch-diameter white or brown mushrooms
2 tablespoons freshly squeezed lemon juice
½ teaspoon dried dill
⅛ teaspoon cayenne

Remove the stems from the mushrooms and save for stock. Clean the mushrooms with a dry cloth or soft brush.

Place a nonstick skillet big enough to hold the mushrooms in a single layer over medium heat. When hot, place the mushrooms, round side down, in the skillet. Sprinkle with the lemon juice, dill, and cayenne, and cook 3 minutes. Turn the mushrooms and cook 1 minute more or until they just lose their chalky, raw look. They will be a light golden brown.

Per serving: 21 calories, 0 g fat, 0 g saturated fat, 4 g carbohydrate, 3 g protein, 1 g dietary fiber, 5 mg sodium. Exchanges: 1 Vegetable

ZUCCHINI WITH HERBS AND LEMON

For all the world this will look as though you've cooked with several sticks of butter, but to my taste, it's better!

SERVES 4

2 medium zucchini (¾ pound)
1 teaspoon nonaromatic olive oil
½ cup finely sliced onions
1 garlic clove, bashed and chopped
¼ teaspoon dried oregano
¼ teaspoon dried basil
¼ teaspoon dried thyme
Salt and freshly ground black pepper to taste
¾ cup low-sodium vegetable stock
   (see page 288)

Pinch of saffron
1 tablespoon freshly squeezed lemon juice
½ teaspoon arrowroot mixed with 1 teaspoon
   water (slurry)

Trim the ends off the zucchini and cut in half lengthwise and then in half crosswise. Set aside.

Heat the oil in a high-sided skillet over medium heat, add the onions, and cook for 1 minute before adding the garlic and herbs. Stir and cook for 3 minutes. Add the zucchini, salt, black pepper, and stock. Cover and cook on medium-high for 7 minutes, until just tender. Stir in the saffron, lemon juice, and slurry. Continue cooking until the sauce is slightly thickened and glossy.

Per serving: 35 calories, 1 g fat, 0 g saturated fat, 6 g carbohydrate, 1 g protein, 1 g dietary fiber, 35 mg sodium. Exchanges: 1 Vegetable

Lettuce

Lactuca sativa

Since lettuce is a native of the Mediterranean area, it is not unreasonable that the emperor Augustus constructed a statue of a physician who had recommended lettuce to treat him of a serious ailment. There's no record of the kind of lettuce that cured Augustus, but according to some sources, it may have been what's known as prickly lettuce, which doesn't play a role in our kitchen garden.

Other than varieties that bring ailing emperors back to robust health, lettuce can be described in four basic styles, plus one miniature or baby:

Iceberg (crisphead): dense, crisp head; white to pale green; rotund

Romaine (cos): tall and crisp; mostly deeper, dark green tops

Butterhead (Bibb): very tender, somewhat juicy broad leaves, with a smooth, even texture

Leaf: open head, separate leaves of mixed colors

Mesclun (spring mix): loose leaf varieties, with sparse more multipronged leaves; colors range from red to speckled, and tastes from mild to peppery

Greenhouse operators, no doubt inspired by Eliot Coleman's amazing work at the Four Seasons Farm in Harborside, Maine, have *almost* flooded the market with their spring mix of lettuce that can be grown year round. This has transformed lettuce into a mixture of leaves that can stand alone without being smothered with a lava flow of bottled dressings!

The soil temperature to remember is 75°F, but this time it's an upper limit because most lettuce seed will not germinate when it's too warm. Remarkably, it will germinate as low as 38°F, so it follows that you can sow in early spring. I like the idea of a bed of mesclun mix that includes arugula, Bull's Blood beet greens, winter red, kale, Pink Petiole, mixed mustard greens, Cherry Belle radish, and salad burnett. (Territorial Seeds do such a mix; the catalog number at this writing is MS480.) A four-grain packet will densely cover a 16-square-foot area. Be sure to cut it while young and always 2 inches above the soil; then it should grow back for a second crop.

The Numbers

For each 100 g romaine (3.5 oz; 1 cup packed): 24 calories, 0.5 g fat, 0 g saturated fat, 4 g carbohydrate, 1 g protein, 1 g dietary fiber, 0 mg sodium

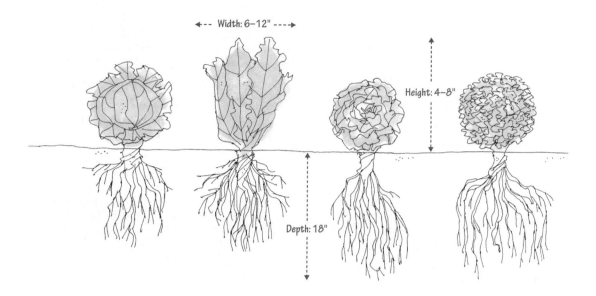

Annual/Cool Season

Water: Light to moderate; irrigation from ground

Sun: Full; partial shade in hot weather

Companion Planting:

PRO: All vegetables except broccoli

CON: Broccoli

Pests: Aphids, beet leafhoppers, slugs, snails

Diseases: Bacterial soft rot, mildews

Notes: For all but spring mix, gather outer leaves first. When a core stem forms, remove the plant. Use scissors to cut 2 inches above the roots and let the plant regrow.

Soil: Well-drained (kept moist) sandy loam; well composted 3 months before planting

Fertilizer: High nitrogen, potassium, and phosphorus with extra bonemeal; fish emulsion every 2 weeks

pH: 6.0–6.8

Varieties:

ICEBERG (CRISPHEAD): Great Lakes, Rouge de Grenobloise (resists bolting)

ROMAINE (COS): Little Gem, Parris Island

BUTTERHEAD (BIBB): Limestone, Boston, Summer Bibb (hot weather)

LEAF: Green Ice, Red Sails

MESCLUN (SPRING MIX): may include arugula, Bull's Blood beet, winter red, kale, Pink Petiole, mixed mustard, Cherry Belle radish, salad burnett, and baby leaf lettuce

Zones: Can be planted in season in all zones.

Planting: Seed ¼–½ inch deep; 6–10 inches apart after thinning

Germinates: 2–10 days

Harvest: Iceberg, 80–90 days; romaine, 80–85 days; butterhead, 40–45 days; leaf, 40–50 days; mesclun, 30–40 days

Rotation: Don't follow artichoke, radicchio, endive

Edible: Leaves

CREAM OF LETTUCE SOUP

This may sound strange, but it's a terrific way to use good lettuce before it bolts and goes bitter.

SERVES 4

4 slices rye bread
1 pound romaine lettuce
1 teaspoon nonaromatic olive oil
1½ cups finely sliced onion
2 garlic cloves, bashed and chopped
2 cups low-sodium vegetable stock
    (see page 288)
2 cups 1% milk
½ teaspoon salt
¼ teaspoon white pepper
½ teaspoon dried dill plus more for garnish
2 tablespoons cornstarch mixed with
    4 tablespoons 1% milk (slurry)
1 tablespoon low-fat plain yogurt

Preheat the oven to 350°F.

Remove the crusts from the bread and set aside for another use. Cut the bread into 1-inch squares. Bake on an ungreased cookie sheet in one layer 10 minutes, until just browned and crisp. Wash the lettuce leaves, discarding the core. Place in a large saucepan, cover, and cook over medium heat 6 minutes. Uncover the pan and stir the lettuce to make sure it is all wilted, and cook for 2 minutes more if need be. Place the cooked lettuce in a blender container and set aside.

Reheat the saucepan over medium-high and add the oil. Sauté the onions for 2 minutes or until they begin to wilt, add the garlic, and continue cooking until soft. Add the onion mixture to the lettuce, and whiz for 2 minutes or until very smooth. If you need a little liquid, add ¼ cup of the stock.

While the vegetables are being pureed, pour the stock and milk into the saucepan over medium-low. When the lettuce and onions are perfectly smooth, stir into the warm liquid. Add the salt, white pepper, and dill. Cover and simmer 7 minutes. Stir in the slurry and heat to thicken.

Serve in warm soup bowls with a dollop of yogurt and a scattering of dill. Pass the croutons.

Per serving: 211 calories, 3 g fat, 1 g saturated fat (4% calories from saturated fat), 38 g carbohydrate, 11 g protein, 4 g dietary fiber, 300 mg sodium. Exchanges: 1 Starch, 2 Vegetable, ½ Fat-free Milk, ½ Fat

MESCLUN SALAD WITH FRUIT

Mesclun is also called spring mix. It is best assembled from a variety of lettuce from your own garden or from a farmers market and eaten on the day it's purchased.

SERVES 6

FOR THE DRESSING
½ teaspoon arrowroot
¼ cup dry white wine*
¼ cup freshly squeezed orange juice
1 teaspoon rice vinegar

FOR THE SALAD

3 oranges, peeled and segmented, reserving any juice for the dressing

6 plums, quartered, pitted, and sliced

¼ cup thinly sliced red onion

3 tablespoons chopped fresh cilantro

3 cups mesclun

I prefer dealcoholized Chardonnay.

Prepare the dressing by combining the arrowroot with the wine in a small saucepan. Stir over medium heat until clear and slightly thickened. Stir in the orange juice and vinegar. Set aside to cool.

Place the oranges, plums, onion, and cilantro in a large salad bowl. When the dressing has cooled, pour it over the fruit and toss to mix well. Set aside until ready to serve.

To serve, toss the mixed greens with the dressed fruit.

Per serving: 72 calories, 0 g fat, 0 g saturated fat, 18 g carbohydrate, 1 g protein, 3 g dietary fiber, 5 mg sodium. Exchanges: 1 Vegetable, 1 Fruit

ROMAINE SALAD

Romaine is my favorite lettuce for sheer crispness, and most of the leaves are darker green, which confirms added vitamin content.

SERVES 4

1 head romaine lettuce, cut (yield 4 cups)

1 cup orange segments

¼ cup chopped green onions

¼ teaspoon salt

¼ teaspoon freshly ground black pepper

1 tablespoon extra-virgin olive oil

1 tablespoon rice vinegar

Remove and discard the battered outside leaves of the romaine. Pull off the leaves and wash carefully. Dry in a salad spinner or colander and cut into bite-size pieces.

Place the lettuce in a large bowl with the orange segments, green onions, salt, black pepper, oil, and vinegar. Toss well and serve.

Per serving: 65 calories, 4 g fat, 1 g saturated fat (14% calories from saturated fat), 7 g carbohydrate, 1 g protein, 2 g dietary fiber, 148 mg sodium. Exchanges: ½ Fruit, 1 Fat

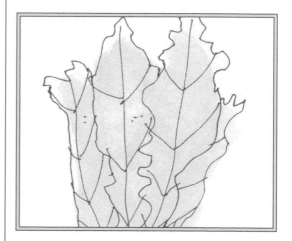

Mâche

Valerianella locusta

This tiny plant—only 3 inches high and up to 4 inches wide—is a relative newcomer to the produce market, and since it's so small, it only takes a couple of months to reach maturity.

Also known as corn salad, it's been well known in Europe since Roman times and makes a great green salad all on its own, but most often it's included in a mesclun (spring) mix. In addition, it can be used as a garnish in place of parsley (as a whole plant when small).

Mâche has a remarkable ability as a groundcover to keep down weeds, so it's especially useful to scratch in a few seeds around garlic, onions, and peppers, and in the midst of a slightly wider spaced strawberry patch.

The soil needs to be 50°F–70°F (no higher) when seeding. Allow for a 3- to 4-inch spacing if you are setting out a special bed (rather than the useful seed-cover crops put out around other crops).

Because of their very shallow roots, you'll need to keep the soil moist and provide partial shade when it gets above 80°F in the summer.

The roots are less than 1 inch, so they are simply cut off at soil level. Then you can turn the soil and reseed for a second—or third—crop, since it grows so rapidly.

The Numbers

For each 100 g (3.5 oz; 1 cup): 21 calories, 0 g fat, 0 g saturated fat, 4 g carbohydrate, 2 g protein, 2 g dietary fiber, 4 mg sodium

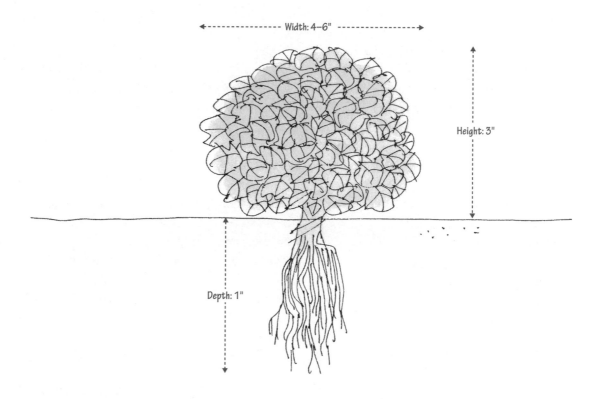

Width: 4–6"

Height: 3"

Depth: 1"

Annual/Tender/Cool Season
Water: Moist soil, deep irrigation
Sun: Full to partial shade
Companion Planting:
PRO: Carrots, onions, strawberries
CON: None
Pests: None (if you've fenced out the rabbits!)
Diseases: None
Soil: Humus-rich, good drainage
Fertilizer: Low nitrogen, phosphorus, and potassium
pH: 6.0–7.0
Varieties: Grosse Graine, Broad Leaf
Zones: 2–6

Planting: Seed ¼ inch deep, 2 inches apart; thin to 4 inches
Germinates: 7–10 days
Harvest: 60–75 days
Rotation: Don't follow radicchio, endive, artichokes
Edible: Leaves

MÂCHE WITH BERRIES

This is a lovely seasonal salad with your own or very fresh local berries. The dressing is deliberately light so as not to overwhelm the tender young leaves.

SERVES 4

4 cups mâche
1⅓ cup strawberries, blackberries, blueberries, or raspberries
¼ cup roughly chopped toasted walnuts

FOR THE DRESSING
¼ cup berry vinegar
2 tablespoons extra-virgin olive oil
¼ teaspoon salt
¼ teaspoon freshly ground black pepper

Place the mâche, berries, and nuts in a large bowl.

Combine the vinegar, oil, salt, and black pepper in a small bowl. Pour over the salad and toss well.

Per serving: 143 calories, 12 g fat, 1 g saturated fat (6% calories from saturated fat), 7 g carbohydrate, 3 g protein, 2 g dietary fiber, 149 mg sodium. Exchanges: 1 Vegetable, ½ Fruit, 2 Fat

MÂCHE, GOAT CHEESE, AND BLUEBERRY SALAD

Mâche can be harvested when quite small as a miniature lettuce. Usually 2–3 small heads can be well washed and served whole. In this case, the colors and tastes are truly elegant.

SERVES 4

8–12 small mâche heads, washed well and left whole
4 tablespoons prepared light ranch dressing
2 ounces crumbled goat cheese
2 ounces pine nuts, lightly pan-toasted
4 ounces fresh blueberries or 2 ounces dried

Toss the mâche heads in the ranch dressing. Carefully fold in the goat cheese, pine nuts, and blueberries.

Serve quite cold as a first course or side salad.

Per serving: 192 calories, 14 g fat, 3 g saturated fat (14% calories from saturated fat), 12 g carbohydrate, 7 g protein, 2 g dietary fiber, 221 mg sodium

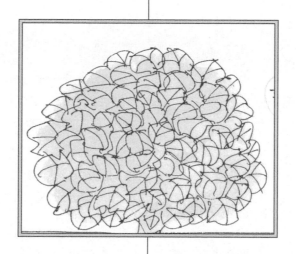

Mustard Greens

Brassica juncea var. *rugosa*

If you've *ever* put a lettuce leaf in a sandwich, like the L in BLT, then prepare to welcome a new arrival with open arms because here comes its splendid replacement: the *young*, tender mustard leaf of the cabbage family.

With its mild bite, fresh mustard greens can take the place of mustard pastes and, in so doing, provide a remarkable instant upgrade to the standard slather of bright yellow mustard. (How's that for a sales pitch?)

The plant itself is a native of the Himalayan regions of India, where some of the oldest written recipes in the world record its cultivation over 5,000 years ago. It grows quite tall—up to 2 feet—though not nearly as high as its cousin the Brussels sprout (see page 96), and needs 10–12 inches of clear soil space in each direction to flourish.

Like most of the bigger, deeper-green leafed plants, they tend to bolt in hot sunny days, so I'm inclined to plant them out for a fall crop, when "the cooler the sweeter" rule comes into play.

If you are fond of rice dishes, such as pilaf, risotto, and fried rice, then finely slice (chiffonade) the leaves and stir them into the very hot rice during the last minutes of cooking. It will truly be a shot to the taste buds—and it looks wonderful.

The Numbers

Mustard greens have excellent levels of antioxidants, vitamins C and E, carotenes, and glucosinolates. But be careful if you are prone to kidney stones.

For each 100 g raw (3.5 oz; 1 cup): 26 calories, 0 g fat, 0 g saturated fat, 5 g carbohydrate, 3 g protein, 3 g dietary fiber, 25 mg sodium

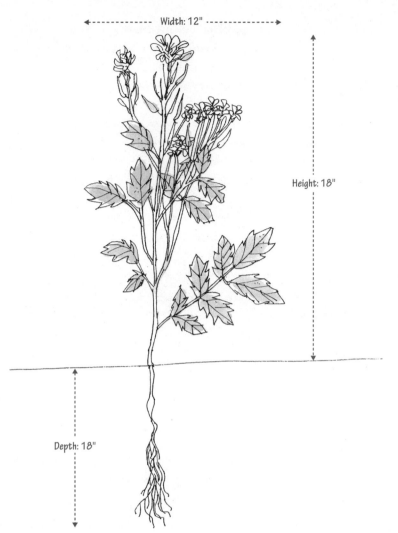

Width: 12"

Height: 18"

Depth: 18"

Perennial/Annual/Cool Season
Water: Keep soil moist, drip irrigation
Sun: Full, shade if over 80°F
Companion Planting:
PRO: Peas, beans, carrots, onions, spinach, lettuce, herbs
CON: None
Pests: Aphids, flea beetles
Diseases: Mildew, white rust
Soil: Moist, richly composted
Fertilizer: High nitrogen, moderate phosphorus, potassium
pH: 5.5–6.8

Varieties: Florida Broadleaf (mild), Osaka Purple (quite robust), Tatsoi (spoon-shaped, dark green leaves)
Zones: 2–8
Planting: Seed ¼ inch deep in late summer (6–8 weeks before first frost) for winter harvest, 1 inch apart; thin to 4–6 inches
Germinates: 4–6 days
Harvest: 30–40 days, when the inner leaves 3–4 inches long (the outer/lower leaves make good compost)
Rotation: Don't follow or precede other cabbage family plants
Edible: Leaves

STEAMED MUSTARD GREENS

These greens make a wonderful accompaniment to black-eyed peas and rice or to ham and cornbread.

SERVES 4

1 pound mustard greens
1 tablespoon freshly squeezed lemon juice

Wash mustard greens in lots of cold water. Remove the stems and chop.

Steam over boiling water 5–7 minutes, until tender and still green. Sprinkle with lemon juice and serve.

Per serving: 30 calories, 0 g fat, 0 g saturated fat, 6 g carbohydrate, 1 g protein, 4 g dietary fiber, 28 mg sodium. Exchanges: 1 Vegetable

CHINESE MUSTARD GREEN SOUP

A delight when you're fresh from the rain-soaked garden. This will warm you through and through with its mild bite.

SERVES 4

4 cups low-sodium vegetable stock
  (see page 288)
1 tablespoon grated gingerroot

2 cups sliced mushrooms
4 cups trimmed and sliced mustard greens, cut
  into ½×2-inch pieces
1 tablespoon low-sodium soy sauce
¼ teaspoon salt
½ teaspoon toasted sesame oil
2 cups cooked long-grain brown rice, hot

Bring the stock and ginger to a boil in a large saucepan. Add the mushrooms and mustard greens, and cook 3 minutes. Stir in the soy sauce, salt, and sesame oil. Place a half cup of rice in each of 4 bowls. Ladle the soup over the top and enjoy!

Per serving: 162 calories, 2 g fat, 0 g saturated fat, 30 g carbohydrate, 5 g protein, 4 g dietary fiber, 458 mg sodium. Exchanges: 1½ Starch, 1 Vegetable

SPAGHETTI WITH MUSTARD GREENS AND VEGETARIAN ITALIAN SAUSAGE

Another great Italian invention for serious fall and winter eating! Great taste, aroma, color, and texture—it is all here in one dish.

SERVES 4

½ pound dry spaghetti
1 teaspoon olive oil
1 cup chopped onion
2 garlic cloves, bashed and chopped
2 low-fat vegetarian Italian sausages,* cut into
  ½-inch pieces

¼ teaspoon fennel seeds

8 cups chopped mustard green leaves (from 2 bunches) or 2 packages frozen

¼ teaspoon salt

¼ teaspoon freshly ground black pepper

1 tablespoon balsamic vinegar

½ teaspoon crushed red pepper flakes

2 tablespoons freshly grated Parmesan cheese

Please be sure to taste first. They almost always come fully cooked. Just check the label—there are both good and awful concoctions, so be careful.

Cook the spaghetti according to the package directions. Drain and keep warm in a colander over a bowl of hot water.

Heat the oil in a high-sided skillet over medium-high. Sauté the onion 2 minutes or until it begins to turn translucent. Add the garlic and cook 1 minute more. Toss in the sausage and fennel seeds, and cook 2 minutes or until lightly browned on the outside.

Stir in the mustard greens, cover, and cook over low about 5 minutes until they wilt but are still bright green. Toss with the spaghetti and season with salt, black pepper, vinegar, and red pepper flakes. Serve with Parmesan cheese sprinkled over the top.

Per serving: 316 calories, 4 g fat, 1 g saturated fat (3% calories from saturated fat), 56 g carbohydrate, 14 g protein, 6 g dietary fiber, 299 mg sodium. Exchanges: 3 Starch, 2 Vegetable

Napa Cabbage

Brassica rapa var. *pekinensis*

Tall, straight, pale yellow, dense, ruffled, crisp, and mild tending to sweet, the incredible Napa cabbage is also known as Chihili or Michihili.

A native of Asia, it was first planted in California's Napa Valley—largely for Chinese and Asian immigrants, but it caught on rapidly and is now widely cultivated. Because of its density, height, and rapid growth, it makes an ideal commercial crop; but without much fuss, it does well in the small kitchen garden pound for pound against other greens.

Because it is crisp and tender and sweet, it makes a perfect bed for salads. It can be tossed in a light dressing and brightened with finely chopped mixed-colored sweet bell peppers and green onions.

Napa also has enough genuine character to withstand a swift stir-fry without losing most of its bulk. It can be a very refreshing main dish when stirred up using the salad ingredients just listed.

I didn't have room this year to try it out, but I'm planning for it in year two as an autumn crop, to be sown in mid-August, with a late September transplanting, to let it sweeten in the cooler evenings and avoid the typical summer bolting.

I've chosen the variety called Tenderheart because it has all the qualities of taste and texture of the larger China Express variety, packed into a miniature dense and crisp head weighing about 2 pounds.

Young leaves have far superior flavor and are best when harvested at about 5 inches tall.

When days are long and hot, expect rapid bolting, so it's best to cut early and use in salads and slaws.

The Numbers

Contains a nutrient initially thought to be vitamin U, now known as the amino acid glutamine, which appears to do a good job in regenerating cells in the gastrointestinal tract.

For each 100 g raw (3.5 oz; 1 cup): 20 calories, 0 g fat, 0 g saturated fat, 3 g carbohydrate, 1 g protein, 1 g dietary fiber, 13 mg sodium

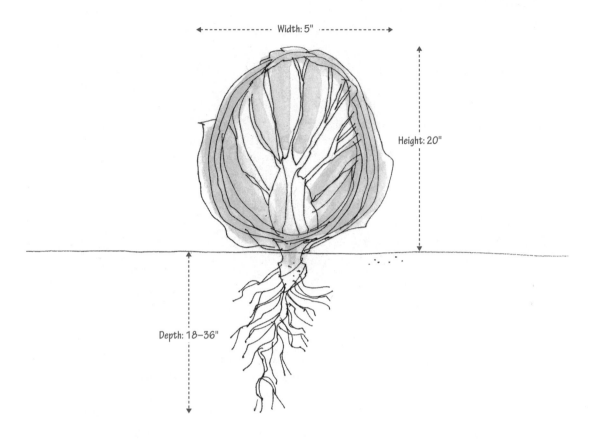

Width: 5"

Height: 20"

Depth: 18–36"

Biennial/Annual/Cool Season
Water: Moderate, frequent
Sun: Full (6 hours minimum)
Companion Planting:
PRO: Beets, lettuce, onions, spinach
CON: Tomatoes, peppers, okra, potatoes
Pests: Aphids, flea beetles, slugs
Diseases: Yellows, clubroot, black root
Soil: Well-drained, rich humus, clay loam
Fertilizer: Heavy feeder
pH: 6.5–7.5
Varieties: Tokyo Giant, Wintertime, pe-tsai, Tender-heart (special for small gardens)

Zones: 3–5
Planting: Seed ¼ inch deep, 10–12 weeks before first frost or midsummer for autumn
Germinate: 4–10 days
Rotation: Avoid following cabbage family
Edible: Leaves

CHINESE NEW YEAR FRESH FISH AND VEGETABLE SOUP

The noodles are a vital part of a New Year's celebration in China. They can be reduced by half if the carbs are a challenge.

SERVES 8

1 pound rice noodles or other flat noodles, such as fettuccine
8 cups low-sodium vegetable stock (see page 288)
4 ounce fresh gingerroot, peeled and slivered
1 teaspoon rice vinegar (optional)
1 teaspoon sesame oil (optional)
1 teaspoon low-sodium soy sauce
1½ pounds firm white fish fillets, such as halibut, orange roughy, or red snapper, cut into 1-inch pieces
1 cup chopped Napa cabbage
2 cups halved fresh snow peas
½ cup shredded carrots
1 cup sliced baby bok choy
¼ cup roasted unsalted chopped peanuts or sesame seeds

Cook the noodles according to package directions.

Heat the stock in a large pot over medium heat, and simmer the ginger in it for 5 minutes. Add vinegar, sesame oil, and soy sauce. Bring the stock to a simmer and add the fish. Bring the stock back to a simmer, cover, and poach the fish about 6 minutes per inch of thickness until done and the flesh flakes easily.

Remove the fish from the stock, transfer it to a plate, and cover to keep warm.

Add the cabbage, snow peas, and carrots to the pot, cover, and cook 7 minutes. Add the bok choy to the pot, cover, and cook 3 minutes more. Gently stir the fish back into the pot. Ladle the soup over the noodles and garnish with peanuts or sesame seeds.

Per serving: 406 calories, 11 g fat, 2 g saturated fat (4% calories from saturated fat), 51 g carbohydrate, 24 g protein, 3 g dietary fiber, 987 mg sodium. Exchanges: 3 Starch, 2 Lean Fish, 1 Vegetable

PHO

Every so often I find a recipe that is so good, I can't imagine a change that would be of benefit. This version of the Thai classic recipe was inspired by Stephanie Lyness, who does excellent recipe development. I have made adjustments to make it vegetable only.

SERVES 6

6 cups low-sodium vegetable stock (see page 288)
4 garlic cloves, bashed
2-inch piece gingerroot, sliced and bruised with a knife
2 star anise pods or 1 teaspoon anise seeds (optional)
3 tablespoons Thai fish sauce or tamari
1 tablespoon low-sodium soy sauce
2 teaspoons sugar

½ pound large white mushrooms, cut into
  ½-inch-thick slices and bundled in a piece
  of cheesecloth
½ pound thick rice noodles
½ Napa cabbage, cut in half lengthwise and
  crosswise into thin strips
2 scallions, sliced
12 large mint leaves, thinly sliced
12 sprigs cilantro, thinly sliced
4 large basil leaves, thinly sliced
1 large lime, cut into 6 wedges

To make the broth, combine the stock, garlic, ginger, anise, fish sauce, soy sauce, and sugar in a chef's pan or large saucepan. Bring to a boil, reduce the heat, cover, and let simmer 10 minutes. Drop the mushroom bundle into the simmering broth and simmer 20 minutes longer. Remove the mushrooms and set aside. Strain the broth and return it to the pan over low heat.

While the broth is simmering, bring water to a boil in a large pasta pan. Pull it off the heat, add the noodles, and let them soak 10–15 minutes until tender. Drain and keep the noodles warm in a colander over hot water.

Add the cabbage to the simmering broth and stir. Divide the noodles among six warm bowls. Place the mushrooms on top of the noodles. Ladle the broth with the barely cooked cabbage over the top. Combine the scallions with the fresh herbs and scatter over each serving. Serve with a lime wedge.

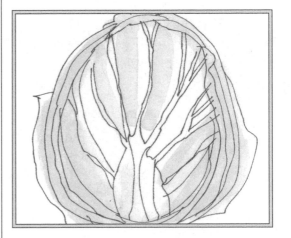

Per serving: 195 calories, 0 g fat, 0 g saturated fat, 40 g carbohydrate, 5 g protein, 3 g dietary fiber, 943 mg sodium. Exchanges: 2 Starch, 1 Vegetable

New Zealand Spinach

Tetragonia tetragonioides

It would appear that Captain Cook's botanical associate Sir Joseph Banks first discovered this fleshy spinach, which is not, in fact, related to the spinach we all know.

Banks suggested that the pods had floated in from somewhere in the South Pacific, taken root, and flourished in the hotter, more humid coasts of Australia and New Zealand, where ordinary spinach would have wilted away.

I decided to follow my planting of common spinach after its spring season (and avoid its bolting in the hot weather) with the more-resilient, denser-leafed New Zealand plant.

It is sown in the spring, when the possibility of a late frost has definitely passed. Unlike spinach, it really loves hot summer weather. Start them off ½-inch deep and 6 inches apart; when they are 2–3 inches high, thin them out. (They work well when small in mesclun-style lettuce mixes.) Eventually they'll need up to 20 inches of breathing room.

New Zealand spinach also works very well as a steaming green because, like chard and kale, it doesn't wind up on the bottom of a saucepan in a deep green shrivel.

The Numbers

For each 100 g raw (3.5 oz; 1 cup): 14 calories, 0 g fat, 0 g saturated fat, 3 g carbohydrate, 2 g protein, 2 g dietary fiber, 130 mg sodium

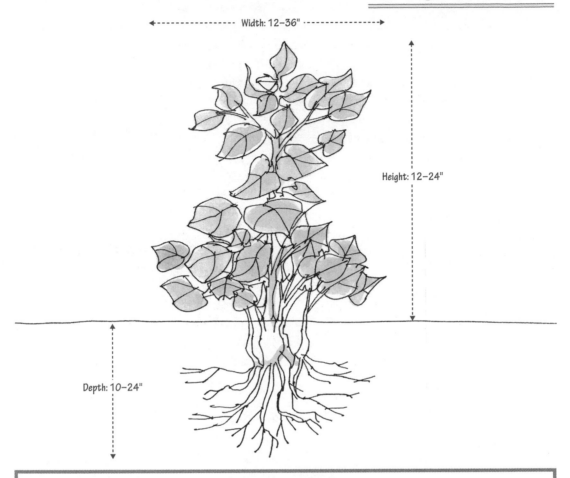

Width: 12–36"

Height: 12–24"

Depth: 10–24"

Annual/Hot Season

Water: Evenly moist; water regularly for rapid, full growth; do not let the soil dry out

Sun: Full; partial shade in afternoon in very hot climates

Companion Planting:

PRO: Strawberries

CON: Avoid planting in shade of tall plants, such as corn or pole beans

Pests: None

Diseases: None

Soil: Prefers moisture-retentive, well-drained soil rich in organic matter; prepare planting beds with aged compost

Fertilizer: Side-dress plants with compost at midseason

pH: 6.8–7.0

Varieties: Maori (the most commonly grown)

Zones: 6 and warmer

Planting: Seed ½ inch deep, and 1 inch apart, at warm time of year. Indoors: 2–3 weeks before last frost in spring for later transplanting; thin to 3–4 inches. Sow in the garden around the date of average last frost in spring.

Germinates: 14–21 days

Harvest: From seed, 55–65 days

Rotation: Do not follow legumes

Edible: Leaves

HOPPIN' JOHN

The classic dish uses collard greens and ham hocks, but I have replaced them with New Zealand spinach, a hardy green that weathers the summer sun, doesn't lose as much bulk when heated as does traditional spinach, and isn't as washed out as long-cooked collards. The ham hock smokiness is replaced with smoked paprika.

SERVES 6

FOR THE PEAS
1 cup dry black-eyed peas
3–4 cups water for soaking (or 5 cups water for quick-soaking)
1 teaspoon nonaromatic olive oil
1 large sweet onion, chopped (2 cups)
3 garlic cloves, bashed and chopped
1 rib celery, chopped (½ cup)
4 cups low-sodium vegetable stock (see page 288)
½ teaspoon dried thyme
2 bay leaves
1 cup raw long-grain white rice
⅛ teaspoon ground cloves
⅛ teaspoon cayenne
1 tablespoon smoked paprika
¼ teaspoon salt (optional)
3 heaping tablespoons chopped parsley

FOR THE SPINACH
½ teaspoon nonaromatic olive oil
½ lemon sliced
1 dried red chile or ⅛ teaspoon cayenne

2 cups low-sodium vegetable stock (see page 288)
8 cups washed and stemmed New Zealand spinach, torn into 2-inch pieces
1 teaspoon freshly grated lemon zest
⅛ teaspoon salt
1 tablespoon freshly squeezed lemon juice

Pick over and rinse the black-eyed peas, then cover them with 3–4 cups of water and soak overnight. To quick-soak, bring to a boil, turn off the heat, and let set, covered, for 1 hour.

Heat 1 teaspoon oil in a 10½-inch chef's pan over medium-high. Sauté the onion 3 minutes, then add the garlic and cook for 1 minute more. Stir in the celery, 4 cups of stock, thyme, bay leaves, rice, soaked black-eyed peas, cloves, and cayenne. Bring to a boil, then reduce to simmer. Add the paprika and cook for 20 minutes or until the rice and peas are tender but not mushy.

While the peas are cooking, prepare the spinach. Heat the oil in a chef's pan over medium-high. Lay the lemon slices and red chile in the pan and cook 2 minutes. Pour in 2 cups of stock and the spinach, and boil gently 3 minutes. Stir in the zest, salt, and lemon juice, and set aside until you are ready to serve.

When the peas are done, taste for salt and add if needed. Stir in the chopped parsley, and you are ready to serve. Divide the spinach among 6 hot bowls. Pour the liquid left in the pan into the rice and pea mixture. Ladle the hoppin' John onto the spinach, and you are ready for a real down-home treat!

Per serving: 258 calories, 2 g fat, 0 g saturated fat, 50 g carbohydrate, 10 g protein, 6 g dietary fiber, 401 mg sodium. Exchanges: 2 ½ Starch, 2 Vegetable

STIR-FRIED MIXED GREENS

This is a delicious way to celebrate the greens. Please leave final step until the last moment before serving. It deserves a standing ovation.

SERVES 4

2 cups collard greens
2 cups Swiss chard
4 cups New Zealand spinach
1 tablespoon extra-virgin olive oil
4 garlic cloves, bashed and chopped
½ cup chopped fresh parsley
¼ cup chopped fresh cilantro
2 teaspoons ground cumin
Juice of 1 lemon (¼ cup)
¼ teaspoon salt

You can do this first step ahead of time. Place the collards in a large steamer over boiling water. Steam 2 minutes, add the Swiss chard, and steam 2 minutes more. Now add the spinach and steam 4 minutes longer. When the greens are tender, turn them out into a sieve and squeeze out the excess liquid with the back of a wooden spoon. Chop roughly.

Just before serving, combine the oil, garlic, parsley, cilantro, cumin, and lemon juice in a large skillet. Warm, add the chopped greens and salt, and mix thoroughly. Serve immediately, while the greens are still bright and beautiful.

Per serving: 59 calories, 4 g fat, 1 g saturated fat (15% calories from saturated fat), 6 g carbohydrate, 2 g protein, 2 g dietary fiber, 265 mg sodium. Exchanges: 3 Vegetable, 1 Fat

Onion

Allium cepa

I should warn you that onions, perhaps more than any other garden crop, are susceptible to both disease and pests, especially if planted as sets, which are immature bulbs (like tiny green onions). If you select small bulbs (about 1 inch or less in diameter), they will take longer, but you should be more successful. Look out for disease-resistant varieties.

I find the derivation of the word *onion* quite delightful. Apparently it comes from the Latin *unio*, whose literal meaning is "single large pearl." I will never look at or handle an onion in the same way again.

Onions are taken at three stages of growth. They reach green onion/scallion stage in up to 35 days and have a stem width of about ½ inch. If intended for such use, they can be planted quite close together (1–2 inches).

Leave them alone (or thin them out to have 2–3 inches of clearance), and they'll reach what is called bunching, when the bulbs are 1–2 inches in diameter.

Leave them completely alone for 3–4 months, and you'll have the mature onion, when the green tops turn brown and dry out. The bulb will be 3–4 inches in diameter.

To avoid crying, chill the onion in the deep freeze for 30 minutes before cutting. This works for me, but then I'm 6 feet 2 inches tall—my eyes are 3 feet away from the onion!

Onions are called photo-periodic plants. Long-day varieties should be planted as early as possible to make use of maximum daylight to form a good-size bulb. Short-day varieties actually need less light, so they go into the ground in the fall. Long days are best when above 36 degrees latitude. A new breed has arrived called day neutral, and guess what? It doesn't matter when you plant those.

The Numbers

Onions are a good source of vitamins C, B$_6$, and K.

For each 100 g raw (3.5 oz; ½ cup): 40 calories, 0 g fat, 0 g saturated fat, 9 g carbohydrate, 2 g protein, 1 g dietary fiber, 4 mg sodium

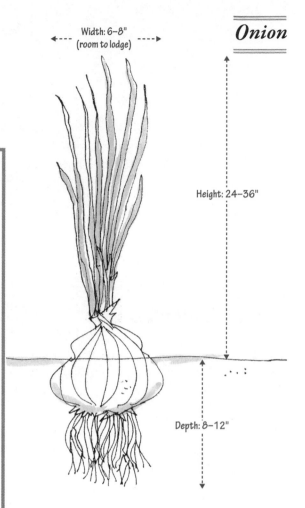

Width: 6–8"
(room to lodge)

Height: 24–36"

Depth: 8–12"

Biennial/Annual/Cool Season

Water: Medium/even, drip irrigation

Sun: Full

Companion Planting:

PRO: Beets, cabbage, carrots, early lettuce, strawberries, tomatoes

CON: All beans, peas, sage

Pests: Japanese beetles, slugs, thrips, cutworms

Diseases: Botrytis, mildew, white rot

Soil: Well-drained, sandy; avoid heavy clay

Fertilizer: Mature compost; moderate nitrogen, phosphorus, potassium; fish emulsion for early growth (when 4–6 leaves appear), then every 2–3 weeks

pH: 6.0–6.8

Varieties:

LONG DAY (14–15 hours of light): Early Yellow Globe, Sweet Spanish

SHORT DAY (10–12 hours of light): Bermuda, Grano Super Sweet

DAY NEUTRAL: Candy, Super Star (mild white), Red Candy Apple (red)

CELEBRITY ONIONS (very sweet): Walla Walla, Vidalia

Plant Care: Check locally for the best advice on suitable varieties, especially those that resist your local diseases

Zones: 3–11

Planting: Indoors, 8 weeks before last frost; seed ¼–½ inch deep

Transplanting: For green onions/scallions, 1–2 inches apart; for bunching, 2–3 inches apart. If started as seed (*very* small), the bulb will be larger and store better. If using bulbs, use those under 1 inch in diameter.

Germinates: 4–12 days

Harvest: From seed, 80–120 days; from transplant, 30–40 days; from scallions from sets, 35 days

Rotation: Don't plant in beds used by garlic

Edible: Bulb and leaves

SWEATING THE ONION

Many people never get the full flavor benefit from an onion because they avoid sweating them, breaking out their volatile oils, at a pan temperature around 350°F. If you use too cool a pan, the water breaks out but not the full flavors that a properly sweated onion can deliver.

CARAMELIZED ONIONS

The sweetness of the onion turns to a caramel when shallow-fried. This couldn't be more simple and is the perfect way to prepare onions for inclusion in many cooked dishes, such as warm salads, spaghetti sauce, or vegetables and rice. And, of course, it is a traditional robust garnish for many foods.

SERVES 4

1 teaspoon olive oil
1 pound onions, peeled and sliced (the sweeter the variety the better)

Heat the oil in a heavy skillet over medium. Add the onions and cook, stirring occasionally, until soft and browned, 20 minutes.

Per serving: 56 calories, 1 g fat, 0 g saturated fat, 11 g carbohydrate, 1 g protein, 2 g dietary fiber, 5 mg sodium. Exchanges: 2 Vegetable

BAKED SWEET ONIONS

Each region has its own celebrity sweet onion, but all will work well with this simple recipe.

SERVES 4

4 medium sweet onions
¼ cup balsamic vinegar
¼ cup water
1 teaspoon arrowroot or cornstarch mixed with 2 teaspoons water (slurry)
1 tablespoon chopped fresh parsley

Preheat the oven to 350°F.

Cut both ends off the onions and peel. Place in a small casserole. Combine the vinegar and water, and pour over the onions. Bake, uncovered, 45 minutes or until tender.

Place an onion on each of 4 hot plates and pour baking liquids into a small saucepan. Stir in the slurry and heat until the liquid is clear and glossy. Serve as a sauce over the onions. Sprinkle the onions with parsley.

Per serving: 73 calories, 0 g fat, 0 g saturated fat, 17 g carbohydrate, 3 g dietary fiber, 5 mg sodium. Exchanges: 3 Vegetable

SAUTÉED ONIONS

An enhanced onion garnish with a definite maple flavor. These onions can be served on their own as a side dish, mixed with other vegetables, spooned over rice or pasta, or even added to baked beans.

SERVES 4

1 teaspoon olive oil
4 medium onions, peeled and sliced
1 tablespoon maple syrup
2 tablespoons balsamic vinegar
¼ teaspoon salt
¼ teaspoon freshly ground black pepper
2 tablespoons chopped fresh basil

Heat the oil in a large high-sided skillet over medium-high. Sauté the onions 2 minutes. Add the syrup, vinegar, salt, and black pepper. Continue cooking, stirring often, 20–25 minutes or until the onions are golden, tender, and cooked down. Stir in the basil.

Per serving: 75 calories, 1 g fat, 0 g saturated fat, 15 g carbohydrate, 1 g protein, 2 g dietary fiber, 151 mg sodium. Exchanges: 2 Vegetable, ½ Carbohydrate

EAST VILLAGE POTATO AND ONION TART

This terrific vegetable tart topped with a rosemary glaze was one of the recipes I brought home from Angelica Kitchen in New York City. The wonderful combination of potatoes and caramelized onions is held together by a soft, luscious chickpea "custard." The tart can be made in a deep quiche dish or pie plate.

SERVES 6

FOR THE CHICKPEA CUSTARD
6 cups cold water
2 cups chickpea flour
½ teaspoon salt
¼ teaspoon white pepper
Pinch of powdered saffron
½ teaspoon Southern France Ethmix (see page 288) or dried thyme
1 teaspoon freshly squeezed lemon juice
2 teaspoons capers

FOR THE TART
1 teaspoon light olive oil
1 pound sweet onions, cut into ½-inch dice (yield 3 cups)
½ teaspoon caraway seeds
1 pound Yellow Finn or other waxy yellow potatoes, peeled and sliced ¼-inch thick
⅛ teaspoon salt
¼ teaspoon freshly ground black pepper
1 teaspoon white wine vinegar
3 tablespoons freshly grated Parmesan cheese
1 teaspoon paprika

FOR THE ROSEMARY GLAZE

½ teaspoon light olive oil

½ cup sliced sweet onions

½ cup sliced shiitake mushrooms (¼-inch slices)

1 teaspoon chopped fresh rosemary

1½ cups low-sodium vegetable stock (see page 288)

1 tablespoon white wine vinegar

1 teaspoon arrowroot mixed with 1 tablespoon water (slurry)

1 teaspoon low-sodium tamari

FOR THE GARNISH

¼ cup water

4 cups frozen peas (or freshly shucked)

2 sprigs mint

1 tablespoon sugar

⅛ teaspoon salt

To make the custard, measure the water into a large nonstick saucepan. Slowly drizzle the chickpea flour into the cold water, beating constantly with a plastic whisk to keep lumps from forming. Bring to a boil over medium heat, stirring often.

Add the salt, white pepper, saffron, and spice mix. Stir to combine. Continue cooking slowly, stirring occasionally, 15–20 minutes or until the custard starts to thicken. Do not allow the mixture to thicken too much; it should be the consistency of pancake batter, not as stiff as polenta.

Remove from the heat and stir in the lemon juice and capers. Set aside.

To make the tart, warm the oil in a large frying pan over medium-high. Cook the onions and caraway seeds for about 10 minutes or

until the onions are wilted and browned. Remove a generous ¼ cup of onions from the pan and set aside for later.

Reduce the heat to medium and add the potatoes to the pan. Season with the salt, black pepper, and vinegar. Cover and cook, stirring often, for 15 minutes or until potatoes are just tender.

Sprinkle 1 tablespoon of the Parmesan cheese over the top of the potatoes and set aside.

Combine the ¼ cup of reserved onions with the remaining 2 tablespoons of Parmesan cheese and the paprika.

To assemble the tart, spray a 10-inch quiche dish or pie plate with cooking spray.

Pour half of the chickpea custard into the dish. Layer the potatoes over the custard, and then add the rest of the custard. Top with the reserved onion mixture. Gently press the onions down into the custard with a rubber spatula. Set aside to let rest for 1 hour.

Preheat the oven to 350°F.

Bake the tart for 45 minutes. Remove from the oven and set aside for 10 minutes to allow the contents to set before serving.

Make the glaze while the tart is baking. Heat the oil in a large saucepan. Sauté the onions until softened, about 2 minutes. Stir in the mushrooms and continue to sauté for another 2 minutes.

Add the rosemary, stock, and vinegar. Boil vigorously until reduced by half, about 15 minutes. Strain the liquid into a small saucepan, discarding the mushrooms and onions.

Add the slurry and the tamari to the saucepan, and stir over medium heat until the mixture clears and thickens. Taste and adjust the seasonings if necessary.

Make the garnish while the glaze is reducing. Bring the water to a boil in a medium saucepan. Add the peas, mint, sugar, and salt. Reduce the heat and simmer for 3–5 minutes until the peas are tender but still bright green. Discard the mint sprigs.

Arrange a bed of peas on each plate. Place a tart wedge on top of the peas. Spoon the rosemary glaze over the tart.

Per serving: 367 calories, 4 g fat, 4 g saturated fat, (10% calories from saturated fat), 57 g carbohydrate, 16 g protein, 10 g dietary fiber, 491 mg sodium. Exchanges: 3 Starch, 2 Vegetable, 1 Fat

BELLA BELLA BEANS

Beautiful, beautiful beans named for the beautiful, beautiful town of Bella Bella on the coast of British Columbia, which we once sailed to.

SERVE 6

FOR THE BEANS
1 teaspoon nonaromatic olive oil
1 cup chopped onion
2 garlic cloves, bashed and chopped
2 cups low-sodium vegetable stock (see page 288)
1 (15.5-ounce) can low-sodium chickpeas, rinsed and drained
6 cups trimmed and torn kale
1 (15.5-ounce) can low-sodium red kidney beans, rinsed and drained
⅓ cup freshly grated Parmesan cheese

FOR THE GARNISH
½ cup fresh oregano leaves
2 limes, cut in quarters
Dried crushed chili pepper flakes to taste
½ cup chopped onion

To make the beans, heat the oil in a Dutch oven over medium-high. Sauté the onion 2 minutes, add the garlic, and cook 1 more minute. Pour in the stock and bring to a boil. Add the chickpeas, kale, and kidney beans. Bring back to a boil, reduce the heat, and simmer 5 minutes.

Stir in the Parmesan cheese and serve in bowls. Pass the oregano leaves, limes, pepper flakes, and raw onions in individual bowls.

Per serving: 192 calories, 3 g fat, 1 g saturated fat (5% calories from saturated fat), 31 g carbohydrate, 1 g protein, 7 g dietary fiber, 183 mg sodium. Exchanges: 2 Starch, 2 Vegetable, ½ Fat

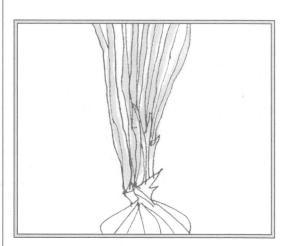

Parsnip

Pastinaca sativa

The parsnip was the root of choice in Europe and very popular in the New World until the late 19th century, when it got replaced by the potato. But it is still my favorite root vegetable. I love it for all kinds of reasons, but mostly for its taste and cooked texture: sweet and nutty and lusciously smooth and creamy.

When cultivating, be careful to thin out the roots early, as they need more space than carrots and a lot more time, which explains why they cost so much more than carrots. All this means they make a good candidate for the home garden.

You'll need to start them as soon as the soil can be worked. The seed can germinate when the soil goes over 40°F. I gave mine a monthly dose of liquid fish fertilizer and left them alone until late fall or winter. I cut off the green tops in the late fall as they wilted and covered the bed with mulch 4 inches deep. The difference in sweetness is remarkable. It's important to dig out this late harvest crop entirely, since they become woody and fibrous if left for a second season.

One other odd fact is that they do not do well when the soil has been recently fertilized or has had a fresh manure application. It's much better to lay on that kind of nourishment a year ahead, so that it matures and the nitrogen levels are lower. Too much nitrogen causes the parsnip to become hairy.

You'll also need to do some digging to give the roots good, even soil density so that they can attain their full potential (up to 10 inches).

The Numbers

For each 100 g boiled (3.5 oz; ½ cup): 71 calories, 0 g fat, 0 g saturated fat, 17 g carbohydrate, 1 g protein, 4 g dietary fiber, 10 mg sodium

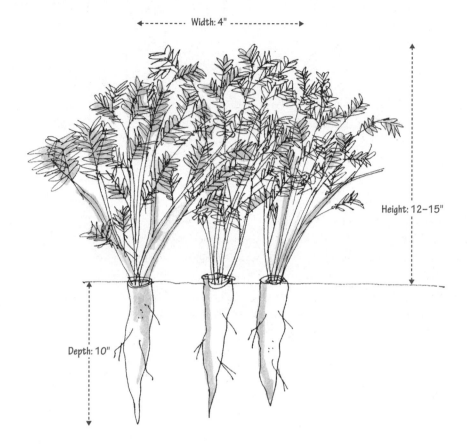

Width: 4"

Height: 12–15"

Depth: 10"

Biennial/Annual/Cool Season
Water: Moderate, drip irrigation
Sun: Partial shade (5 hours of sun a day)
Companion Planting:
PRO: Bush beans, beets, carrots, other root vegetables
CON: Tomatoes, broccoli, cabbage, kale
Pests: Army worms, nematodes, root maggots
Diseases: None
Soil: Sandy, humus-rich, no stones, double dig down to 18 inches
Fertilizer: Low nitrogen, low phosphorus, and potassium
pH: 6.0–6.8

Varieties: White Gem (will grow in any soil), Gladiator (particularly sweet), Cobham (ideal to leave in ground over the winter unless you have really deep frost)
Zones: 3–10
Planting: Early summer for winter harvest; seed ¼–½ inch deep, 1 inch apart; thin to 3–4 inches
Germination: 5–28 days
Harvest: From seed, 95–120 days
Rotation: Don't follow carrots, celery
Edible: Roots

PARSNIPS

Basic Preparation

For several years, I've literally blended parsnips into a sauce that I can characterize only as velvet by simply steaming the youngish, relatively small root until it's very tender and then popping it into a blender with some evaporated skim milk (ratio 1 pound steamed parsnips to an 11-ounce can of milk) and whizzing it for 4–5 minutes until it develops a beautiful sheen. Add salt and white pepper.

I use it in place of a velouté-style sauce over noodles—or whatever you choose—and dust with freshly grated Parmesan cheese just before serving. (One tablespoon of cheese is enough to give the aromatic impression that it really is an Alfredo or Mornay sauce.) The dish can then be put under a hot broiler to "au gratin" it until it is dappled and deliciously golden brown.

You can use this concept of browned (au gratin) velvet sauces with all kinds of foods, from poached fish to cauliflower. If the dish to be dressed is basically white, the au gratin sauce will cover its bland appearance and also provide an interesting texture.

As an alternative to the parsnips, sweet potatoes can be used to get that mac 'n' cheese look!

PAN-ROASTED PARSNIPS

While I had thought this was my absolute favorite way to prepare parsnips, since I've grown and then cooked my own, I know it's the best!

SERVES 4

2¼ pounds parsnips
1 teaspoon nonaromatic olive oil
½ cup roughly chopped onion
1 garlic clove, bashed and chopped
¼ teaspoon salt
¼ teaspoon white pepper
6-inch sprig fresh rosemary
½ cup low-sodium chicken or vegetable stock (see page 288)
1 tablespoon chopped fresh parsley

Peel and cut the parsnips lengthwise into quarters, and slice crosswise into ¼-inch-thick wedges. Pour the oil into a high-sided skillet over medium-high. Add the onions, garlic, parsnips, salt, and white pepper, and stir to mix thoroughly. Sauté 2–3 minutes or until the vegetables just start to brown.

Bury the rosemary sprig in the cooking vegetables, pour in the stock, cover, and cook for 5 minutes or until the parsnips are as tender as you like them. Remove the rosemary and serve with a sprinkle of parsley.

Per serving: 129 calories, 2 g fat, 0 g saturated fat, 28 g carbohydrate, 2 g protein, 6 g dietary fiber, 179 mg sodium. Exchanges: 2 Starch, 5 Vegetable

THAI SPICED PARSNIPS

Just a slight Asian twist with a mild two-star bite!

SERVES 4

2 teaspoons nonaromatic olive oil

1 red chile

2-inch piece gingerroot, peeled and cut into
thin slices

1 pound medium parsnips, peeled and cut into
¼-inch slices

1 cup low-sodium vegetable stock
(see page 288)

¼ teaspoon salt

1 teaspoon arrowroot or cornstarch mixed
with 1 tablespoon Thai fish sauce (slurry)

2 tablespoons chopped fresh spearmint

1 tablespoon toasted sesame seeds

Heat the oil in a high-sided skillet over medium-high. Sauté the red chile and ginger 2 minutes to break out the flavors. Add the parsnips and cook 5 minutes until golden brown.

Pour the stock into the skillet, cover, and cook until the parsnips are tender, about 10 minutes. Add the salt, remove the chile, and stir in the slurry. Heat to thicken and serve topped with the mint and sesame seeds.

Per serving: 126 calories, 4 g fat, 0 g saturated fat, 22 g carbohydrate, 2 g protein, 5 g dietary fiber, 197 mg sodium. Exchanges: 1½ Starch, 1 Fat, 3 Vegetable

Peas

Pisum sativum

The Chinese have been cultivating peas on a grand scale for more than 4,000 years, and it isn't just the snow pea that we usually associate with stir-fried Asian dishes.

Over the years, especially in recent times, we've grafted and otherwise crossbred several ancient varieties and come up with a set of apparently unbeatable characteristics.

The sugar snap pea comes from its rapidly growing bush (easier to harvest mechanically) or trellis (better, in my opinion for the small garden) to the plate, complete with pod and all.

The trellis allows for better air circulation than the bush and reduces Fusarium wilt, which turns the lower leaves brown. Peas don't do well with overhead watering, so my new drip-feed line along with mulch at ground level has managed to keep the roots cool and retain moisture, thus defeating the wilt so far. I discovered the word *inoculant*, which is a liquid used to coat the peas before planting

My soil was about 40°F, which is the low end of the temperature most suited to germination (the upper end is 75°F). But once the plants saw the light, they took off in grand style. I had added a little bonemeal along with my Intrepid fertilizer and couldn't have been more delighted with their fresh-picked sweetness in a lovely early evening stir-fry . . . along with the tendrils that can be snipped from the tops of the vines, about 5 inches above the pods.

There are several varieties of the sugar snap pea, but the one I like best also happens to be one of the nation's most popular, Oregon Sugar Pod II, developed by Oregon State University.

For some reason, many children just don't like peas. Perhaps it's because they are hard to chase around the plate or their little outer shells don't chew up easily. But they have always been well received at our family table—with just a few leaves of fresh mint and a teaspoonful of brown sugar. What child could object?

We also use them to make a bright green version of the velvet sauce I usually make with parsnips (see page 204), but peas must be passed through a fine sieve to remove the shells.

The Numbers

For each 100 g boiled (3.5 oz; ½ cup): 84 calories, 0 g fat, 0 g saturated fat, 16 g carbohydrate, 5 g protein, 5 g dietary fiber, 3 mg sodium

Snow or sugar snap peas per 100 g cooked (3.5 oz; ½ cup): 59 calories, 0 g fat, 0 g saturated fat, 7 g carbohydrate, 2 g protein, 2 g dietary fiber, 12 mg sodium

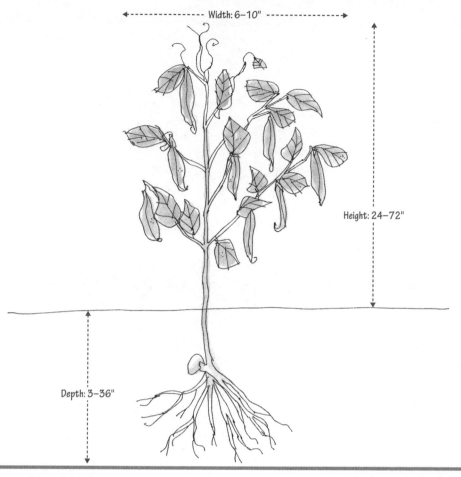

Width: 6–10"

Height: 24–72"

Depth: 3–36"

Annual/Cool Season

Water: Moderate, drip irrigation. Peas don't like really warm weather and shouldn't be handled when wet from dew, irrigation, or rain.

Sun: Full

Companion Planting:

PRO: Beans, carrots, celery, radishes, spinach, strawberries

CON: Garlic, onions, late potatoes

Pest: Aphids, birds, rabbits, thrips

Diseases: Bacterial blight, mildew, root rot

Soil: Sandy loam; good drainage, as heavy, waterlogged soil will produce a poor harvest

Fertilizer: Fish emulsion when 6 inches high

pH: 5.5–6.8

Varieties:

SNOW PEAS: Corgi (for flavor), Oregon Giant (big pods)

ENGLISH PEAS: Dakota (early), Wando (bush pea for small garden)

SUGAR SNAPS: Super Sugar Mel, Super Sugar Snap (pole climber)

Zones: 2–8

Planting: For spring crop, seed ½–1 inch deep, 6–8 weeks before last frost. Sow 2 peas together unless you use the 8 peas to one pole idea—then only one. Plant 2–3 inches apart, thin to 4 inches.

Germinates: 5–7 days

Harvest: From seed, 55–70 days

Rotation: Every other year, to help following crops that need nitrogen fixation, such as kale.

Edible: Peas and pods

ASIAN SNOW PEA SALAD

A lovely bright-flavored salad for early summer when the snow peas are abundant. Depending on the variety, you may have to detach the stalk along with the fine string. The younger they are, the less likely they are to need this fiddle.

SERVES 4

FOR THE DRESSING
¼ cup rice vinegar
2 tablespoons toasted sesame oil
1 tablespoon low-sodium soy sauce
1 teaspoon finely chopped garlic
1 teaspoon grated gingerroot
½ teaspoon hot red pepper flakes
¼ teaspoon salt

FOR THE SALAD
2 cups cooked thin rice noodles
1 cup seedless red grape halves
1 cup fresh (or frozen) snow peas, quickly
    blanched and cooled
½ cup sliced green onions
2 cups salad shrimp or chicken breast pieces
    (can be replaced by mushrooms, sliced and
    briefly sautéed, or tofu)
4 large red leaf lettuce leaves

Combine the vinegar, oil, soy sauce, garlic, ginger, red pepper flakes, and salt in a blender or small bowl and set aside.

Toss together the noodles, grapes, snow peas, onion, and shrimp. Pour the dressing over and mix well. Let sit 30 minutes for the flavors to mingle. Serve on beds of red leaf lettuce leaves.

Per serving: 229 calories, 6 g fat, 1 g saturated fat (4% calories from saturated fat), 21 g carbohydrate, 21 g protein, 2 g dietary fiber, 428 mg sodium. Exchanges: 1 Starch, 1 Very Lean Meat, 1 Vegetable, 1 Fat

GREEN PEA DIP WITH SALSA

A new twist on guacamole, using bright green peas in place of the higher calorie avocado.

SERVES 4

2 cups fresh shelled peas
2 tablespoons freshly squeezed lemon or lime
    juice
1 teaspoon mild chili powder
⅛ teaspoon cayenne (optional)
1 tablespoon minced onion
1 garlic clove, bashed and chopped
⅓ cup prepared salsa

Cook the peas in ½ cup boiling water for 4 minutes, until tender and bright green. Pour into a food processor along with the cooking liquid. Add the lemon juice, chili powder, and cayenne, and pulse until almost smooth. Put into a medium bowl and stir in the onion, garlic, and salsa.

Serve with baked tortilla or pita chips, or jicama slices.

Per serving: 62 calories, 0 g fat, 0 g saturated fat, 11 g carbohydrate, 4 g protein, 4 g dietary fiber, 122 mg sodium. Exchanges: 1 Starch

PEA SALAD WITH CURRY AND ALMONDS

This looks so rich and creamy, you may think it shouldn't be allowed. Yet this luscious first course provides 1½ vegetable servings per person, and check out the nutrition numbers!

SERVES 4

2 cups small new peas
1 cup peeled and chopped jicama
½ cup finely chopped sweet onion
2 tablespoons roughly chopped toasted
    almonds
¼ cup light mayonnaise
¼ cup nonfat plain yogurt
1 teaspoon mild curry powder
Pinch cayenne
¼ teaspoon salt
¼ teaspoon freshly ground black pepper

Place the peas, jicama, onions, and almonds in a bowl.

Combine the mayonnaise, yogurt, curry powder, cayenne, salt, and black pepper. Add to the vegetables and mix well.

Per serving: 118 calories, 3 g fat, 0 g saturated fat, 18 g carbohydrate, 5 g protein, 7 g dietary fiber, 161 mg sodium. Exchanges: 1 Starch, ½ Fat

RISI BISI

Perhaps the second most famous combination of grain and legume—after rice and beans—is this dish, which is a visual delight and a treat for pea lovers. It's also a complete protein combination.

SERVES 4

⅔ cup Arborio or pearl rice
1⅓ cups low-sodium chicken or vegetable
    stock (see page 288)
2 cups fresh small peas, lightly steamed
    (4 minutes)
¼ teaspoon salt
¼ teaspoon freshly ground black pepper
2 tablespoons freshly grated Parmesan cheese

Bring the rice and stock to a boil in a covered saucepan. Reduce the heat as low as possible and cook, covered, 15 minutes or until the rice is tender.

Stir in the peas, salt, black pepper, and Parmesan cheese.

Per serving: 101 calories, 2 g fat, 1 g saturated fat (9% calories from saturated fat), 15 g carbohydrate, 6 g protein, 4 g dietary fiber, 323 mg sodium. Exchanges: 1 Starch, ½ Fat

Peppers

Capsicum annuum

In the first year with my kitchen garden, the bell peppers did very well in more ways than one. As a plant, they flourished—the nights were warm, so I didn't lose blossoms. Almost every flower bore fruit, and eventually those that were supposed to turn color did exactly what their seed packet promised!

Of course it was a tremendous help that we had such a long warm summer. Peppers relish warmth and really don't like it when it rains. All mine began their life indoors and didn't go out until our nights were consistently warmer than 55°F and the plants were 6 inches tall.

When they are mature (with fruit), they can spread out over 15 inches, so it's best to stagger them over at least a 3-foot-wide bed. If it gets really hot (for us, 85°F and above), use a floating cover to provide some shade; too much heat, and you could lose the blossoms essential to produce the fruit.

Two pieces of good advice that I got from my local experts: scratch in a teaspoon of Epsom salt at the base of each plant to give it some extra magnesium, which peppers just love, and keep sweet peppers well separated (at least one bed away) from spicy peppers to avoid cross-pollination.

Normally just growing well would be enough, but they went the extra mile and made my year! I smuggled a couple of red ones into the kitchen and sliced them into a delicious salad with goat cheese, pineapple, pine nuts, and plenty of fresh basil—and waited for the reaction from Treena, who professes to hate peppers. She loved the salad, and when I told her the thin red stuff was peppers, she was enthusiastic enough to suggest we try them broiled, which really is my favorite method.

The Numbers

Commercial crops of these peppers grown via conventional methods can sometimes be quite high in residual chemicals. As yours ripen, they gain red pigment and antioxidants and no chemicals.

For each 100 g raw (3.5 oz; ½ cup): 31 calories, 0 g fat, 0 g saturated fat, 6 g carbohydrate, 1 g protein, 2 g dietary fiber, 4 mg sodium

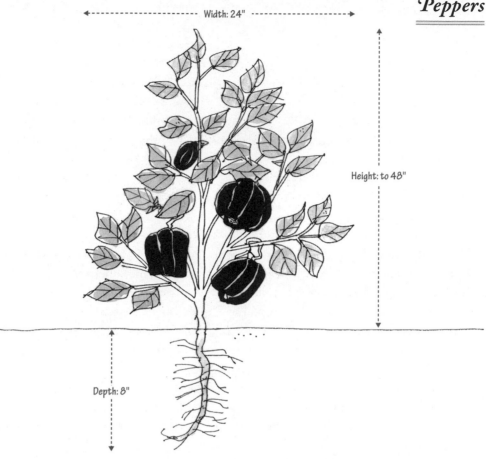

Width: 24"

Height: to 48"

Depth: 8"

Annual
Water: Moderate until fruit forms, then less
Sun: Full
Companion Planting:
PRO: Basil, carrots, eggplant, parsnips, tomatoes
CON: Fennel, kohlrabi
Pests: Aphids, army worms, mites, slugs
Diseases: Rot, blossom end rot, mildew
Soil: Light, well drained, and fertile; good composting before planting out; moderate compost
Fertilizer: Medium to heavy feeders; liquid seaweed at blossom plus 2–3 applications during growth
pH: 5.5–6.8
Varieties:
GREEN: California Wonder

YELLOW: Labrador
ORANGE: Ariane
RED: Ace, Lipstick
Zones: 4–12
Planting: Seed ¼–½ inch deep in spring, when night temperatures are above 60°F; best to start indoors 8 weeks before last frost; plant 12 inches apart
Germinates: 7–10 days
Harvest: From seed, 60–90 days; from transplant, 55–60 days (extra 15–20 days for reds)
Rotation: Don't plant after tomato, eggplant, or potato
Edible: Pod fruits

PEPPER

How to Roast

Peppers have a tough outer skin that can be easily removed after the roasting process to yield a soft, silken flesh, unlike the crispness that you get if you stir-fry peppers with the skin on.

Cut the peppers into strips no more than ½-inch wide to present as flat a skin surface as possible to the radiant heat source, usually an overhead grill or broiler. Place the cut peppers skin side up on a metal cookie sheet. Spray with a little olive oil and place under the broiler for 5–10 minutes or until the skins have begun to blister and turn brown but not black, which will lend the peppers a burned flavor. Turn them immediately into a brown paper bag. Close it up tightly and allow to cool. All things being equal (and they almost never are), you should be able to easily slip the charred skins off and enjoy the smooth luscious slightly caramelized flesh beneath.

COUSCOUS WITH PEPPERS

In a sense, this is a North African salsa, very colorful and full of bright taste and texture. Great with seafood or poultry dishes.

SERVES 6

3 cups low-sodium vegetable stock
   (see page 288)
¼ teaspoon almond extract
1 cup large-grain couscous
3 tablespoons finely diced red bell pepper
3 tablespoons finely diced yellow bell pepper
3 tablespoons finely diced red onion
2 tablespoons freshly squeezed lime juice
½ teaspoon finely chopped cilantro stems
1 teaspoon arrowroot mixed in 2 teaspoons
   water (slurry)
⅛ teaspoon salt
1 tablespoon finely sliced fresh cilantro leaves
½ cup fruity white wine (I prefer
   dealcoholized Chardonnay)

Combine the stock and almond extract in a large saucepan and bring to a boil. Toss in any vegetable trimmings left over from preparing other courses. Simmer for 10 minutes or so. Strain, discard the trimmings, and return the stock to the saucepan.

Stir the couscous into the stock and simmer 20 minutes or until fluffy and dry. If the couscous is too runny, drain the excess liquid. If the couscous is too dry, add up to ½ cup of water or dealcoholized wine. (If you have only alcoholized wine available, boil off the alcohol before adding it to the couscous or it could be harsh.)

While the couscous is cooking, combine the bell peppers and onion in a small bowl. Add the lime juice and cilantro stems and mix.

As soon as the couscous is done, stir in the slurry. (It is important to add the slurry while the couscous is still very hot.) Add the pepper mixture and the salt, and then remove the pan from the heat and cover tightly to keep warm.

When ready to serve, stir in the cilantro leaves and wine.

Per serving: 132 calories, 1 g fat, 0 g saturated fat, 27 g carbohydrate, 3 g protein, 2 g dietary fiber, 260 mg sodium. Exchanges: 1 Starch, 2 Vegetable, ½ Fat

MEXICAN STUFFED PEPPERS

This dish originated on the 1969 Galloping Gourmet *TV show, when my guest from the audience didn't like it! It has since been transformed, so if you are my 1969 guest reading this, let's try it again.*

SERVES 4

4 red bell peppers
1 teaspoon nonaromatic olive oil
1 cup chopped onion
3 garlic cloves
1 jalapeño or chipotle chile (seeds removed if you like it mild), chopped
1 tablespoon chili powder
½ teaspoon ground cumin
1 (15.25-ounce) can diced tomatoes, in juice
1 cup cooked white rice
1 cup fresh, frozen, or canned corn kernels
1 cup cooked or canned pinto beans

Preheat oven to 350°F.

Cut the tops off the peppers, core, and set aside.

Heat the oil in a 10-inch skillet and cook the onion 2 minutes over medium-high, until it starts to wilt. Add the garlic, jalapeño, chili powder, and cumin. Sauté 2 more minutes. Stir in the tomatoes, rice, corn, and beans. Cook until the liquid disappears and the stuffing holds together. Spoon into the prepared peppers and set into a 10-inch greased baking dish.

Bake 1 hour or until the peppers are tender.

Per serving: 248 calories, 3 g fat, 0 g saturated fat, 50 g carbohydrate, 9 g protein, 8 g dietary fiber, 504 mg sodium. Exchanges: 2 Starch, 4 Vegetable

RED, YELLOW, AND GREEN PASTA

This is a splendid and colorful dish, full of crisp textures and flavor. Harvest carefully to have the same colors in your garden at one time. Since that is quite a trick, you may want to fill in a missing color from the store—on this one occasion!

SERVES 4

8 ounces dry orzo or other small pasta
1 teaspoon olive oil
1 cup chopped onion
2 garlic cloves, bashed and chopped
1 red bell pepper, chopped
1 yellow bell pepper, chopped
4 cups chopped fresh spinach
¼ teaspoon salt

¼ teaspoon freshly ground black pepper
¼ cup freshly grated Parmesan cheese

Cook the pasta according to package directions, drain, and cool under cold water. Set aside.

Heat the oil in a high-sided skillet large enough to hold the whole dish over medium-high. Sauté the onion 2 minutes. Add the garlic and cook 1 minute longer. Toss in the bell peppers and cook 5–8 minutes until tender.

Add the spinach just to wilt it. Stir in the cooked pasta, salt, and black pepper. Sprinkle Parmesan cheese over each serving.

Per serving: 283 calories, 4 g fat, 1 g saturated fat (3% calories from saturated fat), 51 g carbohydrate, 11 g protein, 4 g dietary fiber, 144 mg sodium. Exchanges: 2 ½ Starch, 3 Vegetable, ½ Fat

ROASTED RED PEPPER SOUP

If the peppers have done really well and you've left enough to ripen (redden) on the plant, then here's a special soup for the early winter season.

SERVES 6

1 teaspoon olive oil
½ cup diced sweet onion
2 garlic cloves
4 large red bell peppers, roasted (see page 212)
1 (15-ounce) can diced tomatoes, in juice

4 cups low-sodium vegetable stock
  (see page 288)
¼ teaspoon salt
¼ teaspoon pepper
1 tablespoon balsamic vinegar (optional)

Heat the oil in a large saucepan over medium-high. Sauté the onion 2 minutes, and then add the garlic and cook 1 minute more. Add the roasted peppers, tomatoes, and stock, and bring to a boil. Reduce the heat and simmer 10 minutes.

Whiz half the soup in a blender, then pour it back into the pan. Season with salt, pepper, and vinegar. Divide among 6 hot soup bowls and serve with some good hearty, whole-grain bread.

Per serving: 48 calories, 1 g fat, 0 g saturated fat, 8 g carbohydrate, 2 g protein, 1 g dietary fiber, 361 mg sodium. Exchanges: 2 Vegetable

MULTICOLOR PEPPER SAUTÉ

If you love great colors, this dish will delight you. Serve as a side dish to barbecued meats, in omelets, or heaped on small garlic-rubbed toast rounds as bruschetta.

SERVES 4

1 teaspoon olive oil
1 cup sliced sweet onion
2 garlic cloves, chopped
1 red bell pepper, cored and cut into fine strips

1 yellow bell pepper, cored and cut into fine
   strips
1 green bell pepper, cored and cut into fine
   strips
¼ teaspoon salt
¼ teaspoon freshly ground black pepper
2 tablespoons chopped fresh parsley
Spritz of extra-virgin olive oil

Heat the oil in a skillet over medium-high. Sauté the onion 2 minutes or until it starts to wilt but not brown. Add the garlic and bell pepper strips, and sauté about 10 minutes until tender. Stir in the salt, black pepper, and parsley. Spritz with the olive oil just before serving.

Per serving: 60 calories, 1 g fat, 0 g saturated fat, 12 g carbohydrate, 2 g protein, 3 g dietary fiber, 143 mg sodium. Exchanges: 2 Vegetable

SPINACH-STUFFED RED BELL PEPPERS

This side dish looks like an advertisement for Italy, and it tastes that good, too!
SERVES 4

2 large red bell peppers, seeded and cut in half
   lengthwise
3 bunches fresh spinach or 2 (12-ounce)
   packages chopped frozen spinach, thawed
¼ teaspoon salt
¼ teaspoon freshly ground black pepper
¼ teaspoon nutmeg

Place the pepper halves in a steamer and steam 3 minutes over boiling water. Set aside.

Wash the spinach and discard the stems. Chop the leaves and season with salt, black pepper, and nutmeg. Steam until wilted, 3 minutes. (If using frozen spinach, heat in a small saucepan, then season.) Press out the excess water and fill the pepper halves.

Steam the stuffed peppers 3 minutes or until heated through. Cut each half into 2 wedges and serve green side up . . . what else!

Per serving: 87 calories, 0 g fat, 0 g saturated fat, 11 g carbohydrate, 5 g protein, 4 g dietary fiber, 405 mg sodium. Exchanges: 3 Vegetable

Potato

Solanum tuberosum

We live in one of the world's greatest potato-growing valleys, and so I felt I could better use our limited space for plants that have a greater markup at the store.

Then I discovered a yellow potato called German Butterball and a deeply blue tinted organic potato called, of all things, All Blue. So I set out to plant a patch 5x4 feet, using a pound of each variety as seed and hoping for a 10-pound harvest from both. Since these varieties are what one might call designer potatoes, their designer prices in the supermarket—when you can find them—make them a good candidate for the kitchen garden.

For the first-time potato grower, if you want an early new potato size, break off the foliage but leave the tuber in the ground for a couple of weeks to develop a good skin (with its abundant vitamin C), and always serve them unpeeled.

Exactly when to do this depends on how small you want the new potatoes to be; my best suggestion is to delicately excavate the earth bank to see how they are doing. At 1-inch diameters, you may decide to top the greens.

One other handy hint: keep the soil banked up against the green tops to protect the tuber from developing a green skin. This green pigment is actually a low-grade toxin called alkaloid solanine, which can cause digestive distress.

Tradition has it that Escoffier, the famed master chef, used to have potential apprentices who wanted to work in his Savoy Hotel kitchens make him a plain omelet with boiled potatoes—a seemingly simple audition. Yet both can attain perfection only through skill.

The formula for the perfect boiled potato is simple: water, plus 1 teaspoon salt for each quart of water. Add small/new potatoes to boiling water; older and larger potatoes—2 inches diameter and up—are added to cold water, which is then brought to a boil. In both cases, count on about 12 minutes of boiling time. Drain off the water and cover the hot potatoes with a clean absorbent towel, pressed down tightly into the saucepan. Let stand for 10 minutes. The excess water will then steam off and leave the potatoes in a perfect state.

The Numbers

Although there is only anecdotal evidence concerning arthritis and nightshade vegetables (of which potatoes, eggplant, bell peppers, and tomatoes are members), you might be well advised to limit portions of these vegetables if you suffer from arthritis.

100 g baked including skin (3.5 oz; ½ cup): 97 calories, 0 g fat, 0 g saturated fat, 21 g carbohydrate, 3 g protein, 2 g dietary fiber, 14 mg sodium

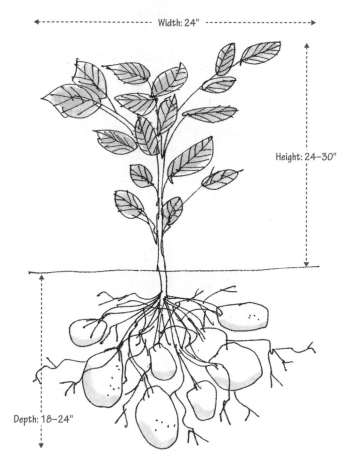

Width: 24"

Height: 24–30"

Depth: 18–24"

Perennial/Annual/Cool Season	FINGERLINGS: Russian Banana
Water: Moist but not saturated	YELLOW: Yukon Gold, German Butterball
Sun: Full	ROUND RED: Norland
Companion Planting:	PURPLE: Purple Viking, All Blue
PRO: Cabbage family, eggplant, beans, marigolds	**Zones:** 3–11
CON: Cucumbers, peas, tomatoes	**Planting:** Sprouted tubers 3 weeks before last frost in 6-inch-wide trenches at 2–4 inches deep, spaced 24 inches apart
Pests: Potato beetles, earwigs, slugs, snails	
Diseases: Black leg, blight, root rot, Verticillium	**Harvest:** From tubers, 90–110 days
Soil: Loose, well-drained sandy loam	**Rotation:** Don't plant after tomato family
Fertilizer: High nitrogen, phosphorus, potassium; add extra potash	**Edible:** Tubers
pH: 5.0–6.5	
Varieties: I've focused my attention on the unusual potatoes to make best use of the kitchen-garden space	

DUFFED POTATOES

My publisher is a devotee of pure white creamed potatoes. I'm hoping he'll like this attempt to compete with the version served at Au Bon Accueil in Paris! At least it will have a lot fewer calories.

SERVES 4

FOR THE POTATOES

4 medium russet potatoes, peeled and
    quartered

½–¾ cup buttermilk

¼ teaspoon salt

¼ teaspoon white pepper

⅛ teaspoon nutmeg

FOR THE SAUCE

1 cup low-sodium vegetable stock
    (see page 288)

Pinch saffron or turmeric

¼ teaspoon salt

1 tablespoon arrowroot or cornstarch
    mixed with 2 tablespoons vegetable
    stock (slurry)

2 teaspoons chopped fresh chives (optional)

Cook the potatoes in boiling water 20–30 minutes or until very soft. Drain, return the potatoes to the pot, put a towel over the top and press it onto the potatoes. Let them sit on very low heat for 15 minutes to dry.

Transfer to an ovenproof bowl. Add ½ cup of the buttermilk and the salt, white pepper, and nutmeg, and mash by hand or with an electric mixer until smooth. Add more buttermilk if the mash is too dry. Keep warm in the oven at 190°F, covered.

To make the sauce, boil the stock in a small saucepan about 10 minutes until reduced by half. Add the saffron and salt. Remove from the heat and stir in the slurry. Return to the heat to thicken and clear.

Divide the potatoes among 4 hot plates. Make a well in the middle of each mound and fill with the sauce, allowing it to spill over just a little. Scatter fresh chives over the top and serve with a nice piece of fish or chicken.

Per serving: 196 calories, 1 g fat, 0 g saturated fat, 42 g carbohydrate, 5 g protein, 4 g dietary fiber, 374 mg sodium. Exchanges: 2 Starch

CELERY ROOT AND POTATO PURÉE

This could become the Mercedes of mashed potatoes if you enjoy the flavor of celery.

SERVES 6

1 small celery root (about 1 pound when
    unpeeled)

2 large russet potatoes

¼ teaspoon salt

4 cups water

¼ cup yogurt cheese (see page 290)

¼ teaspoon white pepper

3 tablespoons finely sliced fresh celery leaves

Scrub the celery root with a vegetable brush. Cut off the top and bottom and discard. Peel the root with a knife, making sure to cut out all the brown spots and any woody parts near the center. Slice thickly and then cut into 1-inch pieces.

Peel the potatoes and cut into 1-inch slices. Put the celery root, potatoes, salt, and water into a medium saucepan. Cover and bring to a boil, then turn down the heat and simmer for 25 minutes, or until the vegetables are very soft.

Strain the vegetables and cover with a towel to dry out for 5 minutes, then mash well. Stir in the yogurt cheese, white pepper, and sliced celery leaves. Cover until ready to serve.

Per serving: 96 calories, 0 g fat, 0 g saturated fat, 21 g carbohydrate, 3 g protein, 3 g dietary fiber, 186 mg sodium. Exchanges: 2 Vegetable

COLORFUL MASHED POTATOES

This is the potato lovers answer to the well-known pasta primavera—an otherwise bland presentation dressed up with lots of colors.

SERVES 6

2 medium Yukon Gold potatoes cut in chunks (yield 2 cups)
1½ cup low-fat milk
2 teaspoons olive oil
1 cup chopped red onion
1 cup chopped carrots
¼ teaspoon caraway seeds
1 cup chopped broccoli

¼ teaspoon salt
¼ teaspoon freshly ground black pepper

Boil the potatoes 10–15 minutes or until very soft. Drain and return to pot, put a towel over the top, and press onto the potatoes. Let them sit on very low heat for 5 minutes to dry. Mash and stir in the milk. Set aside.

Heat the oil in a skillet over medium-high and sauté the onion 2 minutes. Add the carrots and caraway seeds, and cover and cook about 10 minutes until almost tender. Add the broccoli and cook 5 minutes more. The carrots and broccoli should both be just tender and bright in color.

Stir in the mashed potatoes, salt, and black pepper. Heat through and serve.

Per serving: 116 calories, 3 g fat, 1 g saturated fat (8% calories from saturated fat), 18 g carbohydrate, 4 g protein, 2 g dietary fiber, 146 mg sodium. Exchanges: 1 Starch, 1 Vegetable, ½ Fat

Radish

Raphanus sativus

If you still have young children around you, in your role as parent, teacher, grandparent, or—phew, we just made it!—great-grandparent, then radishes are just the thing you want to add to your kitchen garden.

Admittedly, they can have a too-adult taste/texture for the very young—crunchy and a little spicy. However, if you are encouraging your young ones to plant out their own little garden, then these colorful vegetables will come up first and be special companions to carrots, which can be sown at the same time. In other words, there are lots of things happening at once to engage little minds and hands!

You might want to go the whole hog (so to speak) and get a packet each of the various colors: the standard red as well as white, purple, cream, yellow, and even black.

From my very limited experience, if children are involved in planting, watering (and even weeding), and harvesting, they are much more likely to enjoy the adventure of eating.

Because of their small size and rapid growth, radishes make excellent fillers that can be sown directly into spaces that will later be filled by such plants as peppers, cabbage, and tomatoes. By the time these plants mature, your radishes will have been harvested. Remember that the faster they grow, the more tender they will be.

If you harvest the radish at just the right time, the leaves will be tender enough to add to salad (along with other early greens, like beet greens). You might be surprised to learn that small radishes cook up very well in casseroles and stews, where they provide unusual texture and eye appeal.

The Numbers

Radishes are an excellent source of calcium and vitamin C (if used raw; cooking destroys the C content).

For each 100 g raw roots (3.5 oz; ½ cup): 18 calories, 0 g fat, 0 g saturated fat, 4 g carbohydrate, 1 g protein, 0 g dietary fiber, 29 mg sodium

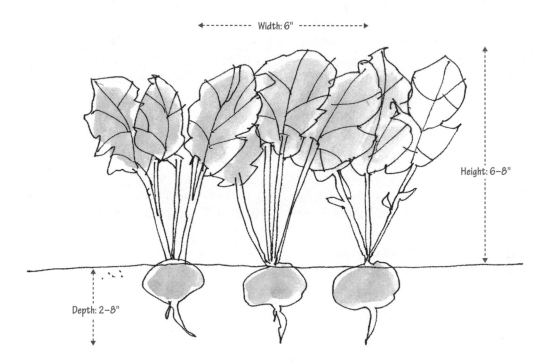

Width: 6"

Height: 6–8"

Depth: 2–8"

Biennial/Annual/Cool Season
Water: Moderate/even, drip irrigation
Sun: Full to part shade
Companion Planting:
PRO: Carrots, beans, beets, peas, peppers
CON: Fennel
Pests: Aphids, white butterflies, nematodes
Diseases: Clubroot, mildew
Soil: Stone-free light soil, drains well but keep moist
Fertilizer: Good compost
pH: 5.5–6.5
Varieties:
SPRING: Red, Comet; white, Burpee White

FALL/WINTER: Long Black Spanish (carrot shaped)
ALL SEASON: Large, long Daikon-style
Zones: 2–10
Planting: Early spring and autumn; seed ½ inch deep, 1 inch apart; thin to 4 inches
Germinates: 4–10 days
Harvest: From seed, 21–35 days; for later fall plantings, 50–60 days
Rotation: Plant in beds previously used for legumes
Edible: Roots and young leaves

MISO SOBA

We enjoyed this dish so much in Japan that we couldn't wait to try it out with the new season's radishes. It could become a rite of passage to mark the start of the growing season.

SERVES 4

1 quart water
1 pound daikon (large Japanese radish), peeled and cut into 1-inch chunks (or 1 pound small red or other colored radishes)
1 medium turnip, peeled and cut into eighths
2 medium waxy potatoes, peeled and cut into eighths
1 small winter squash (I prefer delicata or butternut), peeled, seeded, and cut into 1-inch chunks
12 ounces low-fat extra-firm tofu, cut into 1-inch cubes
8 cups low-sodium vegetable stock (see page 288)
¼ cup low-sodium soy sauce
¼ cup packed light brown sugar
1 (10-ounce) jar gefilte fish in broth
2 tablespoons mustard powder
2 tablespoons arrowroot
½ cup water
2 hard-boiled eggs, shelled
2 tablespoons chopped fresh parsley

Bring the water to a boil in a large saucepan. Drop in the radish, cover, and cook for 10 minutes. Add the turnip, potatoes, and squash, and cook 12 minutes more. Drain, discarding the water, and set aside. This precooking will

ensure a clear broth and good texture for the vegetables.

Pour boiling water over the tofu to cover and let it soak while you do the next step.

Combine the stock, soy sauce, and brown sugar in a heavy Dutch oven and bring to a boil. Drop in the precooked vegetables. Turn the heat down as low as possible and simmer, uncovered, for 60 minutes. The liquid should be reduced by a little more than half, about 3 cups. Then add the drained tofu and gefilte fish with broth. Combine the mustard, arrowroot, and water to make a slurry. Pour into the stew, stirring while it thickens.

Divide among 4 warm bowls. Set half a hard-boiled egg, yolk side up, in each, and scatter chopped parsley over the top.

Per serving: 358 calories, 12 g fat, 1 g saturated fat (3% calories from saturated fat), 38 g carbohydrate, 22 g protein, 3 g dietary fiber, 1,312 mg sodium. Exchanges: ½ Starch, 1 Lean Meat, 1 Vegetable, 1 Fat, 1 Carbohydrate

SIMMERED RADISHES

The color will fade a little in the cooking but can, to a degree, be recaptured with the glossy cornstarch sauce. Please be careful not to use too much cornstarch, as it will goop and become slimy.

SERVES 4

16 red round radishes
1 cup low-sodium vegetable stock (see page 288)

2 teaspoons cornstarch mixed with
   2 tablespoons water (slurry)
¼ teaspoon freshly ground black pepper

Trim the radishes, leaving a little of the green stems and cutting off the root end. Place in a saucepan with the stock, bring to a boil, cover, reduce the heat, and simmer 10 minutes until tender.

Stir in the slurry and boil 30 seconds to thicken and clear. Don't overthicken, please! Dust with black pepper and serve as a side dish.

Per serving: 19 calories, 0 g fat, 0 g saturated fat, 4 g carbohydrate, 1 g protein, 0 g dietary fiber, 49 mg sodium. Exchanges: Free Food

SPRING VEGETABLE SAUTÉ

If the vegetables are small, they may cook a little quicker than indicated here, so be careful not to overcook.

SERVES 4

1 teaspoon olive oil
½ cup sliced sweet onion
1 garlic clove, finely chopped
¾ cup quartered tiny new potatoes
¾ cup baby carrots, cut in half diagonally
¾ cup asparagus pieces
¾ cup sugar snap peas
½ cup quartered radishes
¼ teaspoon salt
¼ teaspoon freshly ground black pepper

1 tablespoon chopped fresh dill or ½ teaspoon dried

Heat the oil in a high-sided skillet over medium-high. Cook the onion 2 minutes, add the garlic, and cook 1 minute more. Stir in the potatoes and carrots, cover, turn the heat to low, and cook about 8 minutes until almost tender. If the vegetables start to brown, add 1–2 tablespoons of water.

Now add the asparagus, peas, radishes, salt, black pepper, and dill. Cook, stirring often, about 4 minutes more until just tender. Try this with a piece of barbecued fish for a complete spring meal.

Per serving: 75 calories, 1 g fat, 0 g saturated fat, 12 g carbohydrate, 2 g protein, 3 g dietary fiber, 199 mg sodium. Exchanges: ½ Starch, 1 Vegetable

Rhubarb

Rheum rhabarbarum

Let's assume for a moment that your garden patch has a quiet side that faces north, a place where you could gather some permanent plantings of tall or large-foliaged vegetables like Jerusalem artichokes (sunchokes), Brussels sprouts, or rhubarb. Their sheer size could block the sun if planted on the east or west.

Here we have another patient plant that's going to take 2–4 years to produce a meaningful harvest, but after that, rhubarb is virtually indestructible for up to 15 years. After the third year, you can divide the crown and plant at least 24 inches apart. The red color can be intensified by cold weather and frosts, which they tolerate quite well.

The best size for harvest are stalks 1 inch in diameter and leaves 24 inches long. To harvest rhubarb, you should bend the stalk, twisting it sideways, and pull—don't cut.

Please don't ever eat the leaves; they contain enough oxalic acid to be toxic.

Rhubarb is very sour on its own, though less so for the varieties Valentine and Strawberry. Because of this, it takes a good deal of sweetening, and that can offset the plant's nutritional advantage. You may want to cook it along with a very sweet fruit, like Bosc pears, and see how you like the natural association.

The Numbers

For each 100 g raw (3.5 oz; ½ cup): 21 calories, 0 g fat, 0 g saturated fat, 5 g carbohydrate, 1 g protein, 2 g dietary fiber, 4 mg sodium

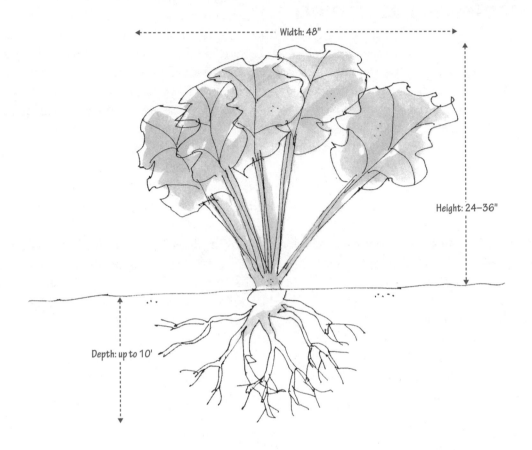

Width: 48"

Height: 24–36"

Depth: up to 10'

Perennial/Hardy/Cool Season
Water: Moderate/even
Sun: Partial shade to full
Companion Planting:
PRO: Okay with other established perennial beds and cabbage family
CON: Legumes, root vegetables
Pests: Aphids, flea beetles
Diseases: Crown rot
Soil: If lots of clay, add sand or gypsum; well-drained, fertile, lots of compost
Fertilizer: Low in nitrogen, phosphorus, potassium
pH: 6.0–6.8

Varieties: Valentine, Strawberry (naturally sweeter); Canada Red (retains color after cooking)
Zones: 3–9
Planting: Early spring, from roots (crowns), 1–3 inches, eventually spaced 3 feet apart
Harvest: Stalks; wait 2 years, then pull; over 4–5 weeks in spring
Rotation: Does not rotate
Edible: Stalks (leaves are toxic)

BUMBLEBERRY STRUDEL

Just outside the city of Victoria on Vancouver Island in British Columbia, Canada, you'll find the village of Oak Harbor and an expanded (to cover all meals) English-style tea shop called the Blethering (which means "endless talking") Place. It is there that I found this admirable dessert.

SERVES 6

FOR THE SAUCE
1 tablespoon honey (fireweed is preferable)
1 cup yogurt cheese (see page 290)

FOR THE STRUDEL
Olive oil cooking spray
1 large Granny Smith apple, peeled, cored, and chopped into ¼-inch dice
2 cups finely sliced rhubarb
1 cup blackberries
1 cup raspberries
½ cup packed dark brown sugar
2 tablespoons freshly grated lemon zest
½ teaspoon ground cloves
8 sheets phyllo dough, thawed (see note on page 148)
½ cup dried bread crumbs
2 tablespoons honey
6 mint sprigs

For the sauce, mix the honey and the yogurt cheese until smooth, and set aside.

Preheat the oven to 360°F. Spray a cookie sheet lightly with olive oil.

For the strudel, combine the apple, rhubarb, blackberries, raspberries, brown sugar, lemon zest, and cloves in a large mixing bowl.

On a flat surface, stretch out a slightly damp dishtowel. Lay a sheet of phyllo dough on top of the towel running lengthwise. Spray lightly with olive oil and repeat with 3 more sheets of pastry. (Keep remaining pastry covered to prevent drying out.)

Sprinkle ¼ cup of the bread crumbs in a strip 3 inches wide down the length of the pastry, leaving 2 inches at either end. Spoon half of the fruit mixture carefully on top off the bread crumb strip.

With the long side of the pastry and fruit filling in front of you, lift the nearest edge of the damp towel and roll the pastry slowly away from you, as you would a jelly roll. Repeat for the remaining pastry and fruit mixture to make a second one.

Place the strudel seam-side down in the prepared pan. With a brush, lightly apply the honey to each roll. Bake for 30 minutes. Lift gently with a spatula to check that the underside is no longer doughy.

When done, place the cookie sheet on a wire rack and let the strudel cool for 15 minutes before slicing. Slice each roll into thirds and serve with a dollop of the yogurt sauce. Garnish with a sprig of mint.

Per serving: 257 calories, 2 g fat, 0 g saturated fat, 55 g carbohydrate, 6 g protein, 4 g dietary fiber, 459 mg sodium. Exchanges: ½ Fruit, ½ Starch

MOLDED RHUBARB STRAWBERRY DESSERT

Simply delicious with low-fat vanilla yogurt and a sprig of fresh mint.

SERVES 8

1 pound rhubarb, fresh or frozen
¼ cup freshly squeezed orange juice
5 tablespoons packed dark brown sugar
2 packets unflavored gelatin
½ cup cold water
1 cup strawberries, sliced

Cut the rhubarb into ½-inch chunks or use frozen rhubarb as is. Place in a saucepan and pour on the orange juice. Bring to a boil, reduce the heat, and simmer 8 minutes or until soft. Stir in the brown sugar.

Sprinkle the gelatin over the water to soften for 10 minutes. Stir into the hot fruit to dissolve. Add the strawberries and mix gently. Pour into a mold or glass 8X8-inch baking pan and chill.

Unmold the dessert by setting in hot water for 30 seconds or until it loosens. Tip onto a plate. Cut in wedges and serve. If you've chosen the glass pan, cut in squares and serve.

Per serving: 60 calories, 0 g fat, 0 g saturated fat, 13 g carbohydrate, 2 g protein, 1 g dietary fiber, 8 mg sodium. Exchanges: ½ Fruit, ½ Carbohydrate

Rutabaga

Brassica napus

It is entirely possible that a carrot and a cabbage found some kind of vegetative bliss in a natural (no human intervention) habitat and had an unusual offspring. At least that's what some well-informed botanists suggest.

The prodigy was, of course, the rutabaga.

Now I happen to really enjoy this root vegetable, regardless of its reasonably unattractive appearance. It's round, light to darker yellow, and squat—a perfect description. It has to be peeled, which, depending on its size, can be an awkward task. Once the skin is gone (and popped into a stockpot), the flesh is fairly evenly golden—much more attractive.

You can eat the leaves (like turnip greens) of the young plant, but I find them an acquired taste and not worth the effort.

As they begin to reach their maximum height of 12–15 inches, it's a good idea to gently bend the stalks over until the tops point to the ground (a little like onions and garlic) so that the energy flowing into the leaf growth is directed into the root. This technique—called *lodging*—promotes growth and sweetness. The vegetable is best when it's about 4 inches in diameter, although the rutabaga can grow up to 8 inches.

They will take a good deal of time to grow—more than 120 days in my case—and, like other roots, do very well after a mild to moderate frost, which again encourages sweetness. If you leave rutabagas to winter, they'll need lots of mulch; and throughout their growth, the soil must be kept evenly moist to prevent cracking.

I used the rutabaga in a special multivegetable soup for some close neighbors. The idea was to gain maximum nourishment at minimum cost and to achieve this by doing enough volume to last for several meals, each of which could be modified with added garnishes to create variety. It really is a perfect dish for tough economic times—or any time, for that matter. (You'll find the recipe for this superb soup on page 230.)

The Numbers

For each 100 g boiled (3.5 oz; ½ cup): 39 calories, 0 g fat, 0 g saturated fat, 9 g carbohydrate, 1 g protein, 2 g dietary fiber, 20 mg sodium

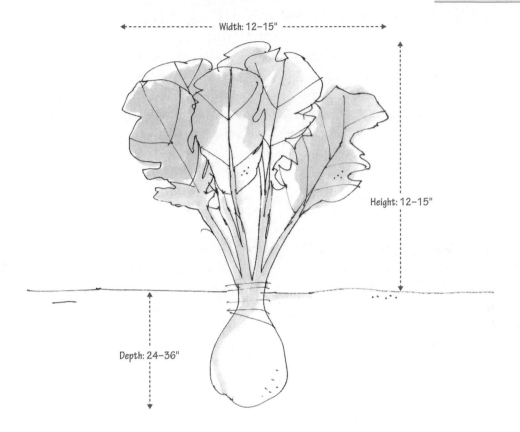

Width: 12–15"

Height: 12–15"

Depth: 24–36"

Biennial/Annual/Cool Season
Water: Moderate
Sun: Full
Companion Planting:
PRO: Beets, carrots, peas, turnips
CON: Potatoes
Pests: Armyworms, cabbage root maggots, flea beetles
Diseases: Black rot, turnip mosaic virus
Soil: Light, sandy loam; good drainage; compost well
Fertilizer: Low nitrogen, moderate phosphorus and potassium (add nitrogen when plants are 5 inches tall)
pH: 5.5–6.8
Varieties: York (smooth, rich), Gilfeather (sweet heirloom)

Zones: 3–10
Planting: Early spring; seed ¼–½ inch deep, 1 inch apart; thin to 6–8 inches
Germinates: 7–15 days
Harvest: From seed, 90–125 days
Rotation: Follow onions/scallions
Edible: Roots, young leaves

KAREENA'S SOUP BASE

Our youngest daughter now has two daughters of her own and lots of reasons to get more vegetables into their young and vibrant lives. Like so many of our neighbors, they wanted something they could make in a reasonable quantity to get ahead of the typical busy day, when, so often, the easy way out was pizza.

I went looking in the fall season for a soup/stew base that could be frozen and nuked back to life in minutes, and then created a list of simple add-ons that took no time and created a sense of variety.

It worked for us and them, and now, I hope, for you.

When the vegetables are in season, this is also an example of good nutrition at a great price. When I tested this, not one of the enhanced soups cost more than $2.00 a portion!

SERVES 30 (EVENTUALLY!)

1½ pounds sweet onions, cut into ½-inch dice (save peelings)

2 ounces grated gingerroot (optional)

5 garlic cloves, crushed (optional)

1½ pounds rutabagas, peeled and cut into ½-inch dice (save peelings)

1½ pounds turnips, peeled and cut into ½-inch dice (save peelings)

1½ pounds carrots, peeled and cut into ½-inch piece (save peelings)

1½ pounds sweet potatoes, peeled and cut into 1-inch dice (save peelings)

1½ pounds parsnips, peeled and cut into 1-inch dice (save peelings)

8 ounces celery, cut into ½-inch pieces

8 ounces Swiss chard stalks, cut into ½-inch pieces (yield 2 cups)

1 quart low-sodium vegetable stock (see page 288)

20 cups cold water

3 tablespoons olive oil

2 tablespoons Greek Islands Ethmix (see page 287) (optional)

2 tablespoons cornstarch mixed with water (slurry; only 1 teaspoon for each portion)

2 tablespoons chopped fresh parsley

Salt to taste

Equipment: *To cook a large amount at one time, you will need a 10-quart saucepan or stockpot (available through a restaurant supply business) and a large, heavy-based frying pan that's at least 10½ inches in diameter. You'll also need quart-size freezer bags.*

First, thoroughly wash all the vegetable peelings and sauté them lightly in 1 tablespoon olive oil over medium-high in a large saucepan. Add the stock and 20 cups cold water. Bring to a boil, reduce to a simmer, and cook 30 minutes. Strain the stock into jugs or bowls and discard the vegetable peelings into the compost. Taste the broth and add just enough salt to begin to make a difference.

Add to the frying pan 2 tablespoons olive oil and sauté the onions until just brown. At this time, you can add the ginger and garlic.

Turn the onions into the large saucepan and set the heat on medium-low.

Now sauté each of the following ingredients, one at a time, until just colored, and tip onto the onions, mix, and let cook together.

This is the order of addition: rutabagas, turnips, carrots, sweet potatoes, parsnips, celery, and chard stalks.

Simmer the vegetables in the stock and add spice mix. Test the carrots after 25 minutes; when they are tender, the rest will be just right.

When done, remove 1 quart of the cooking liquid to a smaller pan, and add the slurry and parsley. Bring to a boil and continue boiling for 30 seconds, to clear the starch taste and thicken the stock. Pour this back into the main saucepan and stir well.

Count 1–1½ cups of the stew per head and add, if you wish, one of the following add-on garnishes. The remaining vegetables and their liquid can be spooned into 1-quart freezer bags, dated, and quick-frozen for later use.

When defrosted and reheated, you will need to repeat the cornstarch thickening to regain the texture and gloss (1 teaspoon per portion is enough).

Add-on Garnishes

1. Red kidney beans—add ¼ cup per serving.

Per serving: 139 calories, 2 g fat, 0 g saturated fat, 27 g carbohydrate, 5 g protein, 7 g dietary fiber, 274 mg sodium. Exchanges: 1 Starch, 2 Vegetable

2. Whole grains—cooked bulgur, quinoa, couscous, barley, or brown rice; add ½ cup per serving.

Per serving with brown rice: 194 calories, 2 g fat, 0 g saturated fat, 40 g carbohydrate, 4 g protein, 6 mg dietary fiber, 90 mg sodium. Exchanges: 1½ Starch, 2 Vegetable

3. Garbanzo beans—add ¼ cup cooked per serving.

Per serving: 157 calories, 2 g fat, 0 g saturated fat, 31 g carbohydrate, 5 g protein, 7 g dietary fiber, 264 mg sodium. Exchanges: 1 Starch, 2 Vegetable

4. Dried fruit—cranberries, raisins, dates, figs, apricots, plums, apples. Add ¼ cup per serving.

Per serving with raisins: 209 calories, 1 g fat, 0 g saturated fat, 50 g carbohydrate, 3 g protein, 6 g dietary fiber, 89 mg sodium. Exchanges: 2 Vegetable

5. Spices—cumin is especially nice, or try one of my Ethmixes (see page 286).

Per serving: 86 calories, 3 g fat, 0 g saturated fat, 18 g carbohydrate, 2 g protein, 4 g dietary fiber, 85 mg sodium. Exchanges: 2 Vegetable

6. Tofu—dice in 1-inch cubes, toss in brewer's yeast, and sauté; add 2 ounces per portion.

Per serving: 121 calories, 3 g fat, 0 g saturated fat, 19 g carbohydrate, 6 g protein, 4 g dietary fiber, 105 mg sodium. Exchanges: 2 Vegetable

Spinach

Spinacea oleracea

I planted my spinach in a partially shaded area (just behind the shed), and I'm so glad I did. We had a shockingly sunny summer for the Pacific Northwest, and with our long days, this made for bolting conditions for these tender plants.

Not only heat can cause bolting but also what I, as a Scot, call stingy planting... that is, planting too close together to maximize growth in a small space. Spinach really needs at least 4 inches clear space for air circulation and no more than 10 hours of sun a day. But even then, temperatures above 75°F are usually bad news, and shade is essential.

When harvesting, start with the outer leaves to encourage growth of the inner leaves and to promote air circulation. If you choose to cut the whole plant, do so 3 inches above soil level and it may grow back for you—mine didn't, but perhaps it was too hot.

I really enjoy these wonderfully flavored tender leaves in salads, especially along with strawberries—a lovely combination. Or I pour a stew or thick soup over a base of fresh leaves, which quickly wilt but still retain that beautiful color.

The Numbers

Dark green leaves are especially valuable from a nutritional standpoint, and spinach certainly delivers more than its fair share. The only possible caution is for those of us who think that one kidney stone is too many. (See also kohlrabi on page 164.)

For each 100 g raw (3.5 oz; 1 cup): 33 calories, 0 g fat, 0 g saturated fat, 4 g carbohydrate, 3 g protein, 2 g dietary fiber, 79 mg sodium

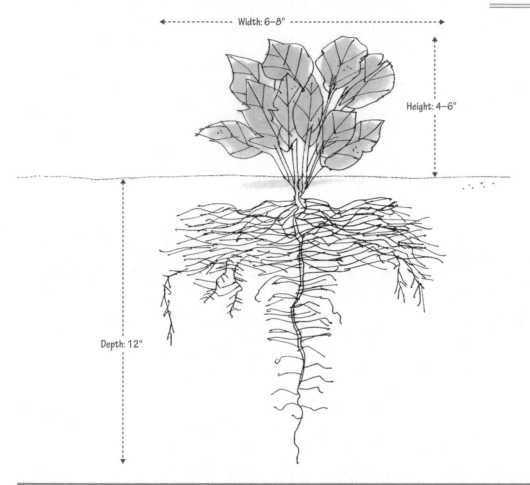

Width: 6–8"

Height: 4–6"

Depth: 12"

Annual
Water: Light/even, drip irrigation
Sun: Full; partial shade in hot weather
Companion Planting:
PRO: Beans, cabbage family, lettuce, onions, strawberries
CON: Any tall plant, including Brussels sprouts, pole beans, corn, rhubarb
Pests: Aphids, slugs, snails, cabbage loopers
Diseases: Curly top virus, spinach blight rust
Soil: Fine sandy soil, well drained
Fertilizer: Lots of compost; moderate nitrogen, phosphorus, potassium; fish emulsion every 1–2 weeks
pH: 6.0–6.8

Varieties: Olympia (for cool areas), Tyee (bolt resistant), Space (semicurly leaves). See also New Zealand spinach (page 192) for warm-weather planting.
Zones: 5–10
Planting: Early spring (4–6 weeks before last frost), when soil is workable; seed ¼ inch deep, 2 inches apart; thin to 4–6 inches to avoid bolting
Germinates: 6–14 days
Harvest: From seed, 40–60 days
Rotation: Don't follow legumes
Edible: Leaves

CRUSTLESS SPINACH RICOTTA QUICHE

This is a wonderful new way to enjoy spinach, and the presentation rivals a good small pizza.

SERVES 6

12 cups (a little more than 1 pound) well-
   washed fresh spinach or 1 (12-ounce)
   package frozen spinach, thawed
2 teaspoons olive oil
½ cup finely chopped onions
1 cup low-fat ricotta cheese
1 cup egg substitute* (or 4 whole eggs), beaten
½ teaspoon dried dill
¼ teaspoon salt
¼ teaspoon freshly ground black pepper
Pinch nutmeg
3 plum tomatoes, seeds and juice removed,
   chopped (yield 1 cup)
1 tablespoon freshly grated Parmesan cheese

I prefer Egg Beaters Southwestern Style.

Preheat the oven to 350°F. Grease a 9-inch pie plate or springform pan.

Steam the fresh spinach about 2 minutes until just wilted. Frozen spinach won't need to be cooked, just thawed. Press the water out of the cooked or thawed spinach and set aside.

Heat the oil in a small skillet over medium heat and cook the onions until soft but not brown. Combine the ricotta cheese, egg substitute, dill, salt, black pepper, and nutmeg in a large bowl. Add the spinach, tomatoes, and onions. Mix thoroughly and tip into the prepared pan.

Sprinkle Parmesan cheese over the top and bake about 30 minutes until set. Let the quiche cool in the pan for 5–10 minutes before slicing in wedges and serving.

Per serving: 102 calories, 4 g fat, 2 g saturated fat (18% calories from saturated fat), 7 g carbohydrate, 11 g protein, 2 g dietary fiber, 342 mg sodium. Exchanges: 1 Lean Meat, 1 Vegetable

SPINACH SAUTÉ ON RICE

Here we have an unusual fried-rice dish filled with aroma, color, and texture. It's almost a wilted salad. Use sun-dried tomatoes that are dry packed, not marinated in oil.

SERVES 4

2 bunches (about 12 ounces) spinach,
   stemmed and thoroughly washed
¼ cup sun-dried tomatoes
1 teaspoon olive oil
1 cup chopped onion
1 garlic clove, bashed and chopped
2 cups thick-sliced mushrooms (⅓ inch)
¼ teaspoon salt
¼ teaspoon freshly ground black pepper
2 cups cooked long-grain white rice
2 tablespoons toasted pine nuts

Cut the spinach leaves in ½-inch strips and set aside for later. Cover the sun-dried tomatoes with hot water and soak 15 minutes. Drain and chop.

Heat the oil in a high-sided skillet over medium-high. Sauté the onions 2 minutes. Add the garlic and reconstituted tomatoes, and cook 1 minute more. Stir in the mushrooms and cook 3–5 minutes until they begin to wilt.

Add the spinach, stirring to mix well. Cover and cook 3 minutes or until spinach wilts but is still bright green. Season with salt and black pepper and spoon over the rice. Scatter the pine nuts on top.

Per serving: 210 calories, 5 g fat, 1 g saturated fat (4% calories from saturated fat), 35 g carbohydrate, 9 g protein, 5 g dietary fiber, 285 mg sodium. Exchanges: 1 Starch, 2 Vegetable, 1 Fat

SZECHWAN SPINACH

A wilted spinach side dish with tremendous flavor.

SERVES 4

8 cups well-washed spinach leaves or 1
   (16-ounce) package frozen spinach, thawed
1 tablespoon low-sodium soy sauce
1 tablespoon rice vinegar
1 teaspoon sugar
1 teaspoon toasted sesame oil
Pinch of dried, crushed chiles
½ teaspoon finely chopped gingerroot
2 green onions (scallions), sliced

Place the spinach in a colander and pour boiling water over the top to wilt the leaves. Drain well.

Combine the soy sauce, vinegar, sugar, sesame oil, chiles, and ginger. Toss with the spinach and green onions to coat well. Stir over medium heat for 2–3 minutes.

Per serving: 38 calories, 1 g fat, 0 g saturated fat, 7 g carbohydrate, 2 g protein, 2 g dietary fiber, 407 mg sodium. Exchanges: 1 Vegetable

Squash (Summer)

Cucurbita pepo

Summer squash obviously love warm weather and warm soil from 65°F–85°F. In our climate, this was a stretch, so I invested in some green mulch plastic sheeting that I found in the Territorial Seed catalog (see References and Resources on page 303). You simply spread it out over the bed of well-composted soil and weigh it down carefully (gardening experts suggest using rebar steel). This keeps the weeds down and greatly increases soil temperature. Cut an X every 36 inches, stagger them across the bed, and plant good starts (grown indoors in at least 2-inch pots, 2 seeds per pot) very carefully (the roots are extremely tender) in each opening.

If you've got the space, they do really well when sown directly into a well-composted bank that inclines south and west, allowing 6 inches between seeds.

I love the way that three vegetables—squash, corn, and beans—can be grown together as the perfect example of a good community. The corn grows up on its own stake (stalk); the beans wrap their tendrils around the cornstalk and climb; the squash hugs the soil in between the cornstalks and keeps down the weeds. Of course, this is much harder to achieve with the plastic mulch and a cooler climate.

To this symbiotic group, add summer savory, which can keep the bean pests at bay and is also a great herb to add to squash, bean, and corn dishes. (I'm told that radishes also keep the bugs at bay. So now we've got five sisters: See what I mean about a community? The common good is the good we can do in common!)

Companion planting allows me to reinforce the idea of FABIS (fresh and best in season). FABIS applies especially when referring to foods that are harvested at the same time and that can be used in one dish, such as a ratatouille or succotash, to celebrate the season in a particular microclimate.

The Numbers

For each 100 g boiled (3.5 oz; ½ cup): 16 calories, 0 g fat, 0 g saturated fat, 4 g carbohydrate, 1 g protein, 1 g dietary fiber, 3 mg sodium

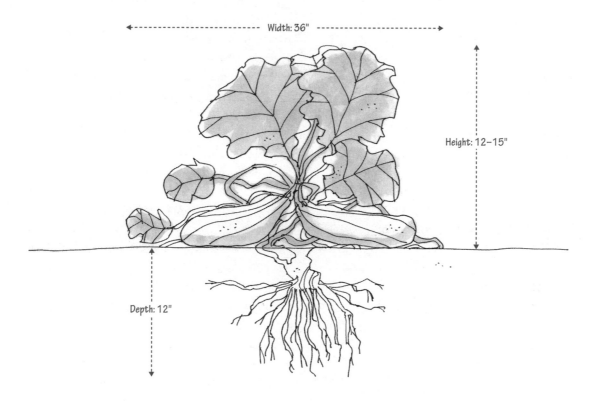

Width: 36"

Height: 12–15"

Depth: 12"

Annual

Water: Heavy, drip irrigation

Sun: Full

Companion Planting:

PRO: Celery, corn, onions, radishes, peas, beans

CON: Potatoes, pumpkins

Pests: Squash vine borers, squash bugs

Diseases: Mildews

Soil: Rich with humus and compost, good drainage

Fertilizer: High nitrogen, phosphorus, potassium

pH: 5.5–6.8

Varieties:

ZUCCHINI: Gold Rush, Space Master, Eight Ball (the latter is really odd: normally green but as round as a pool ball)

SCALLOP/PATTYPAN: Sunburst, Starship

CROOKNECK (YELLOW): Saffron, Horn of Plenty

Zones: 3–7 (for bush varieties); 6–10 (for vines)

Planting: Outdoors, when soil temperature reaches 70ºF; indoors, 3–4 weeks before last frost (2 seeds per 2-inch pot); seed ½–1 inch deep, 12–18 inches apart; thin to 36 inches

Germinates: 7–10 days

Harvest: From seed, 50–60 days

Rotation: Don't follow winter squash, cucumbers, melons

Edible: Fruit

BABY SQUASH SAUTÉ

SERVES 4

1 pound mixed baby squash, such as pattypan
   or yellow crookneck
½ teaspoon olive oil
1 teaspoon chopped garlic
¼ teaspoon salt
¼ teaspoon freshly ground black pepper
2 tablespoons chopped fresh parsley

Wash and trim off the stem end of the squash and dry on paper towels. Cut larger ones in half.

Heat the oil in a skillet over medium-high. Sauté the squash 6–8 minutes until tender. Stir in the garlic, salt, and black pepper. Cook 1 minute longer; sprinkle with the parsley and serve.

Per serving: 30 calories, 1 g fat, 0 g saturated fat, 4 g carbohydrate, 3 g protein, 1 g dietary fiber, 144 mg sodium. Exchanges: 1 Vegetable

FRITTATA PRIMAVERA

This is the same as an open-faced omelet with vegetables throughout. It's one of my favorite brunch meals.

SERVES 2

3 teaspoons olive oil
¼ cup chopped onion

1 garlic clove, finely chopped
½ cup asparagus pieces
½ cup pattypan or yellow crookneck squash
   pieces (½-inch pieces)
½ cup cut sugar snap peas, strings pulled
   (½-inch pieces)
¼ teaspoon dried basil or 1 tablespoon fresh
⅛ teaspoon freshly ground black pepper plus a
   pinch
¾ cup egg substitute*
1 tablespoon low-fat plain yogurt
1 tablespoon freshly grated Parmesan cheese

I prefer Egg Beaters Southwestern Style.

Heat 1 teaspoon of the oil in a 10-inch skillet and cook onion 2–3 minutes or until soft. Add the garlic and cook 1 minute more. Stir in the asparagus, squash, peas, basil, and black pepper, and cook, stirring occasionally, 3–5 minutes until tender but still slightly crisp. Set aside.

Preheat the broiler. Gently fold the egg substitute with the yogurt and another pinch of black pepper. Heat the remaining oil in a heavy-bottom, broiler-safe skillet. Pour in the egg mixture and cook 1 minute until just set on the bottom but still wet on the top. Scatter the vegetables over the top and set in the oven 4 inches from the heat to finish cooking, 2 minutes. Dust the top with Parmesan cheese, cut into wedges, and serve.

Per serving: 155 calories, 8 g fat, 2 g saturated fat (12% calories from saturated fat), 8 g carbohydrate, 12 g protein, 2 g dietary fiber, 234 mg sodium. Exchanges: 1 Very Lean Meat, 1 Vegetable, 2 Fat

STEAMED PATTYPAN

SERVES 4

4 pattypan squash (2½- to 3-inch diameter),
    cut in half top to bottom
¼ teaspoon salt
¼ teaspoon freshly ground black pepper
1 tablespoon chopped fresh basil or
    1 teaspoon dried

Lay the squash halves in a steamer and season with salt, black pepper, and basil. Steam over boiling water 6 minutes or until tender but still firm. A spritz of extra-virgin olive oil wouldn't hurt!

Per serving: 28 calories, 0 g fat, 0 g saturated fat, 6 g carbohydrate, 2 g protein, 2 g dietary fiber, 141 mg sodium. Exchanges: 1 Vegetable

ZUCCHINI FRITTERS

I adapted a classic fritter recipe to a pancake style so that it still delivers all the goodness of the vegetable without the added fat of deep-frying. This could become a great family favorite and can take the place of a starch.

SERVES 4

5 tablespoons pancake mix
¼ teaspoon freshly ground black pepper
¼ cup freshly grated Parmesan cheese
½ cup egg substitute or 2 eggs, slightly beaten
2 tablespoons chopped zucchini
2 tablespoons chopped sweet onion
2 tablespoons diced green chiles, such as
    Anaheim

Combine the pancake mix, black pepper, and Parmesan cheese in a bowl. Stir in the eggs. Add the zucchini, onion, and chiles, and stir to blend.

Heat a nonstick skillet over medium-high. Spray with olive oil cooking spray. Drop the batter into the hot pan with a large kitchen spoon (about ¼ cup). Fry on one side about 3 minutes, turn and cook about 3 minutes more or until the vegetables are tender.

Per serving (2 3-inch cakes) with egg substitute: 66 calories, 2 g fat, 1 g saturated fat (14% calories from saturated fat), 7 g carbohydrate, 6 g protein, 0 g dietary fiber, 271 mg sodium. Exchanges: ½ Starch, 1 Lean Meat

Squash (Winter)

Cucurbita maxima and *C. moschata*

I have two favorite winter squash: the butternut, for which I hunt down the ones with long, narrow (2- to 3-inch-diameter) necks, and the delicata, with its plump cucumber-like shape, yellow and green skin, and sweet pale orange flesh.

Germinating squash plants don't take kindly to frosts, so I kept my starters indoors until after Memorial Day and even then protected them with a glass cloche overnight until they got too big for their britches. You can also use the plastic milk jugs with the bottom cut off as an alternative but decidedly unattractive cloche!

Winter squash attract beetles and borers, so you should invest in row covers to protect them until the flowers bloom. (By the way, if you get a profusion of flowers, they can be dipped in a fine tempura batter and deep–fried, but frankly that's more for folks who love anything deep-fried, as I used to in times now long passed!)

My squash would have done much better if I'd slipped a plank under the just-forming fruit to lift it from the earth. (This coming year I shall try a robust trellis.)

For many people, the cutting up of winter squash can be daunting, especially the harder acorn or hubbard. One way to ease this is to use a microwave. Now here I hesitate to give specific times because ovens vary (and so do squash), so begin at high power for just 2 minutes. Using a large (12-inch) chef's knife, make an experimental cut. Another 2 minutes in the microwave may be needed to soften it up just enough to cut safely.

The Numbers

For each 100 g baked (3.5 oz; ½ cup): 37 calories, 0 g fat, 0 g saturated fat, 9 g carbohydrate, 1 g protein, 3 g dietary fiber, 1 mg sodium

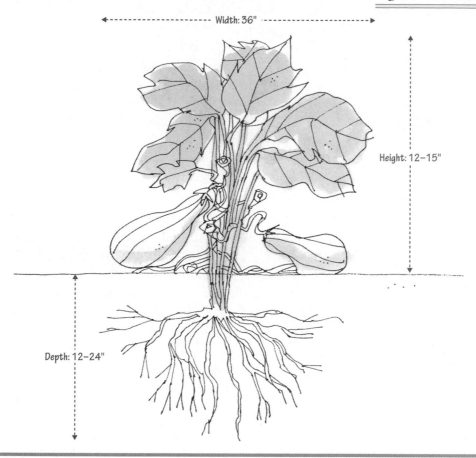

Width: 36"

Height: 12–15"

Depth: 12–24"

Annual
Water: Heavy, drip irrigation
Sun: Full
Companion Planting:
PRO: Celery, corn, onions, beans, peas
CON: Cabbage family, potatoes
Pest: Aphids, cucumber beetles, borers
Diseases: Mildews (downy and powdery)
Soil: Sandy loam, good drainage
Fertilizer: Compost well; high in nitrogen, moderate in phosphorus and potassium; nitrogen only up until flowers appear
pH: 6.5–7.0
Varieties:
ACORN: Heart of Gold, Tuffy

BUTTERNUT: Long Island Cheese
KURL: Uchiki Kuri
HUBBARD: Blue Ballet Delicata (small and sweet)
SPAGHETTI SQUASH
Zones: 3–10
Planting: Indoors, 3–4 weeks before last frost; seed ½–1 inch deep; transplant when soil is 65°F minimum to 2–3 inches; thin to 2–3 feet
Germinates: 4–10 days
Harvest: From seed, 60–100 days; from transplant, 60–80 days
Rotation: Don't follow summer squash, melon
Edible: Fruit

SQUASH (WINTER)

Basic Preparation

I like to use roasted rounds of butternut squash as a booster to modest portions of meat. Peel and cut the squash into even 1-inch disks and roast at 350°F for 45 minutes. Serve as a croûte (base) with smaller portions (about 4 ounces) of meat. The squash gives the traditional centerpiece of the dish greater prominence while reducing the actual amount of meat served.

BUTTERNUT SQUASH BAKED WITH TAMARI

This is an excellent excuse to use the great flavor of tamari, a smoother, more balanced, and more complex variation of soy sauce. It is available in the Asian section of most supermarkets.

SERVES 6

1 butternut or acorn squash, about 3 pounds
1 tablespoon low-sodium tamari or soy sauce
¼ teaspoon freshly ground black pepper

Preheat the oven to 350°F.

Cut the squash in half lengthwise. Scoop out and discard the seeds and pulp. Cut each half, again lengthwise, into 3 wedges. If you are using acorn squash, cut each half into 2 wedges.

Set the squash wedges in a 12-inch greased baking dish. Brush with the tamari and season with black pepper. Coat lightly with olive oil cooking spray. Bake 45 minutes or until the squash is soft. You can brush it with tamari once again before serving.

Per serving: 79 calories, 0 g fat, 0 g saturated fat, 20 g carbohydrate, 1 g protein, 5 g dietary fiber, 108 mg sodium. Exchanges: 1 Starch

BUTTERNUT SQUASH GINGER CHEESECAKE

Here is an unusual use for a vegetable and a kind of pumpkin pie alternative. Butternut squash is used for a molded cheesecake, which does a great job on Thanksgiving for a creative change.

SERVES 12

FOR THE FILLING
1 small butternut squash, cut in half and seeded
2 packets unflavored gelatin
½ cup water
¾ cup packed dark brown sugar
1½ cups 2% cottage cheese
½ teaspoon ground cinnamon
½ teaspoon ground ginger
¼ teaspoon ground cloves
¾ cup yogurt cheese (see page 290)

FOR THE CRUST
18 dried figs, stalk ends removed
1 cup broken ginger snap cookies

FOR THE GARNISH

1 tablespoon finely chopped crystallized
  ginger

Preheat the oven to 350°F.

Place the squash halves face down on a baking sheet and bake 40 minutes. Remove and let cool. Scoop out 2 cups of the flesh for this recipe and freeze the rest for future use.

While the squash is cooking, prepare the crust. Process the figs in a food processor for a few seconds, add the ginger snaps, and continue processing until the mixture clumps together in a sticky ball. Don't process too long or the cookies will lose their texture. Press the crust mixture into the bottom and up the sides of a lightly greased, high-sided, 7-inch springform pan. Dip your fingers into a bowl of cold water to alleviate any stickiness.

To finish the filling, sprinkle the gelatin over the water in a small saucepan and allow to soften for 1 minute. Warm over low heat, stirring, about 3 minutes until the gelatin is completely dissolved. Place the squash, gelatin mixture, and remaining filling ingredients in the food processor and whiz about 2 minutes or until smooth. Pour the filling into the prepared crust, pop it into the refrigerator, and chill about 3 hours or until set.

To serve, unmold the cake onto a platter and slice with a warm knife. Garnish each piece with some crystallized ginger.

Per serving: 181 calories, 2 g fat, 1 g saturated fat (5% calories from saturated fat), 36 g carbohydrate, 7 g protein, 3 g dietary fiber, 192 mg sodium. Exchanges: 1 Carbohydrate, 1 Lean Meat

Strawberry

Fragaria vesca and *F. virginiana*

Okay, so not every plant survived and bore fruit in my first year. My strawberries arrived as crowns (mother plants) obtained by a friend from a farmers market. I planted them in our EarthBoxes alongside some basil plants, the latter doing exceptionally well. The strawberries were not identified as a particular variety, although I suspect they were an alpine or wild strawberry that produces masses of pink flowers and rapidly growing runners. But after so much showing off, they delivered an extremely small collection of tiny *fraise des bois* that would have been a special treat if they'd had any flavor!

This coming year I'm setting them out with more space—12 inches in every direction—in a bed that had winter squash in year one. And I've chosen a variety that I hope will bear just enough to eat from spring through autumn, provided that I pinch off flowers and runners on a fairly consistent basis.

To get more fruit in less space, you can arrange the bed in a series of mounds 10 inches across and 12 inches apart and about 4 inches high. By doing this, you should get less vigorous runners, and the longer-lasting (day neutral) varieties should keep on producing berries all summer long.

Be sure to mulch with straw under the fruit and close to the roots to keep down root rot. (Could this be the derivation of the word *straw-berry*?) Pinch off early blooms and runners to increase the size of the fruit.

What appeals to me most—other than the flavor that I should get by growing my own—is that mine will be chemical free. Strawberries are one of the worst offenders in sucking up and retaining added inorganic materials.

The actual fruit of the strawberry are the tiny seeds. The cone-shaped berry is described as a false fruit—something like our economy when we get a bubble?!

So what if I got used to buying strawberries every time I shop, I just like them on my cereal along with blueberries. I don't really notice the cost, or even if they come from South America. I just like berries, even if they don't taste like our local varieties. However, have I lost the taste for what is fresh and best in season?

Answer: I could grow my own and eagerly anticipate the coming of each season and its special treats.

The Numbers

For each 100 g raw (3.5 oz; ½ cup): 32 calories, 0 g fat, 0 g saturated fat, 7 g carbohydrate, 1 g protein, 2 g dietary fiber, 1 mg sodium

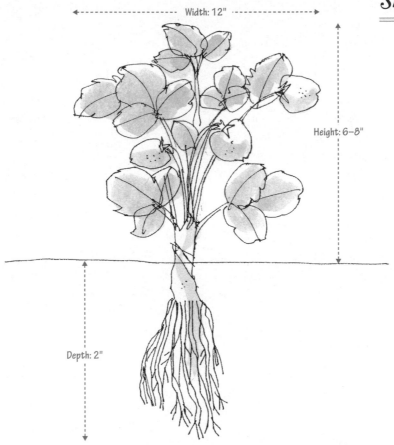

Width: 12"

Height: 6–8"

Depth: 2"

Perennial
Water: Moderate, drip irrigation
Sun: Full to partial shade
Companion Planting:
PRO: Melons
CON: Broccoli, cabbage family
Pests: Birds and mice
Diseases: Botrytis fruit rot, leaf scorch
Soil: Well drained, acidic
Fertilizer: Light nitrogen, phosphorus, and potassium; don't overfeed—tends to produce excessive growth that can lead to fruit rot
pH: 5.5–7.0
Varieties:
EVERBEARING (DAY NEUTRAL): Alexandria, Fort Laramie, Quinault (early summer through autumn)

SINGLE CROP: Allstar, Benton, Earliglow (late spring, early summer)
CULTIVATED WILD: Yellow Alpine, Pineapple Cross, Rugen
Zones: 3–10
Planting: Indoors, 8 weeks before setting out in spring; outdoors, after last frost; seed ⅛–¼ inch deep; crowns, just above soil level; 12–14 inches apart
Germination: 7–14 days
Harvest: June through September on West Coast; June to July on East Coast
Rotation: Don't follow beet, corn, tomato, pepper, pea
Edible: Fruit

STRAWBERRY SUNSHINE

The best way to enjoy the full riches of a home-grown, freshly harvested berry is to eat it by hand with a simple dip made of 1 cup of low-fat vanilla yogurt sweetened with 4 teaspoons of soft dark brown sugar.

Per ¼ cup serving of dip: 50 calories, 1 g fat, 1 g saturated fat (18% calories from saturated fat), 8 g carbohydrate, 3 g protein, 0 g dietary fiber, 40 mg sodium. Exchanges: ½ Carbohydrate

STRAWBERRY JALAPEÑO SALSA

SERVES 4

3 cups sliced fresh strawberries
1 apple, cored and chopped
1 jalapeño chile, chopped (leave the seeds in if you like it hot)
1 tablespoon packed dark brown sugar

Combine the strawberries, apples, jalapeño, and brown sugar. Serve immediately with cold meats.

Per serving: 73 calories, 0 g fat, 0 g saturated fat, 18 g carbohydrate, 1 g protein, 4 g dietary fiber, 1 mg sodium. Exchanges: 1 Fruit

TRIFLE-STYLE SUMMER PUDDING

Welcome to one of my childhood memories—a combination of two great English desserts.

SERVES 10

1½ cups fresh or frozen unsweetened raspberries
1½ cups fresh or frozen sliced rhubarb
1½ cups fresh or frozen unsweetened strawberries, sliced
1½ cups fresh or frozen blueberries
½ cup sugar
2 packets unflavored gelatin
3 tablespoons cold water
3 tablespoons boiling water
20 Italian ladyfingers (savoiardi)

FOR THE CUSTARD
3 tablespoons cornstarch
6 tablespoons sugar
2 cups 2% milk
1 teaspoon vanilla extract
1 cup egg substitute (or 4 egg yolks)

Combine the fruit in a large saucepan. Add the ½ cup sugar and bring just to a boil, to break out the juice and dissolve the sugar. Set aside to cool. Sprinkle the gelatin over the cold water in a small bowl to soften for a few minutes. Add the boiling water to completely dissolve the gelatin. Stir into the berries.

Arrange 2 ladyfingers in each of 10 individual stemmed dessert glasses. Divide the berry mixture among the glasses, with the cookies sticking upright. Leave about 1 inch space at the top of each dish for the custard.

To make the custard, combine the cornstarch and sugar in a small bowl. Stir in ½ cup of the milk to make a slurry. Heat the remaining milk in a heavy saucepan over medium-high until small bubbles form around the edge or a skin starts forming on the top. Add the slurry and vanilla, stirring constantly while it comes to a boil. Remove the pan from the heat, allow to cool slightly, and gently stir in the egg substitute. Pour the custard evenly over the berry mixture in each dish and chill 2 hours or more until set. Garnish with a mint sprig or an edible flower, such as a pansy or violet, if you wish.

Per serving: 204 calories, 2 g fat, 1 g saturated fat (4% calories from saturated fat), 41 g carbohydrate, 9 g protein, 3 g dietary fiber, 98 mg sodium. Exchanges: 2 ½ Carbohydrate, ½ Lean Meat

STRAWBERRY BANANA FRUIT LEATHER

Here's a way to create a healthy snack for the entire family that avoids the sometimes huge sugar content of commercial leathers.

SERVES 8

3 cups strawberries
1 ripe banana
2 tablespoons frozen orange juice concentrate
2 tablespoons honey
1 teaspoon freshly squeezed lemon juice

Line a 12×17×1-inch baking pan with plastic wrap.

Whiz the strawberries, banana, orange juice concentrate, honey, and lemon juice in a blender until very smooth. You can do this in batches if need be. You should have 2 cups of puree.

Preheat the oven to 140°F.

Pour the puree into the prepared pan and spread with a spatula, making the edges thicker than the middle. Bake with the oven door slightly open for about 6 hours or until just barely sticky. Cool, roll the long way, and cut into 8 2-inch pieces. Store in the fridge for up to a week—but your kids will probably eat it before the week is through.

Per serving: 71 calories, 0 g fat, 0 g saturated fat, 18 g carbohydrate, 1 g protein, 2 g dietary fiber, 2 mg sodium. Exchanges: 1 Fruit

Sweet Potato

Ipomoea batatas

We have lived in southern Texas (Kerrville—where else?) and in Arizona, and while we've enjoyed our days in the South, we wouldn't swap the Pacific Northwest summers with anyone, anywhere, *except* to have enough consistent warmth to grow sweet potatoes!

Notwithstanding this moderate temperature drawback, I'm going to risk growing these beauties next year because the process—described by my new pal Stephen Albert in his *Kitchen Garden Grower's Guide*—sounds like such fun (providing one has a small greenhouse). The big secret for cooler weather growth is to use what are called *dry varieties.*

Stephen recommends beginning with what he calls *slips* or *draws* or *seed roots*. You get these by putting a small sweet potato in a glass jar half filled with water, so that one third of the tuber remains under water. Put it in a sunny spot until it sprouts, keeping water at the same level. When the sprouts reach 6 inches, pull them off the bulb and set them in water (or a potting solution) or damp soil, to root and grow into a starter plant suited to transplanting at about 5 inches tall.

Harvest the tubers when the leaves go yellow. Dry them in the sun before storing at 55°F–60°F for 4–6 months.

Oh yes, and then there's the issue of what is the difference between a sweet potato and a yam?

A yam is, in fact, a different plant genus (*Dioscorea*) with a somewhat similar appearance. To add to the confusion, the *batatas* species from Peru via the Caribbean is often called a yam. The sweet potato is one of the Americas' greatest gifts to the world. Nutritious, delicious—surely it is the king, or perhaps queen, of all root vegetables.

The Numbers

For each 100 g baked (3.5 oz; ½ cup): 90 calories, 0 g fat, 0 g saturated fat, 21 g carbohydrate, 2 g protein, 3 g dietary fiber, 36 mg sodium

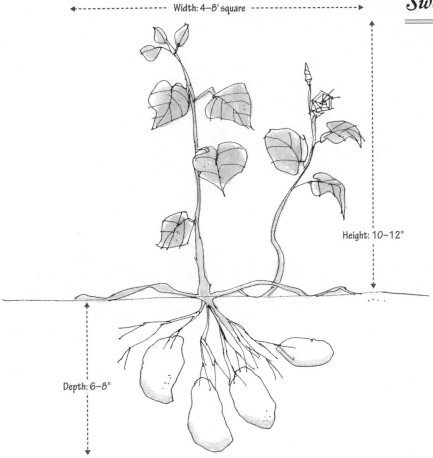

Width: 4–8' square

Height: 10–12"

Depth: 6–8"

Perennial/Annual/Warm Season

Water: Low

Sun: Full

Companion Planting:

PRO: Marigolds (this is a personal observation—seem to help ward off common pests)

CON: Beets, parsnips

Pests: Aphids, flea beetles, wire worms

Diseases: Fungus (black rot, root rot)

Soil: Well-drained sandy loam

Fertilizer: Good compost; low nitrogen, phosphorus, potassium (avoid high nitrogen—it pays the leaf and robs the root)

pH: 5.0–6.5

Varieties:

MOIST VARIETIES (WARM WEATHER): Allgold, Jewel, Vineless Puerto Rico (soft, sugary, yellow orange flesh)

DRY VARIETIES (COOLER WEATHER): Onokeo, Waimanalo Red, Yellow Jersey

Zones: 6–12

Planting: 2 weeks after last frost, when soil is at least 70°F–85°F; slips, 2–3 inches deep, 10–12 inches apart in raised ridges

Harvest: From slip, 150–175 days; from transplant, 100–125 days

Rotation: Don't follow other root crops; don't plant in same bed for 4 years

Edible: Swollen root (tuber)

BAKED SWEET POTATO MOUSSE

I concocted this combination of oranges, raisins, and allspice to complement, but not mask, the sweet potato's creamy sweetness. The result is akin to a delicately textured mousse packed with interesting flavors.

SERVES 6

¼ cup freshly squeezed orange juice
1 tablespoon raisins
3 tablespoons packed dark brown sugar
⅜ teaspoon ground allspice
2 pounds sweet potatoes, peeled and roughly chopped
⅛ teaspoon salt
½ cup yogurt cheese (see page 290)
½ teaspoon freshly grated orange zest
1 tablespoon slivered almonds

FOR THE GARNISH
Edible flowers, such as pansies, nasturtiums, and bachelor buttons

Preheat the oven to 400°F. Spray a 10-inch round ovenproof baking dish with cooking spray.

Warm the orange juice in a small saucepan over medium heat. Add the raisins, 2 tablespoons of the brown sugar, and ⅛ teaspoon of the allspice. Mix and set aside to let the raisins soak while the potatoes are cooking.

Put the potatoes and salt in a large saucepan, cover with water, and bring to a boil. Boil 15 minutes or until very soft. Drain the cooking liquid and return the potatoes to the pan. Cover the potatoes with a clean dishtowel and place over very low heat for 5–10 minutes or until the potatoes have a dry, floury appearance.

Mash with a potato masher and add the yogurt cheese, remaining ¼ teaspoon of allspice, and orange zest. Drain the raisins, reserving the liquid, and set aside to use for garnish. Add the liquid to the potatoes and stir until smooth.

Spread the mashed potatoes in the prepared baking dish. Press the potatoes with the tines of a fork to create a ridged texture, and sprinkle the top with the remaining 1 tablespoon of brown sugar and the almonds. Bake 15 minutes, until a thin-bladed knife will come out clean.

To serve, scoop a portion of the potato mousse onto a dessert plate and top with a few of the plumped raisins. Set an edible flower alongside.

Per serving: 231 calories, 1 g fat, 0 g saturated fat, 30 g carbohydrate, 2 g protein, 2 g dietary fiber, 92 mg sodium. Exchanges: 2 Carbohydrate

MASHED SWEET POTATOES

Some plants contain many calories and great nutrients. Because of this, a smaller portion can provide great benefits. You'll find this portion small but so delicious!

SERVES 4

4 small to medium orange sweet potatoes
2 teaspoons fresh thyme or ¾ teaspoon dried

¼ teaspoon salt
¼ teaspoon freshly ground black pepper

Peel and cut the sweet potatoes into ½-inch slices (you should have about 2 cups). Cook in a steamer over boiling water about 16 minutes until tender. When they are very soft, tip into a bowl and mash with a fork or potato masher. Stir in the thyme, salt, and black pepper, and serve.

Per serving: 99 calories, 0 g fat, 0 g saturated fat, 23 g carbohydrate, 2 g protein, 2 g dietary fiber, 59 mg sodium. Exchanges: 1½ Starch

Combine the seasonings in a small bowl and sprinkle over the top. Roast 30 minutes.

Per serving: 128 calories, 19 g fat, 0 g saturated fat, 28 g carbohydrate, 1 g protein, 4 g dietary fiber, 13 mg sodium. Exchanges: 1 Starch

SPICY ROASTED SWEET POTATO WEDGES

SERVES 4

1 pound orange sweet potatoes
½ teaspoon olive oil or olive oil cooking spray
¼ teaspoon ground cumin
¼ teaspoon mild chili powder
Dusting of smoked paprika

Preheat the oven to 350°F. Grease a baking sheet.

Peel the sweet potatoes and cut in thin wedges lengthwise. Place in the prepared pan and brush or spray with oil.

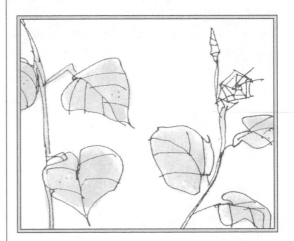

Tomato

Lycopersicon esculentum

If anyone ever needed a reason to grow their own kitchen garden, it would surely be to get a tomato that tastes truly wonderful: a combined sweetness with a balanced acidity and a glorious just-picked aroma, somewhat like a geranium in full flower.

Tomatoes are perennials but grown, for the most part, as annuals. And in our part of the world, growing them at all can be a problem because rainfall can cause heavy blight in the fall. Mine did very well, at least from my perspective, which is colored by never having grown one before.

The fabled Brandywine plant produced only three fruits—one ugly and two picture perfect and delicious. (Although I asked our local experts why this might be, I did not get any kind of meaningful answer.)

By far the best tasting was an orange cherry tomato called Sun Gold, which flourished and bore lots of fruit. Meanwhile, the small lemon yellow pear-shaped variety, Yellow Pear, split early, its skin too tender for its rapid growth.

The fruit of the plants nearest the evening sun, Early Girl, were large, deeply colored, and abundant.

The other plant I liked, Russian Paste, is useful for Italian plum-style (Roma) tomato sauces and for drying.

My greenhouse varieties didn't do as well as those set out in the raised beds with a sturdy trellis, where I warmed the soil using green plastic mulch. I let the greenhouse plants climb sticks and strings, but they quickly became home to hundreds of whiteflies, which I was told could be hosed off with a good pressure shower of fresh water. That technique worked for only a while and seemed to damage the lower leaves. Later I used diluted neem oil, which worked much better.

I had planted them too close to each other in the EarthBoxes and hadn't tapped them each day to self-pollinate.

In the coming years, I'm going to focus on three varieties: Brandywine, Sun Gold cherry, and Russian Paste. The latter two I will bring indoors (the greenhouse) and let them grow up a coarse garden string. And this time I will do better with daily tapping close to the flowers to help self-pollination (done by the wind and insects outside) and will diligently remove the suckers that grow out of the crotch of each leaf stem. (My pals tell me to do this once a week without fail and in that way concentrate energy toward the fruit.)

The Numbers

For each 100 g (3.5 oz; ½ cup): 18 calories, 0 g fat, 0 g saturated fat, 4 g carbohydrate, 1 g protein, 1 g dietary fiber, 5 mg sodium

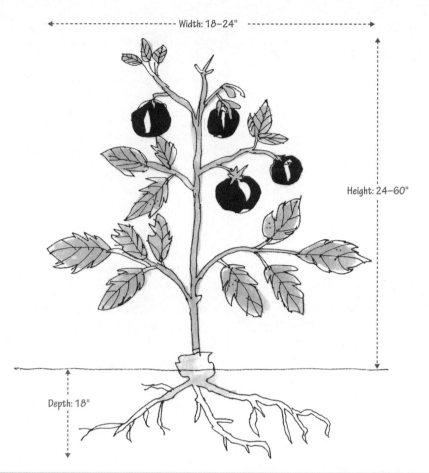

Width: 18–24"

Height: 24–60"

Depth: 18"

Tomato

Perennial/Annual

Water: 1–2 inches per week (light to moderate consistent drip irrigation)

Sun: Full (6 hours minimum)

Companion Planting:

PRO: Basil, cabbage family, garlic, onions

CON: Corn, dill, potatoes

Pests: Aphids, whiteflies, slugs, snails

Diseases: Alternaria, early blight; look out for resistance codes on seed packages or starts: *V*, Verticillium wilt; *F*, Fusarium wilt; *N*, nematodes; and/or *T*, tobacco virus

Soil: Light, loose, and with good drainage; add bonemeal to each planting hole

Fertilizer: High phosphorus, potassium; moderate nitrogen; fish emulsion every 3–4 weeks

pH: 5.5–6.8

Varieties: My picks for the home garden include Sun Gold (cherry tomato), Early Girl (for early harvest), Russian Paste (very dense flesh, few seeds good to make a paste), Viva Italia (blight-resistant hybrid, great for bottling and sauce making), and Brandywine (heirloom)

Zone: 3 and warmer

Planting: Seed ½ inch deep, indoors, allowing at least 12 inches for roots and around stem, 6–7 weeks before last frost, 18 inches apart; thin to 36 inches

Germinates: 5–7 days (best at 85ºF)

Harvest: From seed, 50–90 days

Rotation: Don't follow potato, eggplant, pepper

Edible: Fruit

FRESH TOMATO SOUP

SERVES 4

1 teaspoon olive oil
½ large yellow onion, chopped
1 garlic clove, crushed
1 teaspoon dried basil
1 teaspoon dried oregano
8 Roma tomatoes, cored, blanched, skinned, seeded, and chopped
1 cup water
¼ teaspoon salt

Heat the oil in a medium saucepan over medium-high. Sauté the onions, garlic, basil, and oregano for 5 minutes. Add the tomatoes, water, and salt. Bring to a boil, reduce the heat, and simmer 15 minutes. Don't sieve or puree; serve just as it is.

Per serving: 63 calories, 1 g fat, 0 g saturated fat, 9 g carbohydrate, 2 g protein, 2 g dietary fiber, 181 mg sodium. Exchanges: 2 Vegetable

GRILLED PORTABELLA MUSHROOMS WITH TOMATO JALAPEÑO SAUCE

This is one of my special-occasion side dishes, usually served with a red meat or game, but it could also become an appetizer with a watercress or arugula garnish.

SERVES 6

FOR THE MUSHROOMS

2 garlic cloves, bashed and finely chopped
¼ teaspoon cayenne
⅛ teaspoon ground allspice
¼ teaspoon salt
1 teaspoon olive oil
1 tablespoon freshly squeezed lemon juice
6 medium portabella mushrooms, cleaned with stems removed

FOR THE SAUCE

½ teaspoon light olive oil
2 cups roughly chopped sweet onion
3 jalapeño chiles, cored, seeded, and roughly chopped
6 small (or 4 large) Italian plum tomatoes, such as Roma, quartered
⅛ teaspoon salt
⅛ teaspoon ground allspice
1 bay leaf
1 tablespoon arrowroot mixed with ½ cup dealcoholized red wine or water (slurry)

Combine the garlic, cayenne, allspice, salt, olive oil, and lemon juice in a bowl. Place the mushrooms in a shallow dish and brush with the garlic mixture. Set aside while you make the sauce.

To make the sauce, warm the oil in a medium frying pan over medium heat. Sauté the onions 3–5 minutes until slightly browned. Stir in the jalapeños, tomatoes, salt, allspice, and bay leaf. Reduce the heat to low and cook 10 minutes. Press the tomato sauce through a sieve into a saucepan, discarding the pulp. Add the slurry to the sauce and stir over medium heat until thickened. Remove from the heat and keep warm until ready to serve.

Preheat the grill or broiler.

Grill or broil the mushrooms about 3 minutes per side. Cut the mushrooms into slices and fan out on 6 plates. Stir any juices from the broiler pan and cutting board into the tomato sauce. Spoon the sauce over the mushrooms.

Per serving: 90 calories, 0 g fat, 0 g saturated fat, 17 g carbohydrate, 5 g protein, 5 g dietary fiber, 261 mg sodium. Exchanges: 3 Vegetable

TOMATO AND SWEET CORN WITH BALSAMIC SAUCE

The classic salad uses tomato, basil, and mozzarella cheese. I've used fresh sweet corn as a colorful flavorful alternative to the higher fat mozzarella.

SERVES 6

FOR THE SALAD
2–3 ears fresh corn, shucked
3 large ripe tomatoes

FOR THE SAUCE
¼ cup unsweetened apple juice
2 tablespoons balsamic vinegar
¾ teaspoon arrowroot

FOR THE GARNISH
9 large basil leaves (to be sliced)
6 sprigs basil

To prepare the salad, drop the ears of corn into a pot of rapidly boiling water and cook 5 min-

utes. Remove from the heat and immediately immerse in ice water to chill. When cool enough to handle, cut the kernels from the cobs. Discard the cobs and refrigerate the kernels.

Core the tomatoes by cutting a shallow cone around the stem. Cut each tomato in half lengthwise, top to bottom, and lay the tomato halves, cut side down, on a cutting board. With a sharp knife held parallel to the cutting board, cut thin slices across each tomato from the blossom end toward the stem end, stopping just before you cut all the way through. Make about six slices, discarding the top slice, which is completely covered with skin. Repeat with all tomato halves and set aside until ready to serve.

To prepare the sauce, combine the apple juice, vinegar, and arrowroot in a small saucepan. Stir over medium-high heat until the sauce thickens and turns glossy. Set aside to cool.

To serve, scatter the corn on individual salad plates. Lay a tomato half in the center of each plate and press down gently to fan out the slices. Drizzle about 1 tablespoon of the sauce over each tomato. At the last minute, slice the basil leaves into thin strips and sprinkle over top of each plate. Lay a sprig of basil at the base of the tomato fan.

Per serving: 67 calories, 0 g fat, 0 g saturated fat, 16 g carbohydrate, 2 g protein, 2 g dietary fiber, 10 mg sodium. Exchanges: ½ Starch, 1 Vegetable

Turnip

Brassica rapa var. *rapa*

I've had great blessings in my professional life both on and off television. First has been Treena and her production skills, and second has been every one of my food assistants, from Barbara to Patricia to Anne to Robert and finally to Suzanne Butler, with whom I've made more than a thousand television shows.

I mention this because turnips were what brought Suzanne's remarkable gifts to my attention!

I visited her small-town deli called Red Bread back in the early 1990s. She was reserved at first but then revealed the object of her unreserved enthusiasm: the first of the season's young, tender turnips. I remember her face flushed with delight, and I was equally taken aback. I'd *never* considered a turnip as worthy of such unbridled praise!

Therefore, how could I have a kitchen garden without turnips?

Turnips can be started in early spring, when the soil is at least 40°F. With 12-inch leaves and a 2- to 3-inch root in 30 days, you can easily go for a second and even third planting to coincide with the early winter frost, when they are at their very best and sweetened by their exposure to the cold.

After my first season, I discovered the sensational Tokyo Kobaku variety—those smooth, white, golf-ball-size orbs of flavor that are truly excellent.

Just one added note: when making a truly great vegetable stock, always add turnip, as its flavor makes a remarkable contribution to the stock.

The Numbers

For each 100 g boiled (3.5 oz; ½ cup): 20 calories, 0 g fat, 0 g saturated fat; 4 g carbohydrate, 1 g protein, 4 g dietary fiber, 29 mg sodium

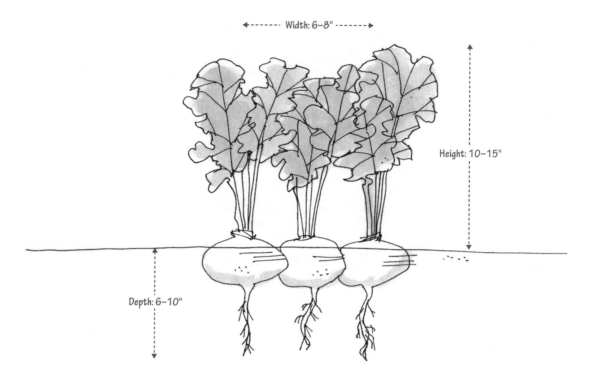

Width: 6–8"

Height: 10–15"

Depth: 6–10"

Biennial/Annual/Cool Season
Water: Moderate
Sun: Full to light shade
Companion Planting:
PRO: Bush beans, peas, tomatoes, peppers
CON: Potatoes
Pests: Cabbage root maggots, aphids
Diseases: Few and quite rare
Soil: Loamy soil with good drainage
Fertilizer: Compost with green manure; bonemeal/phosphorus to increase yield; low nitrogen, phosphorus, potassium
pH: 5.5–6.8

Varieties: De Milan (early), Purple Top White Globe (heirloom/winter crop), Tokyo Kobaku (small white)
Zones: 3–12
Planting: Early spring, 4–6 weeks before first frost; seed ½ inch deep, 2 inches apart; thin to 8 inches
Germinates: 3–10 days
Harvest: From seed, 30–50 days; best when greens are 12 inches and the root 2–3 inches; can be kept in the ground at 35°F–80°F, but only those planted for winter crop; spring plants must be taken young (30–40 days)
Rotation: Don't follow cabbage family
Edible: Root and leaves

PUREED ROASTED TURNIPS

Roasting gives turnips an extra sweetness (less moist). This is quite an unusual treat—especially with the smoked paprika and parsley for both color and flavor.

SERVES 4

6 medium turnips, peeled and cut in quarters
Salt and black pepper to taste
Chopped fresh parsley to taste
Dusting of smoked paprika

Preheat the oven to 375°F.

Set the turnip wedges in a baking pan and coat lightly with olive oil cooking spray. Roast 30 minutes or until soft. You can season with a little salt and black pepper and serve them whole as a vegetable side dish. Or puree them and use as a thickener for a soup or stew. Whether serving whole or pureed, garnish with parsley and paprika.

Per serving: 33 calories, 0 g fat, 0 g saturated fat, 8 g carbohydrate, 2 g protein, 2 g dietary fiber, 78 mg sodium. Exchanges: 1 Vegetable

SCOTTISH IRISH VEGETABLE STEW

The traditional Scottish Irish stew is made with lamb but also features all of the vegetables that I've chosen to include in this version. When removing the meat, there is a great need for added robust flavor—and the turnip becomes essential.

SERVES 6

4 small (2-inch-diameter) turnips, cut into ½-inch pieces
2 tablespoons tamari
1 teaspoon olive oil
1 medium onion, coarsely chopped
1 pound parsnips, cut into 2-inch pieces
1 pound yellow potatoes, peeled and cut into ½-inch pieces
2 medium carrots, peeled and cut into ½-inch pieces
18 small boiling onions, blanched and peeled
½ cup pot barley
½ teaspoon freshly ground black pepper
5 cups low-sodium vegetable stock (see page 288)
18 whole white mushrooms, to match onion size
1 pound fresh spinach leaves, washed and stemmed

Sprinkle the turnips with the tamari; let set for 15 minutes.

Heat the oil in a high-sided skillet over medium. Sauté the chopped onion 1 minute. Add the turnips, potatoes, carrots, boiling onions, and parsnips. Sauté 4 minutes; browning is not necessary. Add barley and black pepper, and pour in the stock. Bring to a boil and simmer 40 minutes, until carrots are tender. Stir in the mushrooms and cook 5 minutes more.

Line 6 bowls with raw spinach leaves, pointed end up. Ladle the stew into the lined bowls and serve.

Per serving: 273 calories, 2 g fat, 0 g saturated fat, 59 g carbohydrate, 5 g protein, 18 g dietary fiber, 200 mg sodium. Exchanges: 3 Vegetable, 1 Starch

and blend at high speed. Stir the puree into the reserved liquid. Freeze in 1-cup freezer bags.

Per serving: 40 calories, 1 g fat, 0 g saturated fat, 8 g carbohydrate, 1 g protein, 2 g dietary fiber, 53 mg sodium. Exchanges: 3 Vegetable

VEGETABLE PUREE

Because this puree delivers what I call "lay-ered" flavors, it adds greatly to simple stews, soups, and sauces by enhancing both taste and texture. I usually use it 1 cup at a time—and freeze the rest in 1-cup containers.

MAKES 4 1-CUP SERVINGS

1 teaspoon nonaromatic olive oil
1½ cups chopped onion
2 garlic cloves, bashed and chopped
1 teaspoon grated gingerroot
1 cup chopped carrots
1 cup chopped celery
3 medium turnips (¾ pound each), peeled and chopped
2 sprigs parsley
¼ teaspoon freshly ground black pepper
5 cups water

Heat the oil in a Dutch oven over medium-high. Sauté the onion 2 minutes. Add the garlic and ginger, and cook 1 minute more. Toss in the carrots, celery, turnips, parsley, and black pepper.

Pour in the water. Bring to a boil, reduce the heat, and simmer 25 minutes or until the vegetables are tender. Drain the vegetables, reserving the liquid. Place the vegetables in a blender

The Herb Garden

You will find no surprises in my initial herb selection. To venture beyond the traditional list is to throw the door open to a bewildering array of herbs, many quite unsuited to the kitchen. These, then, are culinary and often used in popular recipes.

My herbs grow outside the "critter defenses" and predate the new garden by more than five years. Our ever-present rabbits, deer, and moles have left these plants alone, so we have set aside a partly shaded morning sun area, and everything except basil has thrived. (Basil needs full sun all day in a wind-sheltered spot.)

The soil is a fertile mix of sand and clay loam, without any added compost. The pH is 6.5, which, I was told, is perfect for most herbs. I've added a swift spray of fish-based liquid fertilizer once a month as a *side* dressing (not *on* the plants).

After the last frost in the spring, I divided the clumps and set them apart to gain both air circulation and root space. When they got too big, I transplanted some into small pots to give away. I leave the watering to once a week and take that day to check for weeds.

All the taller herbs are at the back and graduate toward the "ground huggers" in the front, so nothing is overshadowed. I found some beautifully colored and naturally textured flagstones, and divided up the herbs with these natural stone barriers. They provide a sure-footed walkway on rainy days.

The whole herb garden is close to the kitchen door and well lit, in case I need a last-minute picking on a pitch-dark night!

As to their use?

Fresh-snipped herbs go brilliantly in both salads and soups, and as a garnish to almost everything. Herbs are not unlike perfumes in their appeal—some you'll love, others not so much. Only through use will you get the needed confidence to use them abundantly and well!

One very important use is to see them as a partial replacement for salt, with or without citrus and berry fruits and their juices. All of us can do better by reducing salt (sodium) content, and the best solution that I know of is to use herbs, citrus, and spices to add aroma, texture, and taste to foods that normally seem to attract liberal salting.

I have also sown edible flowers among my herbs to add both color and taste to dishes. I grow these in the main fenced garden, again for colorful splashes, because I like to break up the sense of order that comes with carefully planted rows of vegetables as well as attract bees and butterflies.

Basil

Ocimum basilicum

The powerful aroma from this luscious salad herb is one of the reasons I had to grow it. Then there's that clove/anise flavor and its ease of germination and early growth in the greenhouse—although a sunny window box will do just as nicely. I waited for 70°F soil temperatures before setting it out in raised beds.

We did a couple of EarthBoxes with four small plants a side that eventually filled the boxes to overflowing. We had a warm summer, and the basil plants became a little long-legged and began to flower early. Because this means losing some of the volatility of the leaves, I made it a daily practice to nip the flowers in the bud.

Don't put the plants out too early, and do give them the sunniest most sheltered spots—both in the herb garden and around the garden alongside some of your edible flowers.

I harvested the lot in late August and made up some pesto in bulk, using 2 cups basil, ¼ cup pine nuts, 4–6 garlic cloves, and ¼ cup grapeseed oil, which I whizzed together until relatively smooth in a food processor. I froze the pesto in ice cube trays (1 tablespoon a cube) to defrost and mix with extra-virgin olive oil and good grated Parmesan cheese for pasta dishes. I use about 1 tablespoon of pesto for each portion of pasta.

When we don't make our own bread (which is mostly the case nowadays), we buy Health Nut (whole-grain bread) and make sandwiches with goat cheese, basil leaves, and sun-ripened vine tomatoes seasoned with sea salt and freshly ground white peppercorns—it's hard to imagine anything better!

Whenever I make a vegetable stir-fry, I'll scatter in a cupful of basil leaves *just before* serving to keep their aroma intact.

Unless a recipe calls for the leaves to be sliced, as in a chiffonade (very finely diced), simply tear them apart, because the pressure of the blade will crush the sensitive leaf, and it blackens quickly. Torn leaves retain their color much longer, but you still need to leave this step until the last possible moment.

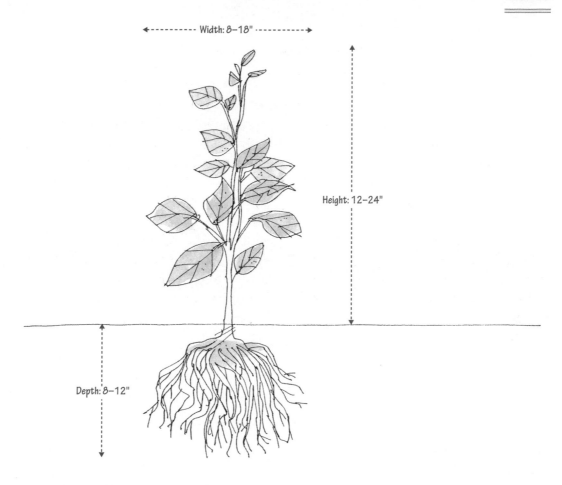

Width: 8–18"

Height: 12–24"

Depth: 8–12"

Annual/Warm Season
Water: Light
Sun: Full
Companion Planting:
PRO: Tomatoes, peppers
CON: Cucumbers, snap beans
Pests: Slugs, snails
Diseases: Botrytis
Soil: Rich humus
Fertilizer: Low feeder
pH: 6.0–6.5

Varieties: Genovese (green leaf), Dark Opal (purple leaf), and a wide variety of scented culinary basil, including lemon and cinnamon
Zones: 4–10
Planting: Seed ⅛ inch deep, 10 inches apart
Germinates: 7–14 days
Harvest: 50–60 days
Rotation: Don't follow marjoram or oregano (keep them apart in the bed)
Edible: Leaves

Chive

Allium schoenoprasum and A. *tuberosum* (garlic chive)

I've had an untidy clump of chives that has been struggling in the midst of a sea of dandelions for 7 years. They'd still come up regardless of frost, snow, and below-zero periods, but they didn't look very *happy* until I learned of their need to be divided every 3 years. So in the fall I dug them up, used pruning shears to cut vertically through the shallow roots, and spread out my clump into six parts, set 6–8 inches apart.

This year I'm going to companion plant the chives with carrots, which I'm told will help the carrots avoid a common fungus. In any event, the idea of purple chive blossoms bobbing about in a bed of bright green carrot tops seemed too good to pass up.

I've had two types of chives for years: the one with purple flowers and thin, empty stems (Ruby Gem), and the larger solid strap-like stemmed garlic (Chinese) chive, with a pure white edible flower that really has a garlic lilt to its taste.

I use both types in mixed-egg dishes: scrambled, omelets, frittatas, and even savory pancakes. Another major use is with pasta and potatoes as a final garnish. The garlic chive is especially good with pasta and makes a brilliant addition to an otherwise all-green salad.

The fine, slim, bright green stalks are a perfect garnish to elegant Asian-styled dishes, where there's a lot of open plate space; just two chive stems casually crossed can say more than words will ever say about your ability to finish in beauty.

And while on the subject of beauty, I happened across an unusual companion planting suggestion: chives flourish in the company of roses. Since making this discovery, I intend to try this myself and find yet another reason to see plants as a kind of community that celebrates diversity.

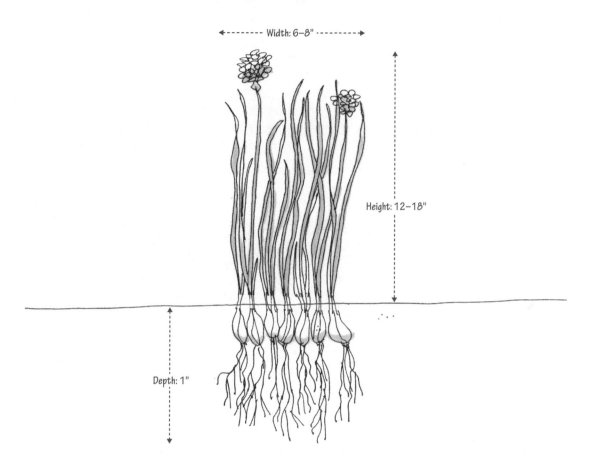

Width: 6–8"

Height: 12–18"

Depth: 1"

Perennial
Water: Low
Sun: Part
Companion Planting:
PRO: Tomatoes, peppers, carrots, roses
CON: Beans, peas
Pests: None
Diseases: Fungus
Soil: Good humus content, well drained
Fertilizer: Fish fertilizer 2–3 times a year

pH: 6.0–7.0
Varieties: Ruby Gem (purple), Forescate (red flowers), Chinese (garlic; white)
Zones: 3–9 (garlic chive, 4–8)
Planting: Seed ½ inch deep, thin to 6 inches apart
Germinates: 7–14 days
Harvest: From seed, 75–90 days
Rotation: None (except for dividing every third year)
Edible: Stems and flowers

Cilantro

Coriandrum sativum

Now here's the plant that some love and some hate; the haters declare that it tastes like soap—or even bugs, although I would be hard-pressed to find anyone who could legitimately make that comparison!

To be fair, it does have a strange, somewhat unattractive aroma in its early leaf form, before it goes to seed and produces the extraordinary spice seed *coriander*, which is widely used in curry powders.

I've become a fan through an appreciation of Tex-Mex foods as well as classic Mexican dishes, where cilantro plays a major part both as a garnish and in great fresh salsas.

Just squeezing a fresh lime (or Meyer lemon) over a quartered avocado and sprinkling it with chopped cilantro is enough to justify a valued spot in the herb garden.

In late summer, as the seeds form, you can bind a bunch together and place them upside down in a large jar and let the whole thing dry out. The coriander seeds drop off the drying plant, and you've got your second harvest—the spice coriander.

You can also dig up the roots, dry them, and whiz them up into a powder just before using them to flavor soups and sauces. The aroma is remarkably complex and a great mystery waiting to challenge your gourmet friends: "And now . . . which herb did I use to flavor this?" I can almost guarantee they won't get it!

Try coriander seeds freshly ground (treated like peppercorns in the peppermill) over beets, onions, potatoes, and lentils. (Lentils are a superb high-fiber food, and by adding ground coriander and garnishing with the fresh leaves, we may have found a perfect starch dish for those who live with diabetes!)

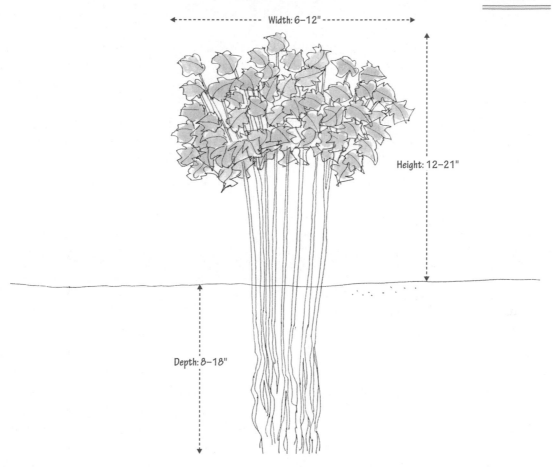

Width: 6–12"

Height: 12–21"

Depth: 8–18"

Annual/Hardy
Water: Lightly drip irrigation; earth needs to be moist
Sun: Full
Companion Planting:
PRO: Fruit trees
CON: None
Pests: None
Diseases: None
Soil: Rich humus, well drained
Fertilizer: Very low feeder; don't add nitrogen, which causes plants to grow more and yield less flavor

pH: 6.0–6.7
Varieties: Santo (slow to bolt)
Zones: 2–9
Planting: Outdoors after last frost; seed ½ inch deep, 2 inches apart; thin to 6–8 inches
Germinates: 7–10 days
Harvest: 65–75 days; may need a light fabric shade in hot weather; best when 6-inch stems
Rotation: None
Edible: Leaves, stems, roots (dried and ground) and seeds (coriander)

Mint

Mentha suaveolens (apple mint); *M. × gracilis* (golden apple mint)

Queen Elizabeth I of England delivered an edict that every Englishman that partakes of sheep meat shall take with it a bitter herb as a penance. The herb selected was mint.

At the time, there was a brisk and profitable export trade in wool, but apparently the Brits had taken a fancy to lamb and were upsetting exports by putting the cart before the horse, so to speak!

Eating mint, which is an excellent digestive, is fine with the stronger-flavored, less tender mutton, but mint with lamb, especially when pickled in malt vinegar, wasn't only a penance—it was in one fell stroke the best example of how *not* to use herbs.

An herb, of any kind, is culinary perfume. Its purpose is to complement but never overwhelm the main ingredient. Mint goes well with beans, carrots, eggplant, potatoes, and peas.

In the herb garden, you must take steps to control mint's invasive nature. We put bricks ends down (to about 12 inches) to create a defined box just 2 feet square—quite enough for our purposes. You can also cut it right back in midsummer for a lovely fresh fall-to-winter crop.

Divide the plant in spring and autumn. Stem cuttings root easily in vermiculite—keep good air space or ventilation.

I listed two mint species by their botanical names in the header to this description, but I would be remiss not to include some exotic mints that you may wish to try in your garden. Peppermint and spearmint are obvious, but much less likely is the extraordinary chocolate mint (*Mentha × piperita* 'Chocolate') and bergamot mint (also called orange mint), which is remarkable when served as a garnish to iced tea.

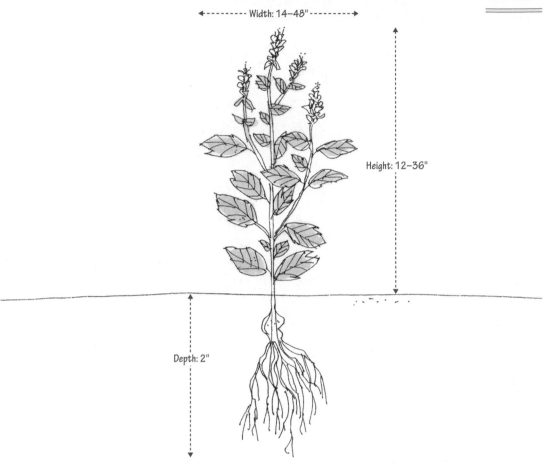

Width: 14–48"

Height: 12–36"

Depth: 2"

Perennial
Water: Moist but not soaked
Sun: Full
Companion Planting:
PRO: Peppers, tomatoes
CON: None
Pests: Aphids
Diseases: Verticillium wilt
Soil: Common garden soil is fine
Fertilizer: Low feeder
pH: 6.0–7.0
Varieties: Apple mint (*Variegata*), pineapple mint,

golden apple mint, Vietnamese mint (good for food), chocolate mint, bergamot (orange) mint
Zones: 5–9
Planting: Seed ¼ inch deep in spring; from root stem-tip cuttings in water or moist soil, spring to summer
Germinates: 7–10 days (seeds)
Harvest: 60 days
Rotation: Permanent (sometimes you wish it was not!)
Edible: Leaves

Nasturtium and Edible Flowers

Tropaeolum majus

Have you ever wondered how botanists come up with such extraordinary and mostly unpronounceable names for plants? I've finally come upon one I get, and it's almost humorous!

Nasus tortus, one name given to the nasturtium, means "convulsed nose" and refers to that odd-shaped beak of a flower that droops backward to the soil. My convulsed nose did brilliantly at the sunny end of a row of cabbages, flanked on either side with green onions, like organic sentries. I separated the cabbage from the nasturtiums with a buffer zone of mesclun lettuce, basil, and arugula.

I love the flat disc leaves for their peppery almost arugula taste, and the flowers dress a salad or garnish a main dish brilliantly with yellow, orange, and red shades. The droopier or longer the nose, the sweeter the flower. Very long ones can garnish a dessert.

It's just one of several edible flowers that you might want to plant in the odd bare patch throughout your raised beds—just to get some splashes of natural color amid all the greens.

Nasturtium does have the reputation for attracting aphids, which is actually not such a bad thing if you can get them all in one place (like having a Starbucks for aphids). At least it'll keep them out of my tea shop!

I did a whole border of alyssum around the tomatoes and peppers and basil, which wound up keeping the lower hanging fruit from touching down in the dirt!

This coming year, I'm setting out a range of edible flowers that will include pansies, begonias, calendula, daisies, geranium (I use the leaves only), Johnny-jump-ups, lavender, marigold, and an old-fashioned deep red rose (it makes an intriguing jam).

It seems that many flowers work, but only a few should not be eaten, including lily-of-the-valley, sweet pea, oleander, and foxglove. Please check first to ensure that a flower is, indeed, edible, and never eat anything that has been grown or protected by inorganic chemicals.

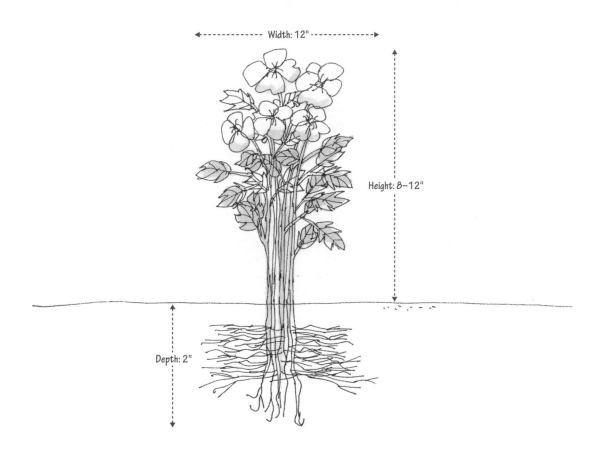

Width: 12"

Height: 8–12"

Depth: 2"

Annual
Water: Moist, not saturated
Sun: Full
Companion Planting:
PRO: Good for most plants (attracts aphids away from tomatoes)
CON: Cabbage family
Pests: Cabbage maggots, flea-beaten aphids
Diseases: None
Soil: Sandy loam, well drained
Fertilizer: Light fertilizer at planting; don't compost heavily

pH: 6.2–6.8
Varieties: Copper Sunset
Zones: 5–10
Planting: Seed 1 inch deep, 2–3 inches apart, after last frost
Germination: 9–12 days
Harvest: 50 days
Rotation: Avoid following cabbage family
Edible: Leaves and flower

Oregano

Origanum vulgare; O. × *hirtum*

There is some confusion about two commonly used herbs that crop up in hundreds of Mediterranean-style dishes: marjoram and oregano.

They are almost interchangeable in the way they are used in cooking and how they are grown. However, oregano tends to be more assertive—and, for some, almost harshly so. As a result, it's often called wild marjoram. It grows prolifically on the barren stony Greek mountainsides and takes its name from *oros*, meaning "mountains," and *ganos*, "meaning joy."

When tasted side by side with oregano, marjoram is less powerful and, if anything, slightly sweet. Unlike its heartier cousin, it grows amid lush pastures and is often called pot marjoram because of its use bunched with other herbs in meat and poultry stews.

I tend to use oregano in Italian and Greek dishes and marjoram in southern French and Spanish recipes, but frankly the two are, for all practical purposes, the same.

One way to think about both of them is their FABIS factor. They tend to come up fresh and best in season alongside tomatoes, sweet bell peppers, and eggplant, so it's no surprise that local folks in these regions put them together and created special recipes that have become justifiably famous: Provençal basquaise (marjoram), marinara sauce (oregano), and so on.

I grow oregano and marjoram as far apart as possible in my herb garden to reduce the risk of cross-pollination. While the mild differences between the two may seem like splitting hairs, for me discovering and distinguishing these subtle differences is what's such fun!

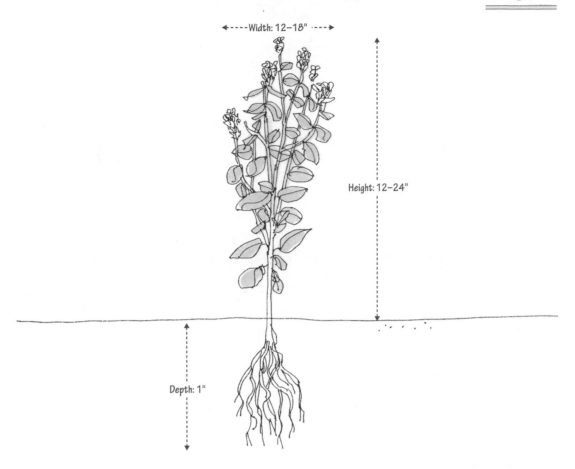

Width: 12–18"

Height: 12–24"

Depth: 1"

Perennial/Hardy
Water: Light
Sun: Full
Companion Planting:
PRO: All vegetables
CON: Not close to marjoram
Pests: Aphids
Diseases: Root rot
Soil: Well drained
Fertilizer: Low compost; fish emulsion 2–3 times per season
pH: 6.0–7.0

Varieties: Aureum (creeping gold), Kaliteri (silver, gray leaves, spicy taste), White Anniversary (tender for sauces)
Zones: 5–9
Planting: Seed (indoors on soil surface) 4 weeks before last frost, then set out after last frost; thin to 18 inches
Germinates: 10–21 days
Harvest: From seed, 50–60 days
Rotation: None (perennial)
Edible: Leaves and flowers

Parsley

Petroselinum crispum (curly leafed); *Petroselinum crispum* var. *neapolitanum* (flat-leafed Italian)

In my earlier professional kitchen days, a chef asked me to chop some. I busily picked off the curly tops when he yelled, "It's parsley, not a poodle!" I replied, "This is how our chef instructor at Brighton Tech School for Hotel Management told us how to do it."

The next moment there was a swish and a dull thud, and a 12-inch carbon steel Sabatier knife buried itself in the wooden kitchen wall just above my head. "I said chop it," yelled the chef, who I later learned had been a circus knife thrower. I chopped at lightning speed and have never looked back.

One little trick: when you're done chopping a small heap—say 1 cupful—put it in a dry cloth towel, screw it up in a ball shape and run it under cold water, wring every last drop out of it and turn the bright green flecks into a small bowl, then leave it to dry out in the refrigerator, where it's easy to get at for garnishes.

As a garnish, I use the flat-leaf Italian parsley as uncut sprays and the curly as chopped. The stalks of both finely chopped are a fine addition to omelets and scrambled eggs.

Now for the garden! Parsley isn't easy to start from seed; in fact, some old wives' tales suggest that it "Goes down to the devil seven times before it comes up."

It does, in fact, take almost as many weeks to germinate (5–6 weeks), but it can be hastened with an overnight soak in warm water, and it's useful to use a thermal insulated mug to retain the warmth.

I've learned to keep a pair of garden scissors in a lidded plastic container in the herb garden for ready use. It really does pay to snip all herbs and not tear or bend and break their stems. As with other leafy plants, always cut from the outside, 2–3 inches up from the soil, and the center will gain from the extra energy. You'll notice a tall flower stalk developing; cut this as it forms—you want leaves, not flowers.

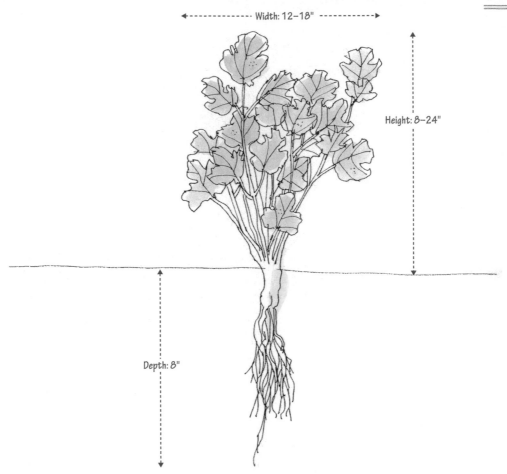

Width: 12–18"

Height: 8–24"

Depth: 8"

Biennial/Annual
Water: Keep moistened, occasional watering in dry conditions
Sun: Full
Companion Planting:
PRO: Sweet corn, peppers, tomatoes
CON: Carrots, celery
Pests: Loopers, mites
Diseases: None
Soil: Sandy loam, well composted, good drainage
Fertilizer: Heavy feeder; fish emulsion 3 times per season

pH: 5.5
Varieties: Giant of Naples (flat leaf), Moss Curled (curly leaf)
Zones: 2–10
Planting: Seed ¼ inch deep, thin to 8 inches; early spring before last frost
Germinates: 35–42 days
Harvest: From seed, 70–90 days
Rotation: Keep location for annual use
Edible: Leaves and stalks

Rosemary

Rosmarinus officinalis

Rosemary is one of my all-time favorites, and fortunately, it grows abundantly around our house. Yet there is an old wives' (not husbands') tale about this herb: if it grows well, then the wife is the one in charge.

Our plants grow tall and wide, so they are placed at the back of the herb patch. Like other pungent herbs, this one repels small insects, butterflies, carrot flies, and ticks. So you may want to plant a couple of starts in your raised-bed areas at one end on the north or east side, so that their size doesn't rob other plants of the sun.

It's a brilliant flavor companion to all meats but especially, to my taste, with lamb. It has a multitude of uses. When your plant (and marriage?) has strengthened, you can strip off the spiny leaves and use the stems for skewers. I put rosemary and orange zest in low-fat egg custards to compensate for the removal of fat—it works really well.

If you grill, you can add both rosemary and fennel branches to the coals just at the last few minutes of cooking to add a smoky flavor that is really different. The aromatic smoke glaze is a real winner, and it's pretty spectacular!

Finally, if you boil or steam rice—especially brown rice—you can add a rosemary branch to the water and pick up a heady background scent to what otherwise can be pretty dull stuff!

You may also want to pair rosemary with peas, potatoes, pumpkin, spinach, and tomatoes. (Wrap a branch in cheesecloth so that it's easier to remove before serving.)

You will see from the zones (8–10) that this herb doesn't like extreme heat or cold. Because of this, you may wish (if you live where it gets really cold) to buy a lightweight container, at least 12 inches in diameter, and grow your rosemary in light, well-drained soil. Be sure to punch holes in the container and buy a drip tray to catch excess water when you bring it indoors for the winter. We are in Zone 7, and our rosemary did well for 6 years; *then* came our deep freeze, and our trusted bush died, which apparently gave me the chance to reclaim my husbandly role!

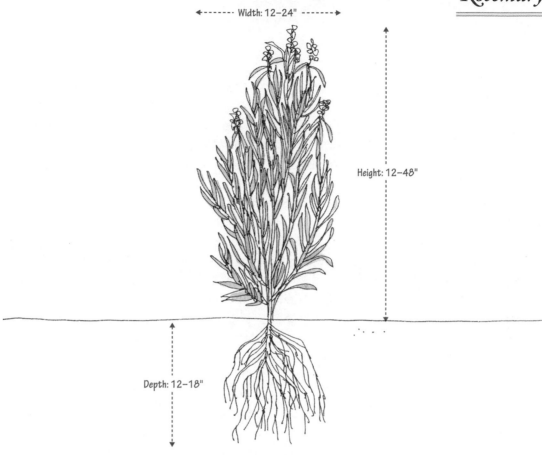

Width: 12–24"

Height: 12–48"

Depth: 12–18"

Perennial
Water: Light
Sun: Full
Companion Planting:
PRO: Cabbage family
CON: Cucumber family (gourds; gherkins)
Pests: Mealy bugs, scales (an insect that sucks plant juices and can promote mold)
Diseases: None
Soil: Light, sandy, well drained

Fertilizer: Fish emulsion 2–3 times a season
pH: 6.5–7.0
Varieties: Rexford (for culinary), Spice Island (4 feet tall), Roman Beauty (small)
Zones: 8–10
Planting: Cuttings ¼ inch deep, 24 inches apart
Germinates: 18–21 days
Harvest: From cuttings, 60 days
Rotation: Permanent
Edible: Leaves

Sage

Salvia officinalis

Since sage, like rhubarb, comes from Siberia, it is what I would call robust! Sow in late spring, and allow it to grow for an entire season without harvesting, as it needs to mature. In the autumn, cut it back and cover well with mulch. The next year it will burst forth with great flavor. Every third year, simply divide it in early spring.

Sage has a powerful almost overwhelming aroma, and yet the leaves are actually quite mild—milder and in the same flavor range as rosemary. Because of this factor, the fresh leaves are often added to a dish at the last moment, or buried within vegetables, meats, or poultry to be touched by its scent.

There is, for example, a great Italian veal dish called saltimbocca that marries air-dried ham (prosciutto) with fresh sage leaves and uses thin slices of veal to encompass these flavors like a sandwich. A truly wonderful example of the benefits that sage can bring

Perhaps the greatest, or most popular, use is the dressing (or stuffing) for poultry. For some years now I've used a small onion and a small orange—both stuck with four cloves holding four sage leaves each—as a roasting seasoning, put inside the bird in place of the dressing and discarded before serving.

I make the dressing separately, using 2 cups whole-grain bread (cubed) moistened with ¼ cup *good* chicken stock, 1 tablespoon chopped fresh sage leaves, ¼ teaspoon fresh thyme, ¼ teaspoon sea salt, ¼ cup dried cranberries, and one diced Bosc pear. All of this goes into a small loaf pan and is baked alongside the roasting bird for at least 40 minutes.

I do this because I'm nervous about the potential for blood to move into the stuffing and potentially breed bacteria in its warm, moist well-insulated center! (The onion and orange are discarded but give a great flavor to the bird.) Also, the dressing itself is much lower in fat in that it doesn't absorb it from the bird.

Now, all this is for carnivores, and this book is 99.9 percent vegetable and fruit oriented, so what to do? I make the dressing just described with a vegetable stock and use it to stuff winter squash. It can be placed in a halved acorn squash or even a small delicata, covered with foil, and baked with, obviously, no fear of flesh contamination.

If you have a special reason to start your sage bush from seed (such as a friend who has a particularly aromatic variety unable to be found as a starter), then you'll have to do this on a sunny windowsill (or greenhouse). Sage doesn't germinate outdoors very well. It needs a soil temperature of 55°F–80°F and takes 7–21 days to show signs of life. If you start from seed, let the plant develop without harvesting in the first year.

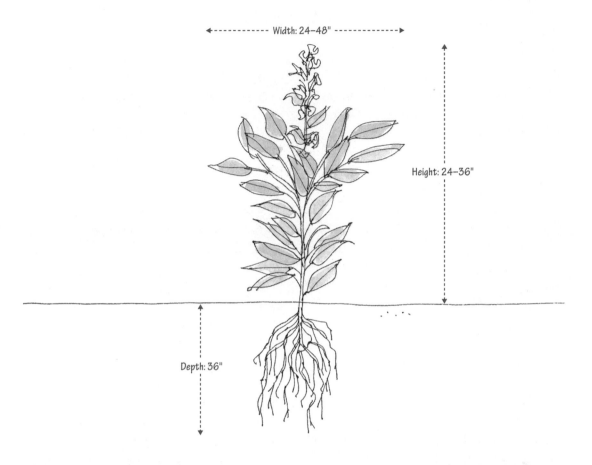

Width: 24–48"

Height: 24–36"

Depth: 36"

Perennial
Water: Light
Sun: Full
Companion Planting:
PRO: Broccoli, cabbage family
CON: Cucumber family
Pests: None
Diseases: None
Soil: Well-drained, loam
Fertilizer: Light feeder; fish emulsion twice per season
pH: 5.5–7.0
Varieties: Common garden, blackcurrant, pineapple, tricolor (for a great multicolor floral display in the garden), Greek (too strong from culinary use)
Zones: 4–8
Planting: Seed (indoors on soil surface) 6–8 weeks before last frost, then set out after last frost; thin to 24 inches apart
Germinates: From seed, 7–21 days
Harvest: From seed, 75–80 days
Rotation: Replace completely (or divide) every 4 years; don't follow cabbage family
Edible: Leaves

Summer Savory

Satureja hortensis

There are two kinds of savory: summer and winter. The winter variety can be coaxed into becoming a low hedge and is named *Montana pygmaea* in its dwarf variety, which is low enough (4–5 feet tall) to see over to talk with neighbors but not good enough for the kitchen, as it is coarse, dry, and bitter.

However, both varieties of savory have this one remarkable and useful quality: they are natural insect repellents. In some locations, they appear to keep down the leaf bugs and weevils that typically go after beans. And if you crush either type of savory, the moist paste can be used to ward off mosquitoes and/or bring some relief to wasp or bee stings.

Like most seed-sown herbs, these are sown directly on a moist surface. They need both moisture and all the light they can get. Be sure you get really fresh seeds, no more than one-season old. If you've already got a plant growing, you can either divide it or take a cutting. If you are using a container, make sure it's a good 6 inches deep.

Again, like other flowering herbs of reasonable height (8 inches and above), watch out for flower stalks and cut them back before they bloom, to strengthen the aromatic qualities of the leaves.

There's a wide range of uses for summer savory, beginning with every bean dish you've ever thought of. Somehow the peppery—almost mint-like—flavor works very well. If you've ever made your own sausages from scratch or bought plain (low-fat) sausage meat, then add summer savory and celebrate!

If you enjoy really complex tossed salads, then adding a few fresh leaves will provide a wonderful peppery taste.

And if all this wasn't enough, in the midsummer it will break out into a choice of three colors of tiny flowers—pink, white, and lavender—that simply smother the plants and bring in the bees to get everything up and running.

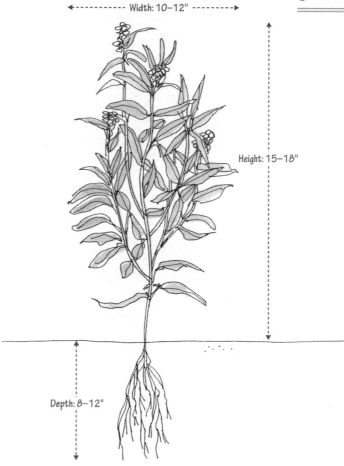

Width: 10–12"

Height: 15–18"

Depth: 8–12"

Annual
Water: Light
Sun: Full
Companion Planting:
PRO: Beans, sweet corn
CON: None
Pests: None
Diseases: None
Soil: Sandy, well-drained loam
Fertilizer: Light feeder

pH: 6.5–7.0
Varieties: Aromata (best for culinary use)
Zones: 5–9
Planting: Seed ¼ inch deep (seeds must be *fresh*), or cuttings ¼ inch deep (best to use tip cuttings); plant out after last frost 10 inches apart
Germinates: 7 days
Harvest: From seed, 60–70 days
Rotation: Can follow any crop
Edible: Leaf

Tarragon

Artemisia dracunculus

I'm not a great fan of the Crusades, but they did do one great service: in the midst of their pillaging, the crusaders discovered and brought back to the West the herb tarragon, without which many of the great French classic dishes would not be possible.

The French have an incredible buttery sauce, béarnaise, that owes its anise-type flavor to French tarragon. It was this sauce that helped me see how the same herb could elevate fish and poultry and many vegetables, like asparagus, broccoli, carrots, peas, and tomatoes, to an entirely new level.

A great way to use the herb is to create a tasty vinegar for use in salad dressings: Wash and dry the herb and place in a clean (sterilized) jar about one quarter full. Top it off with Japanese rice wine vinegar, seal, and keep in a cool dry place. Please don't try this with oil, as there is a rare but possible risk of *Clostridium botulinum* with any raw plant kept in oil.

There are two varieties of tarragon: French and Russian. Although the original comes from Siberia and the Middle East, the Russian should be avoided as a culinary herb because it lacks the essential estragole that provides the licorice flavor.

Tarragon isn't grown from seeds, only cuttings and starts. It annoyingly wilts in warm to hot weather, so zones 9 and above should be avoided. It's also more comfortable in moist but not wet soil that is never less than pH 5. As with the other herbs, cut back in the late fall, mulch deeply, and divide every third year to keep it vigorous.

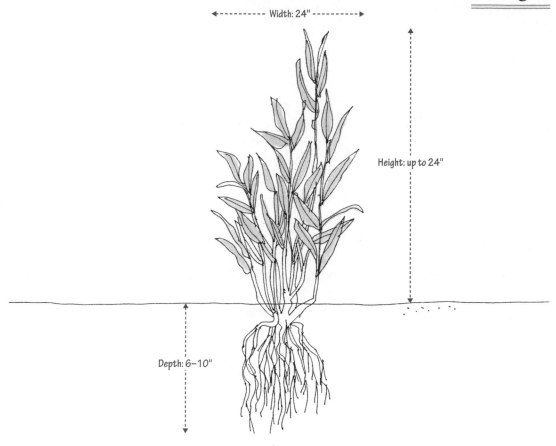

Width: 24"

Height: up to 24"

Depth: 6–10"

Perennial	**pH:** 6.5–7.0
Water: Low	**Varieties:** French (for culinary purposes); Russian and Mexican are unsuitable for cooking due to bitterness
Sun: Full	
Companion Planting:	**Zones:** 4–8
PRO: All vegetables	**Planting:** Cuttings 18 inches apart; divide and replant every third year in the spring
CON: None	
Pests: None	**Germinates:** 5–10 days
Diseases: Mildew	**Harvest:** From transplant, 60 days
Soil: Rich, sandy, very good drainage	**Rotation:** Don't follow sunflowers
Fertilizer: Light feeder; fish emulsion 2–3 times per season	**Edible:** Leaf

Thyme

Thymus vulgaris; T. citriodorius

We have friends who planted lemon thyme between fairly wide-spaced paving stones in a garden patio. It's gradually grown into every space and looks fantastic. It's remarkably resilient, and on a warm evening, the crushing it gets underfoot sends up the most delicious aromas, not unlike the chamomile planted amid the grassy lawns of Buckingham Palace, which smells like green apples as you take tea during a midsummer visit . . . or so I'm told.

This is a ground-hugging herb—never taller than 9 inches, and half that for the creeping *T. citriodorius* (lemon thyme).

There are more than 60 varieties listed, and while I haven't tried them all in the kitchen, so far the combination of citrus/lemon and mint flavors have captured my enthusiasm, and I now use it exclusively.

Since lemon thyme won't grow from seeds, you have to resort to one of two propagation techniques: division or layering. *Division* is simply easing an established plant out of the ground and cutting vertically through the roots to separate a clump. Both sides are then replanted with a 6- to 8-inch space all around.

Layering is a gardening art form that involves growing a stem as long as possible. Then (while the root is still buried), strip off the leaves and lay it on the soil. Dig a small shallow hole/trench, scrape the underside of the stem with a knife, then fill the trench with sand and peat moss. Press the scraped stalk into the sand and hold it there with a U-bent piece of wire pushed down like a staple. The roots should grow out from the wound. You can prop up the end of the stalk on a small stake to get it looking upward!

Of course, you can also buy your starts from a good nursery, but be sure that it's lemon thyme.

Plant it in front of the taller herbs, which logically belong at the back of a bed, and it'll be easy to harvest.

You can get great success using it on asparagus, beans, broccoli, carrots (along with nutmeg), sweet corn, eggplant, potatoes, spinach, and tomatoes.

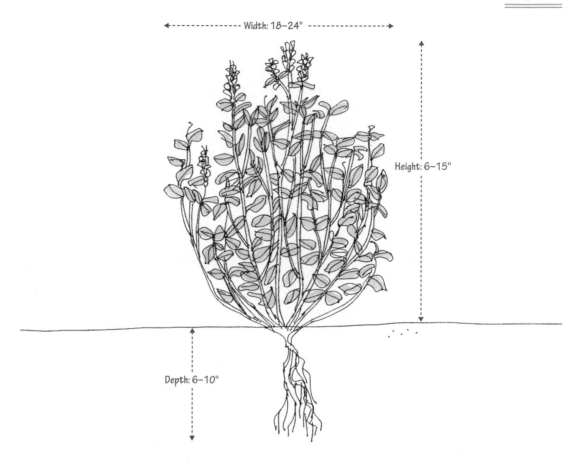

Width: 18–24"

Height: 6–15"

Depth: 6–10"

Perennial/Hardy
Water: Light
Sun: Full
Companion Planting:
PRO: Cabbage family
CON: Cucumber family
Pests: Aphids
Diseases: None
Soil: Light, well drained
Fertilizer: Some feeding (light) and fish emulsion 2–3 times per season
pH: 5.0–5.7

Varieties: Lemon thyme, orange thyme (both good culinary herbs)
Plant Care: When the tiny underbrush leaves dry out, snip down to main stems 3 inches above soil level to re-grow the top leaves
Zones: 4–10
Planting: Seed ¼ inch deep, after last frost; can be divided in the spring; thin to 6–12 inches
Germinates: 8–12 days
Harvest: From seed, 70 days
Rotation: Permanent
Edible: Leaf

Basic Recipes

The following section includes the basic recipes, including the ingredients for my Ethmix spice mixtures. In addition, I have included recipes for several whole-grain/starch dishes—even though they cannot be grown in a kitchen garden—because they are integral to a completely well-balanced diet.

ETHMIX RECIPES

The apparent lack of time has become a very real factor for the survival of cooking from scratch and has promoted the increasing availability of convenience and processed foods.

As a result, over my many years of creating recipes, I have been advised by my editors and publishers to limit the number of ingredients in any recipe to eight or so. My problem with this goal is that I seek to replace large amounts of salt, fat, sugar, and refined starch with layers of taste, aroma, color, and texture, *and for this I use a variety of herbs, spices, and citrus, which pushes the number of ingredients in most recipes beyond the critical eight!*

As an alternative, I chose to combine the following enhancers into just one ingredient, which I call an Ethmix *(for "ethnic mixtures," such as the famed Herbes* *de Provence or Chinese Five Spice). I offer Eth-mix for sale only directly, and because of this limited availability, I've provided the recipes so that you can create your own mixings. All are available at $6.95 a bottle plus shipping and handling. Order by phone at 360-387-3807 or by fax at 360-387-1898.*

BALI
¾ teaspoons ground bay leaves
4 teaspoons ground ginger
3 teaspoons ground turmeric
1½ teaspoons dried onion
1½ teaspoons dried garlic
1½ teaspoons freshly ground black pepper
6 teaspoons hot red pepper flakes

GERMANY
16 whole juniper berries
1 teaspoon dried Cascade hops
1 teaspoon dried morel mushroom powder
4 teaspoons dried chives
2 teaspoons horseradish powder (wasabi)
2 teaspoons caraway powder
8 teaspoons dried marjoram
2 teaspoons ground white pepper

GREEK ISLANDS
4 tablespoons dried oregano
6 teaspoons ground fennel seeds
6 teaspoons dried lemongrass
¾ teaspoon freshly ground black pepper

HARISSA
3 teaspoons caraway seeds
1½ teaspoons ground cumin
6 teaspoons powdered coriander
12 teaspoons hot red pepper flakes

INDIA
5 teaspoons ground turmeric
2½ teaspoons dry mustard
5 teaspoons ground cumin
5 teaspoons ground coriander
1¼ teaspoons ground red pepper (cayenne)
2½ teaspoons ground dill seeds
2½ teaspoons ground cardamom seeds
2½ teaspoons ground fenugreek seeds

MOROCCO
5 teaspoons freshly grated nutmeg
5 teaspoons ground cumin
5 teaspoons ground coriander
2½ teaspoons ground allspice
2½ teaspoons ground ginger
1¼ teaspoons ground red pepper (cayenne)
1¼ teaspoons ground cinnamon

NORTHERN FRANCE
10 teaspoons dried tarragon
1¼ teaspoons powdered bay leaf
5 teaspoons dried thyme
½ teaspoon ground cloves
10 teaspoons dried chervil

NORTHWEST ITALY
8 teaspoons dried oregano
4 teaspoons dried basil
4 teaspoons ground fennel seeds
4 teaspoons rubbed sage
2 teaspoons dried rosemary

PACIFIC NORTHWEST
3 tablespoons hot red pepper flakes
2 tablespoons crushed dried dill
2¾ teaspoons ground ginger
2¾ teaspoons ground anise

POLAND

4 teaspoons caraway powder

1½ teaspoons dried marjoram

3 whole juniper berries

⅛ teaspoon ground cloves

¾ teaspoon white pepper

SCANDINAVIA

4½ teaspoons horseradish powder (wasabi)

2¼ teaspoons caraway seeds

3 tablespoons dried parsley

2¼ teaspoons dried morel mushroom powder

2¼ teaspoons dried seaweed

1 teaspoon ground white pepper

½ teaspoon ground allspice

4¼ teaspoons sea salt

½ teaspoon dried dill weed

SHANGHAI COASTLINE

3 tablespoons hot red pepper flakes

2¾ teaspoons ground ginger

2¾ teaspoons ground anise

SOUTHERN FRANCE

2½ teaspoons dried rosemary

2½ teaspoons dried basil

5 teaspoons rubbed sage

1¼ teaspoons powdered bay leaf

5 teaspoons dried marjoram

5 teaspoons dried oregano

THAILAND

10 teaspoons dried lemongrass

5 teaspoons galangal

1½ teaspoons ground red pepper (cayenne)

1¼ teaspoons dried spearmint

5 teaspoons dried cilantro

2½ teaspoons dried basil

VEGETABLE STOCK

This low-sodium recipe does better than using odd trimmings, which in turn does better than using plain water! (Please note: I consider the turnip to be essential.)

MAKES 4 CUPS

1 teaspoon nonaromatic olive oil

1 onion, chopped

2 garlic cloves, bashed

½ teaspoon freshly grated gingerroot

½ cup coarsely chopped carrot

1 cup coarsely chopped celery

1 cup coarsely chopped turnip

¼ cup coarsely chopped leeks, white and light green parts only

3 sprigs parsley

½ teaspoon black peppercorns

5 cups water

Pour the oil into a large stockpot over medium, add the onion and garlic, and sauté for 5 minutes. Add the rest of the ingredients and cover with the water. Bring to a boil, reduce the heat, and simmer 30 minutes. Strain through a fine-mesh sieve and cheesecloth. Use immediately or date and freeze for later use in 2-cup quantities.

Per serving: 12 calories, 1 g fat, 0 g saturated fat, 0 g carbohydrate, 0 g protein, 0 g dietary fiber, 1 mg sodium. Exchanges: Free Food

PIE CRUST

This crust reduces the calories from fat but still provides a flaky tender crust that is best used as a pie topper—not top and bottom! You can make enough for two tops or a bottom if you must!

1½ cups cake flour
1 teaspoon sugar
⅛ teaspoon salt
2 tablespoons nonaromatic olive oil
¼ cup unsalted stick butter, frozen for
    15 minutes (easier to cut)
1 teaspoon vinegar
4 tablespoons ice water

Combine the flour, sugar, and salt in a food processor. Pour in the oil and pulse until mixed. Cut the butter into small pieces and add to the flour mixture. Pulse 10 times or until the mixture is full of lumps the size of small peas.

Pour in the vinegar and ice water. Pulse 10 more times or until the dough begins to hold together. Gather into 2 equal balls, wrap separately, and refrigerate at least 30 minutes before rolling out.

Alternatively, you can make this dough by hand. Combine the flour, sugar, and salt, and stir in the oil. Add the butter and mix with a pastry cutter or two knives until the size of small peas. Add the vinegar and ice water, and mix with a fork just until it starts to hold together. Gather into 2 balls, wrap, and refrigerate at least 30 minutes before rolling out.

Per serving (¹⁄₁₆ recipe): 78 calories, 5 g fat, 2 g saturated fat (11% calories from saturated fat), 10 g carbohydrate, 2 g protein, 0 g dietary fiber, 52 mg sodium. Exchanges: ½ Starch, 1 Fat

ITALIAN BREAD WITH OLIVES AND ROSEMARY

I've included this rustic homemade bread because a vegetable-only meal is greatly improved with such a chewable side dish.

SERVES 12

1 teaspoon dry yeast
1 cup warm water
⅝ teaspoon salt
½ teaspoon dried oregano
½ teaspoon dried basil
1 teaspoon dried rosemary
2–2¾ cups all-purpose flour
2 sweet onions, cut into 1-inch pieces
2 red bell peppers, cut into 1-inch pieces
3 garlic cloves, peel on
1 teaspoon olive oil
12 sun-dried tomato halves, cut into strips
12 black olives, pitted and quartered
Pinch kosher or sea salt

Sprinkle the yeast over the warm water in a large bowl and let set until creamy, about 10 minutes. Stir in ½ teaspoon of the salt, the oregano, basil, and rosemary. Add 2 cups of the flour and mix thoroughly, adding more flour until you have a nice medium firm dough. Turn out onto a floured surface and knead until the dough is smooth and springy, at least 5 minutes. Place the dough in an oiled bowl, cover, and allow to rise 1½–2 hours in a warm, draft-free place until doubled in volume.

Preheat the oven to 425°F.

Toss the onions, peppers, and garlic with ½ teaspoon of the oil in a baking dish. Sprinkle with the remaining ⅛ teaspoon of salt. Bake 25 minutes or until the vegetables are tender and just browned and the garlic is soft. Cool before using. Peel the garlic and cut into small pieces.

Reduce the oven temperature to 400°F. Grease a 10-inch ovenproof skillet or pie pan.

Spread the dough into a large rectangle. Scatter the vegetable mixture evenly over the top. Add the sun-dried tomato pieces and black olives and fold in the sides. Knead the vegetables into the dough until they are well distributed throughout. Put the dough in the prepared skillet. Allow it to rise about 30 minutes until almost doubled in size.

Make deep dimples into the slightly risen dough with your fingertips. Brush the remaining ½ teaspoon of oil over the top and scatter on a pinch of kosher salt. Bake 30 minutes or until golden brown. Cool on a rack for 10 minutes before cutting.

Per serving: 116 calories, 1 g fat, 0 g saturated fat, 24 g carbohydrate, 3 g protein, 2 g dietary fiber, 91 mg sodium. Exchanges: 1½ Starch

YOGURT CHEESE

Strained Yogurt

I'm loath to overstate the value of any one food or idea. However, the consistent use of yogurt cheese instead of butter, margarine, or cream has made a huge difference in my family's consumption of calories from saturated fat. In our case, the actual savings over one year amounts to more than 40,000 calories, or about 11 pounds of body fat!

MAKES 16 1-TABLESPOON SERVINGS

1 (32-ounce) tub of nonfat plain yogurt that contains no thickeners (such as gelatin, starch, or cornstarch) of any kind*

*I've found that Dannon makes one that's almost always readily available.

Place a yogurt strainer or a colander lined with absorbent kitchen toweling, inside a larger bowl (to catch the whey). Turn the yogurt into the strainer or lined colander, and cover and place in the refrigerator for 12 hours or overnight. About 50 percent of the whey drains away, and you are left with yogurt cheese that is quite firm.

OTHER WAYS TO USE YOGURT CHEESE BESIDES IN THE RECIPES:
Add soft light margarine (with no trans-fatty acids) in equal proportions with the yogurt cheese to create a spread. Or use ⅔ yogurt cheese and ⅓ margarine for even less fat and fewer calories.

Mix with maple syrup to serve alongside a slice of pie.

Substitute for sour cream with a baked potato, adding fresh ground pepper and chives.

Serve as a sauce with poached chicken, using the yogurt cheese and chicken stock thickened with cornstarch, and garnished with capers, pimiento, and a dash of parsley on the top.

Per serving: 12 calories, 0 g fat, 0 g saturated fat, 2 g carbohydrate, 1 g protein, 0 g dietary fiber, 17 mg sodium. Exchanges: Free Food

Grains and Starches

BARLEY WITH LEEKS

If you are someone who has followed my work (and profound changes) over the years, you will know that the acronym TACT means taste, aroma, color, and texture—the basic elements of food pleasure. Texture is last but not least. In fact, the reason why fats are so well liked is because of their texture or sense of mouthroundfulness. So texture is vital! I use pot barley, not the more refined pearl barley, to add texture. I brew up a batch of the following recipe and keep it frozen in 1-cup portions. It also works wonders with soups that can do with more body.

MAKES 12 PORTIONS

1 teaspoons olive oil
2 leeks, white and light green parts only, cleaned and roughly chopped
4 garlic cloves, bashed and finely chopped
3 cups pot barley
6 cups filtered water
1 teaspoon salt

Heat the oil in a medium or large saucepan over medium heat, and sauté the leeks and garlic 5 minutes. Rinse the barley in a strainer and stir into the leeks. Add the water and salt, and bring to a boil. Reduce to simmer and cover. Cook 45 minutes (30 minutes for pearl barley); barley should still be slightly resistant to the teeth.

Per serving: 117 calories, 1 g fat, 0 g saturated fat, 23 g carbohydrate, 4 g protein, 5 g dietary fiber, 144 mg sodium

BOIL 'N' STEAM BROWN RICE

I have never been a great fan of brown rice. It always seemed so stodgy and broken by over-cooking. Then we found this long-grain brown rice, used my old boil 'n' steam method for long-grain converted white rice, and it worked well. It does take an extra 10 minutes or so, though, so we always make double and freeze the un-used portion. Brown rice is a better choice for diabetics, who need to slow down the conver-sion to sugars.

MAKES 4 ¾-CUP SERVINGS

1 cup long-grain brown rice
5 cups filtered water
½ teaspoon salt

Put rice in a strainer or sieve and wash well under running cold water. In a medium sauce-pan, bring the water and salt to a boil. Add the rice, reduce the heat to medium-low, and cook 30 minutes.

In a second pot, bring water to a boil and place a hand sieve on top. When the rice is finished boiling, turn it into the sieve, cover tightly, and let steam for 8–10 minutes.

Per serving: 171 calories, 1 g fat, 0 g saturated fat, 36 g carbohydrate, 4 g protein, 2 g dietary fiber, 306 mg sodium

COUSCOUS

North African Durum Semolina Grains

This classic starch consists of dry, fluffy, tiny granules, and most commercially available types are, in fact, presteamed and dried, and can be made in less than 6 minutes. Varieties distinguished by larger granules take longer to cook and don't have the same fine texture but are equally good. Couscous does a fine job of soaking up gravy and can also form the base of an excellent light-starch salad. It is usually cooked in water, but I greatly prefer using veg-etable stock.

One cup dry will make 3½ cups cooked. I use ½ cup of lightly packed cooked couscous for a side dish, and a full cup for a salad base.

SERVES 6–7

1¾ cups low-sodium vegetable stock (see page 288) or water
1 cup couscous
1 teaspoon salt (if water is used)

Bring the stock to a boil in a small saucepan. Add the couscous and stir four or five times. Remove from the heat, cover, and allow to plump up for 5 minutes. With a fork, gently tease the mix to separate the grains.

Per ½ cup serving: 99 calories, 0 g fat, 0 g saturated fat, 3 g protein, 20 g carbohydrate, 3 g protein, 31 g dietary fiber, 28 mg sodium

LENTILS IN A CUMIN-FLAVORED BROTH

We really love lentils, and more so now that we've visited India. Dahl is a deeply seasoned lentil dish served in India as often as rice or beans are served in Mexican traditions. It's important to use a good stock at a slow simmer and to catch the lentils when just done—before they begin to mush. They are helpful for folks with diabetes because their high fiber content slows down the conversion to sugar.

SERVES 4

1 cup lentils (green, brown, or red)
1½ cups low-sodium vegetable stock
    (see page 288) or water
1 teaspoon ground cumin
Salt to taste

Wash the lentils well and spread them out to dry. Discard any broken or discolored pieces. Measure the remaining ingredients.

Bring the stock to a boil in a medium saucepan. Pour the lentils slowly into the boiling water and reduce the heat to a simmer. Cover and cook 40 minutes. In the last 10 minutes, add the cumin. Taste and add salt only if really necessary!

Per serving made with water: 169 calories, 1 g fat, 0 g saturated fat, 28 g carbohydrate, 14 g protein, 15 g dietary fiber, 3 mg sodium

QUINOA

Pronounced keen-wa, *this seed grain, which has been cultivated in South America for more than 5,000 years, is a very attractive starch alternative to the standard potato, pasta, or rice. It also provides an excellent base for a combined salad. Note: Leftovers freeze well.*

MAKES 4 ½-CUP SERVINGS

1 cup water
¼ teaspoon salt
1 cup quinoa
1 tablespoon chopped fresh parsley or cilantro
2 teaspoons wild mushroom powder (optional)

Bring the water and salt to a boil in a medium saucepan. Add the quinoa all at once. Stir once to get the seeds off the bottom of the pan. When the water comes back to a boil, turn the heat to low, cover, and cook 14 minutes or until the grain absorbs all the liquid. Stir in the parsley. Add the powdered wild mushrooms for flavor if desired.

Per serving: 106 calories, 3 g fat, 0 g saturated fat, 27 g carbohydrate, 6 g protein, 3 g dietary fiber, 148 mg sodium

Sharing the Harvest

A Commitment to Community

My kitchen garden is a metaphor for our community. The soil is like a gathering place; the seeds are words we use to communicate. The wiser the words, the better we grow to understand what is true, and it is shared truth that governs the actions that can lead to a peaceful community.

I'm deeply committed to community.

All my adult life I've tried to sow a few good words to encourage my neighbors to eat together, to share good things, and to find joy in their journeys.

I've watched, with sadness, as life pressures and the more rapid pursuit of happiness by way of countless diversions have limited the time we seem prepared to spend with one another over the family dinner table. I didn't see this from some kind of ivory tower; it surrounded me, as I too was swept along in a mud slide of commercial opportunism.

I really wanted out, and struggled

graham and Treena are here!

for the high ground, where surely there must be some respite? But always the tyranny of the urgent required me to meet deadline after deadline.

Now that you have plowed (not a bad use of words?) through this book, you may be ready to put your own spade into the earth and take our seed-like words of encouragement. But do please start small; even one EarthBox can provide a whole new meaning to the word *delight*, both in achievement and in taste. And at the risk of going off into some utopian vision, I strongly believe that no matter how small your first step, the reward will be so meaningful that you may eventually decide to devote more time and resources to such an amazing pursuit.

Since I began this book, my life has changed. The time I've spent with plants has increased the time I spend with people, both in shared gardens in our community and at each other's tables, where we rejoice over fresh food lovingly prepared rather than engage in some kind of *Iron Chef* competitiveness.

But surely, way above and beyond all the direct benefits of personal achievement and better-tasting, more nourishing meals has been the pure joy of sharing the abundance with others in our community who have been adversely affected by recent economic hard times and hostile surroundings. On so many levels, the fact is that the greater our consumption of vegetables and fruit, the better our ability to handle the toxic environment in which we now live.

Why on earth (literally) would we not want our neighbors to share in our blessings? Surely that's what a neighborhood means.

When we lived in Hawaii, I planted a lawn with St. Augustine grass, which is well suited to the tropical heat. It is planted in clumps, about 12 inches apart on bare earth. Each clump sends out runners that reach its neighbor, and together, in their outreach, they thatch. The earth is soon covered with a verdant carpet that makes the best use of moisture and shade and that requires much less maintenance than a standard lawn.

Consider yourself a small clump of St. Augustine grass: find a neighbor who has just enough space to grow a few experimental plants and encourage each other, back and forth, as you thatch a new, more rewarding way of life. And if you live in an urban setting without a plot of land to call your own, ask your city parks and recreation department where you might be able to join with others whose kitchen gardens are already taking root, or visit the American Community Gardening Association website at www.communitygarden.org and find yourself on the map.

Nowadays life is too full of critics and has too few contributors. But if you are inclined to give me a piece of your mind or to proffer some friendly advice that we can add to the store of local knowledge, please contact me through my website, www.grahamkerr.com.

Damage Control

What now seems like a great many years ago, I lead a small team to the island of Dominica following a hurricane disaster in 1979. It was during this relief effort that I met a French biodynamic agronomist who showed me what the hurricane had done to his prized crops. Most had weathered the storm. "What do you do about pests?" I asked. "I grow enough for them," he replied. "You see these holes?" He held up a large cabbage leaf to the light. "Well," he added, with the kind of lopsided grin that only a Frenchman can manage, "the holes help them cook quicker!"

Of course they don't, but his real point was that small holes or chewed leaves or even blotches and bruising should not send warnings to avoid eating the plant. *In fact, it could be the reverse!*

We are so accustomed to perfect produce that the merest blemish can cause rejection. Our modern standard dictates that every plant on display (under special halogen bulbs) in our supermarkets must radiate reflected light and sparkle with abundant life—chock-full of vitamins, minerals, and good life promises. But to achieve this standard, we have a range of chemicals that control everything that can possibly threaten perfection.

In my earlier experience, we used the acronym LISA, which stood for low-input sustainable agriculture. Our goal back then was to use as many local materials as possible, so that the first growth would lead only to soil improvement and never depletion and erosion. In short, it would be *sustainable* rather than deliberately *organic*.

There are some who would call this a slippery slope because it avoids the absolute standards that "organic" claims. They caution that once there is input, then it's fair game for all manner of dangerous nasties.

While this may be true for professional farmers, who, by protecting their crops, are defending their very livelihood, it should not be the case for home kitchen gardeners, whose customers are their family, friends, neighbors, and loved ones.

And so it was that I chose the most natural routes possible to be sustainable.

I knew I'd have to deal with two main enemies: pests and diseases.

For pests I could use chemicals that are called *systemic*. In other words, they are absorbed into the plant through its leaves, stems, or roots and carried throughout the plant by its sap. These chemicals come in different time-lapse formulations:

- Biodegradable: 1–2 weeks to 1 month

- Relatively persistent: 1–2 years

- Persistent: several years (mostly discontinued)

graham decides not to crop dust his garden...

I've chosen to use only biodegradable products and to give treated plants a 6-week breather before harvest (a simple date written on a stake can ensure that this is done).

I then had to decide how to administer the chemical. Once again, I had choices: dusts, sprays, granules, and baits. I chose immiscible oil mixed to a specific rate of flow—namely 60 seconds, this being the lightest and safest for plant use.

Now came the more probable causes of plant damage . . . disease, and there's a bunch of them. Once again the solutions come in four main categories that deal with fungal diseases:

- Protectant: prevents spores from growing

- Fungistatic: prevents further growth of existing fungi

- Eradicant: kills existing fungi

- Antibiotic: kills fungi and bacteria

I purchased a very practical hand-pumped compression sprayer, which I use for fish fertilizers and the occasional liquid dishwashing detergent (1 teaspoon per 1 gallon), to help in spreading the concoctions over the leaves to provide a proper coating.

I always strain the mixtures through cheesecloth before using the pump sprayer to remove small particles that can "glue up" the fine-spray nozzle.

Finally, I wear rubber gloves, a long-sleeved shirt, an old pair of gardening slacks, goggles, a battered straw hat, and a simple but effective respirator mask. I'm almost ready for a dance up the yellow brick road!

Now . . . given all these precautions, wouldn't you want to avoid their use?

I do have one extra fallback aid, and that's a telephone number to call if I have the slightest question before I use anything: 1-800-858-PEST.

And Now for the Other Way

It has been said forcibly, by experienced gardeners, that the healthier the plant is, the less likely it will suffer a major threat. The obvious source of ill health is the quality of the soil and its appropriate pH and mineral balance. For this you need regular soil testing (or your own tester) and a well-thought-out plan of rotation that you record year after year, bed by bed.

Insects can fly into your space, and when they are evident, you can protect with floating row covers set over wire hoops that permit light and air to continue to reach the plants but fend off your flying friends.

Tiny whiteflies and especially aphids can be attracted to orange-colored sticky boards, sold commercially or made yourself. Some are even biodegradable, complete with their load of bugs!

You can also import your own good insects and let them loose, to savage the lesser plant-eating varieties. Ladybugs are a great example; they love aphids and mites. Praying mantis are purchased in egg boxes; when they hatch, they'll eat anything in sight (within reason). Unfortunately, they are also partial to ladybugs! (See References and Resources.)

You may also want to follow up and conduct an Internet search for pheromones, which are an insect aphrodisiac that attracts oversexed leaf eaters into traps baited with insecticide.

All of these ancient and modern ways will help you win the natural wars you will encounter. But remember: the best thing you can do if it looks really sick is to pull it up, put it in a resealable plastic bag, and take it to your nearest local county extension service agent.

Garden Supplies and Books

GARDEN.COM
A wide range of garden supplies, accessories, and books.
www.garden.com

Greenhouses

CHARLEY'S GREENHOUSE AND INDOOR SUPPLIES
Offers the most extensive selection of quality hobby greenhouses, equipment and greenhouse supplies in the United States.
800-322-4707
www.charleysgreenhouse.com

GREENHOUSE GARDENER'S COMPANION
An excellent resource for everything to do with greenhouse gardening, and beyond.
www.greenhousegarden.com

Herbs

RICHTERS HERBS
Huge selection includes medicinal herbs.
905-640-6677
www.richters.com

Not Just for Kids

KIDSGARDENING.ORG
Under the auspices of the National Gardeners Association, this organization provides parents and teachers with information, resources, and inspiration to introduce children to gardening.
800-408-1868
www.letsgetgrowing.com

Pest and Insect Control

ARBICO ORGANICS
Sustainable supplies for pest control and other organic gardening needs.
800-827-2847
www.arbico.com

Seeds and Plants

THE GOURMET GARDENER
International seeds and edible flowers.
913-345-0490
www.gourmetgardener.com

HUMMERT INTERNATIONAL
Features a wide range of seeds.
800-325-3055
www.hummert.com

JOHNNY'S SELECTED SEEDS
Excellent catalog of offerings, especially
vegetables.
207-437-4301
www.johnnyseeds.com

SEED SAVERS EXCHANGE
A good resource for heirloom seeds, this non-
profit organization of gardeners is dedicated
to saving and sharing heritage varietals.
319-382-5990
www.seedsavers.com

TERRITORIAL SEED COMPANY
An excellent resource for seeds, live plants,
and garden supplies.
541-942-9547
www.territorialseed.com

*And finally, for those of you who haven't had enough of Graham Kerr—
the rampant enthusiast—visit my website at www.grahamkerr.com.*

INDEX